Also by Norman Gelb:

Scramble
Less than Glory
The British
Irresistible Impulse
Enemy in the Shadows

The
Berlin Wall

The
Berlin Wall

Kennedy, Khrushchev, and a Showdown in the Heart of Europe

Norman Gelb

𝕮imes BOOKS

The photographs in this work are used courtesy of Presse- und
Informationsamt der Bundesregierung, Federal Republic of Germany;
United States Information Service, United States Mission Berlin;
and Norman Gelb.

Library of Congress Cataloging-in-Publication Data
Gelb, Norman.
The Berlin wall.
Bibliography: p.
Includes index.
1. Berlin wall (1961–   )   2. Berlin question (1945–   )
3. World politics—1955–1965. 4. United States—
Foreign relations—Soviet Union. 5. Soviet
Union—Foreign relations—United States. I. Title.
DD881.G45   1987   943.1'550876   86-5898
ISBN 0-8129-1218-7

Designed by Mary Cregan
Manufactured in the United States of America

9 8 7 6 5 4 3 2
First American Edition

For Mallary, who arrived with the Wall

Contents

The
Berlin Wall

1
The Wall

GRIM and forbidding, the Wall snakes through the city of Berlin like the backdrop to a nightmare. In certain respects that's exactly what it is. Tears have been shed here, curses uttered, threats snarled, blood spilled, lives snuffed out. The Wall has been standing a long time now—more than two decades. It has become part of the political architecture of modern times, a concrete barrier planted across the middle of the biggest city between Paris and Moscow, a dramatic statement as well as a grotesque edifice. It is an awkward thing, outlandish and unloved, a numbing fact of life, a fortification thrown up in panic to keep people in rather than out.

What follows is the story of the Berlin Wall and the circumstances surrounding its erection. But it is more than just an account of the splitting of a city. It is also a story of power politics and thermonuclear threat. It was played out in Washington, Moscow, London, and Paris as well as Germany. Berlin was, after all, the place described by Soviet Premier Nikita Khrushchev as "the testicles of the West. When I want the West to scream," he said, "I squeeze on Berlin." It was the place about which President John F. Kennedy growled, "If Khrushchev wants to rub my nose in the dirt, it's all over." Berlin was where the Cold War began with a Soviet blockade, where Soviet and American tanks faced each other virtually snout-to-snout for the first time, and where the grisly game of nuclear brinkmanship was introduced.

For a brief moment the Berlin Wall was the focus of the world's attention. Spawned in an atmosphere of bluster and defiance, it generated a mood of deepest anxiety and despair. Hawks and doves everywhere debated its significance and consequences. In Moscow the Soviets, who had authorized its erection in violation of international agreement, kept nervous watch as this most remarkable, most presumptuous urban redevelopment scheme of all time—chopping a city in two—was implemented. They needn't have worried. Despite rumors of secret American connivance, the White House, State Department, Pentagon, and Central Intelligence Agency, expecting something else, struggled but failed to fix on a suitable response. Deplored and reviled but unchallenged, the Wall stood and grew.

Swarms of journalists and news photographers descended on Berlin to see and record the erection of what people quickly designated either the Wall of Shame or the Wall of Peace, depending on where they stood ideologically. Pundits and politicians, generals and spymasters converged on it like impious pilgrims come to marvel at a blasphemous miracle. People marvel at it still and wonder, Did its erection halt a downhill tumble toward a war that might have engulfed the globe, or would the world be a better place today had it been immediately, unceremoniously, defiantly demolished?

The great Wall of Berlin is more than just an emotionally charged geopolitical spectacle. Made of reinforced concrete, standing ten to thirteen feet high, it is a remarkable structure. Meandering through the heart of the metropolis, turning corners, winding and bending, it hacks the old capital of Germany into two distinct entities and then curls to enfold the western half of Berlin in its concrete embrace. If straightened, the Wall would measure 103 miles, which is greater than the distance between New York and Philadelphia, or London and Calais.

But there is more to the Wall than just this wall. Behind it, one hundred yards deeper into Communist territory, is another concrete barrier almost as formidable. The leveled area between the two is a desolate, dangerous no-man's-land, patrolled by kalashnikov-toting guards, dotted with free-fire machine-gun emplacements, and sown in places with landmines. It is punctuated with 285 elevated watchtowers, more suited to prison camps than city centers, and by a series of dog runs where ferocious, long-leashed Alsatians effectively run free. It is not a safe place to be.

To reach the Wall from the East, a person would have to scale the interior concrete barrier and evade the guards, dogs, minefields, automatically triggered guns, and strategically positioned devices designed to set off sound alarms and light signals. If that person reached the border undetected, he would have to get a firm grip on the Wall to lever himself over, despite the thick, smooth-surfaced, ungrippable cement tubing affixed to its top to prevent people from doing just that. Some who have remarkably gotten that far have been foiled by this last refinement.

Floodlights and searchlights are positioned along the Wall to illuminate it at night. Specially reinforced obstructions have been erected at the handful of official border-crossing points to discourage people from crashing through in vehicles, which a daring few did during the Wall's early days.

All this vigilance is not directed against criminals. The objects of these extraordinary precautions are the people of East Germany. When the Iron Curtain was lowered by the Communists along the border between East Germany and West Germany after World War II, Berlin—though deep within Communist East Germany—was spared this division. It remained under joint control of the victorious Soviets, Americans, British, and French, each with their own sector of the city, each with their own military garrison stationed in that sector, but with right of unrestricted movement throughout the German capital guaranteed by East–West agreement.

That meant that East Germans, seeking more from life than they believed was being offered to them in their Communist homeland but unable to cross the Iron Curtain directly into West Germany, could still find a way out. They could make their way to East Berlin—which was the Soviet Sector of the city—and then cross without fuss or ceremony into West Berlin, where the dividing line between the American, British, and French sectors had become largely irrelevant, where freedom of speech, belief, and mobility was protected by law, and which was recovering from the war's devastation at a dazzling pace. American correspondents in Berlin at the time called the East Germans' crossover the "five-cent subway ride to freedom." Having come across, the refugees could stay in West Berlin or, if they wished, they could be flown out to West Germany to waiting jobs and new lives well beyond reach of the Communists from whom they had fled.

They came in the thousands over the years, tens of thousands, hundreds of thousands, millions. So great was the flight that the continued existence of the Communist East German state was threatened. The Wall was erected around West Berlin to stop the exodus and thereby save the Soviet Union and its East European empire from the consequences of an East German collapse.

Many things have happened since that summer night in 1961 when the city was rent asunder. Much has changed. But East Berlin is still walled off from West Berlin. The people behind the Wall are still being shielded from the temptations and distractions so glitteringly displayed just a few minutes away. They are still locked in.

Not all people in East Berlin and East Germany have accepted this situation. Despite all the obstacles, many have managed to get through, over, or under the Wall since it was built. But more than three thousand East Germans are known to have failed in their effort to escape and to have been arrested by the *Vopos* (*Volkspolizisten,* or People's Police) for trying to cross over into West Berlin. At least sixty persons are known to have been shot dead in the attempt. How many more have lost their lives or have been wounded trying to escape is just a guess. The East German authorities do not publicize such things. People wounded and caught are led or carried away by the border guards. Rarely is news of their subsequent fate made public. However, it is known—through observation from afar and reports brought across by successful escapees and western visitors— that dozens of persons have been wounded in abortive, often foolhardy bids to break through to West Berlin.

The Wall has regularly been strengthened, with points deemed penetrable reinforced and other sections merely tidied up. There is continuous maintenance along its entire length. So efficient has this maintenance been that escape attempts have by now practically ceased, though a reckless or desperate person still occasionally tries to go through, and occasionally succeeds. Not long ago, an East Berlin border guard was jailed in West Berlin for shooting dead another guard before fleeing over the Wall. He said he had not wanted to kill the man, only disable him so that he could make his getaway without fear of being shot himself. Two East Germans soared over the Wall on a pulley attached to a steel cable strung from the roof of a building in East Berlin and fixed by a friend to a car hidden behind a West Berlin house. The East German authorities are continually alert for new schemes, new devices, new subterfuges for getting over the Wall. Not for nothing have they outlawed hang gliding.

While writing this book, I experienced the curious feeling of going down a distant, winding road I had been down before, at least part of the way. In fact, I had. I went to Berlin as correspondent for the Mutual Broadcasting System a little more than a year before the Wall was built. I remained in the city for two years, till the Wall crisis just about petered out, before I was shifted to London. For practically that entire period, it was one hell of a story to cover. The city was, at the time, politically turbulent, emotionally charged, and unceasingly eventful. I have sought in the following pages to capture the drama of that traumatic moment as well as tell the story of the Wall and the circumstances that led to and grew from the construction of that gruesome monument to human discord.

2
The Stage
Is Set

SHORTLY after 1:00 A.M. on August 13, 1961, the roar and rumble
of heavy vehicles broke the silence of otherwise deserted streets in
the Soviet Sector of Berlin. Roused from sleep, people looking down
from their windows saw convoys of trucks and troop carriers speed-
ing toward the line dividing East Berlin from West Berlin. More
convoys followed, and still more. Within two hours thousands of
steel-helmeted East German troops and armed police were deployed
along the border. A particularly strong contingent was positioned in
and near Potsdamer Platz, which was the busiest crossing point
between the two parts of the city during the day. Even along normally quiet stretches of the border line, crisp commands rang out
through the warm night as East German officers moved their men
into place. Guards with automatic weapons were posted at crossing
points between the eastern and western sections of the city. Machine
gun positions were set up. Border patrols were assigned and dispatched. Work details set about digging up cobblestones, jackham-
mering holes into pavement, and chopping down trees, clearing
a way for barbed wire that was to be strung along the line that
had divided East Berlin from West Berlin since the end of World
War II.

Until that night the line had been marked off primarily by signs informing people in English, Russian, French, and German that they were passing between East and West in the city. Paying little regard to those signs, tens of thousands of Berliners crossed and recrossed the border every day going to work, visiting relatives and friends, going to the movies or theater, or just sauntering. Now, however, the East–West agreement on freedom of movement throughout Berlin was being unilaterally shattered. A physical barrier was rising in the middle of the city to mark the spot where the Berlin Wall would soon stand. East German troops and police were already clamping down on crosstown traffic and briskly turning back west-bound East Berliners.

Through the night, East German army trucks rattled through East Berlin, carting more bales of barbed wire and additional cement posts on which the wire was to be strung. Through the night, people living along the border peered apprehensively down at the bizarre nocturnal scene. By morning Berlin had been effectively split in two. In addition to the East German forces deployed along the city-center border, two divisions of Soviet troops had ringed the city, serving notice that Moscow was backing up this blitz operation. The Berlin Wall was about to thrust the world into crisis. That crisis had been brewing for a long time.

Fifteen-and-a-half years before the Wall went up, as World War II drew toward an explosive close in the winter of 1945, Soviet troops battling their way to Berlin reached the Oder River, a mere thirty-five miles east of the city. There they were brought to a halt. As the Germans desperately struggled to forge a defensive line between the Red Army and their capital, Soviet commanders were ordered by Moscow to stay put and consolidate their positions. They were to wait for their supply lines to catch up with them, for their units to regroup, and for orders commanding them to crash through to the Berlin nerve center of Adolf Hitler's Third Reich.

The Soviet commanders were mystified. It was true that their supplies were running short, their tanks were having to cope with the mud of an early thaw, and many of their units had been decimated. But their goal—the capital of the hated enemy—was so close and their men, having built up a head of steam, were eager to push forward to seize it. Soviet leader Joseph Stalin had other things in mind. Stalin realized that the fall of Berlin would end the war. He therefore held his Berlin-bound troops in check while his other armies pressed forward to overrun as much of German-occupied East and Central Europe as possible before the end of the war and thereby guarantee Soviet control of the region.

Stalin was confident his troops could take Berlin whenever he gave the order. His forces were less than an hour's car-drive away, while the western Allies were a safe three hundred miles from the city. In addition, the Americans were still recovering from the Battle of the Bulge, the daring but ultimately abortive German Christmastime counteroffensive in the Ardennes. While they sorted themselves out, there was still Budapest for Stalin's troops to take, and Prague and Vienna.

Prime Minister Winston Churchill had also begun examining the prospects for the postwar world. The British leader was convinced that whoever captured Berlin would have a trump card to play when hostilities were brought to an end. He and his generals proposed that the western Allies roar across the north German plain to take the city with the kind of thrust operation that the Germans had earlier used to devastating advantage.

Everyone knew that the capture of Berlin was the primary objective of the Allied forces—or so it seemed. General Walter Bedell Smith, chief of staff to Supreme Allied Commander Dwight Eisenhower, declared, "From the day our invasion broke over the beaches of Normandy, the goal of every Allied soldier had been Berlin. The Supreme Commander, the staff and all the troops shared a driving ambition to seal the defeat of Nazi Germany by seizing the capital of the Reich itself." A planning memorandum at Supreme Headquarters Allied Expeditionary Forces (SHAEF) had been unequivocal: "Our main objective must be the early capture of Berlin." Eisenhower himself had called Berlin "the main prize."

Two crack American paratroop divisions were in advanced training for a drop on Berlin at short notice to support a ground assault on the city. Newspaper headlines in the United States and Britain blared out reports of the diminishing distance between Allied forces and Hitler's Berlin headquarters. A popular American song crowed "We'll Be Singing Hallelujah, Marching Through Berlin!"

Nevertheless, Eisenhower was not much taken with the idea of racing his forces forward to take Berlin. As a strategist, he inclined toward a broad front advance by his armies rather than the narrow thrust attack that the British preferred. Though a broad advance would make movement toward the German capital a much more protracted operation, it was less risky. With the forces under his command still a good distance from the city and the Soviets practically within artillery range of Hitler's Berlin bunker, talk of the western Allies taking Berlin did not overly impress him. If the Soviets were capable of capturing the German capital more easily—and it seemed they were—there was no reason to engage in a race with them.

To Americans at the time the Soviets seemed to pose no threat whatsoever. On the contrary, Americans saw them as gallant allies who shared their desire to wind up this ugly war as soon as possible and who would join with them in guaranteeing that peace, harmony, and justice would prevail in the postwar world. Getting to Berlin before the Soviets, just to be there first, would not be warfare but a shabby, pointless form of politics, and American soldiers fighting a war did not play politics—shabby, pointless, or any other kind.

Eisenhower shared Bedell Smith's view that "battles are fought to defeat armies," as if war were simply a military exercise, remote from other considerations. The supreme commander considered that his mission—his "crusade"—was to destroy the enemy forces, thereby sealing the defeat of Germany and ending the conflict. And that was all! Though he was prepared to concede that Berlin had symbolic significance, he turned his attention to what he believed was a more pressing matter.

A flurry of reports told of German elite forces converging on the mountainous region to the south, in southern Germany and western Austria. There, it was said, the Nazis intended to hold out indefinitely with new miracle weapons at their disposal and an abiding faith in their Führer. This alpine bastion proved to be nothing more than fantasy, existing only in the feverish daydreams of a handful of Nazi leaders whose grotesque world was crumbling about them. General Omar Bradley later wrote, "Not until the campaign ended were we to learn that this Redoubt existed largely in the imaginations of a few fanatic Nazis. It grew into so exaggerated a scheme that I am astonished that we could have believed it as innocently as we did." In addition, what was left of German military capabilities was highly exaggerated in the reports Eisenhower and his aides received. Instead of gathering elite troops to man this "National Redoubt," the Germans were piecing together whatever forces they could find—including elderly Home Guard, Hitler Youth units of teenagers, army labor battalions, untrained headquarter staff personnel, stranded navy personnel, and planeless airmen—to reinforce the defensive lines facing the Soviets on the Oder.

American military intelligence was completely duped. On the basis of misinformation fed to him Eisenhower decided that rather than head for Berlin, which he now dismissed as "only a geographic location," his troops, once they reached the Elbe west of the capital, would turn south along the river to link up with advancing Soviet troops well away from Berlin. Hitler's remaining forces would thus be split in two, making them easier to take on and finally crush completely.

That was the plan as winter began to give way to spring. However, in March a dramatic transformation on the field of battle raised tactical questions. The Soviet forces east of Berlin were still where they had been at the end of January, on the Oder, and the Germans were busily bolstering their defenses against them. At the same time it was evident that the Germans were rapidly losing both the ability and the will to challenge the onrushing armies of the western Allies, now fully recovered from earlier setbacks. Resistance to American and British forces was disorganized and crumbling fast after the Germans failed to blow up the bridge at Remagen, permitting American forces to get across the Rhine without the delay and huge casualties that had been anticipated. There were still battles to be fought. But American and British troops were encountering far less resistance than had been expected as they surged across the rubble of western Germany. German soldiers were surrendering to them in droves, sometimes whole units at a time, sometimes even by telephone to front-line headquarters positions. Countless others simply shed their uniforms, threw away their rifles, and drifted homeward. With the Rhine well behind them, the forces of the western Allies faced no major obstructions on the road to Berlin except the River Elbe.

Eisenhower had sixty divisions to throw against the German capital if he wanted to do so. There were more than enough supplies to meet any situation in the field. German airfields east of the Rhine had been quickly adapted to receive Allied transport planes, which were ferrying in two thousand tons of supplies each day. It could no longer be said that the Soviets were best placed to capture Berlin.

The British did not hesitate to hammer that point home. In view of America's far greater contribution of troops and supplies in the fight against Nazi Germany, they were prepared to accept American military leadership in the war. But they had ideas of their own on how the war should be run. Having fought longest against Nazi Germany and, during some dark, worrying months, having stood alone in that struggle, the British had hoped that their troops would have the privilege of administering the death blow to Hitler's Reich by taking Berlin. They were riled when that privilege was denied them by Eisenhower, who diverted the Berlin-bound forces under the command of Field Marshal Sir Bernard Montgomery, Britain's most popular war hero and the victor of El Alamein, northward to capture the north German ports and liberate Denmark. To learn in addition that Eisenhower was contemplating letting the Soviets capture the German capital when it seemed that the Americans could easily get there first, left Prime Minister Winston Churchill dumbfounded and furious. Capturing Berlin was no longer a matter of national pride. It concerned the long-term fate of Europe and the world.

Devoutly anti-Communist, profoundly suspicious of Soviet intentions, Churchill insisted that international political considerations had to be taken into account on the battlefield as the war approached a climax. Like Stalin, the British leader knew that the shape of the postwar world would be strongly influenced by developments in the final stages of the conflict. Allies might share a common objective in a war, but each country had interests and aspirations of its own. Agreements had been reached with Moscow, but there was no guarantee that they would be honored any more than the Nazis honored the prewar nonaggression pact they had signed with the Soviets. There would be much bargaining, much haggling, much jockeying for position. All sorts of factors neglected in the heat of battle could turn out to be of critical importance.

It had been pointless to raise questions about the fate of Berlin when the forces of the western Allies had barely begun making their way in that direction. But with western troops now scudding across Germany as fast as their tanks and trucks could take them, Churchill strongly challenged Eisenhower's contention that Berlin was of secondary significance. How could it be when the very name Berlin had become synonymous with Nazi Germany? There was still time. Berlin was within reach. Churchill insisted it could and should be taken by the western Allies—by the Americans if not the British.

His arguments made little impression on Eisenhower. The supreme commander remained haunted by a vision of an invulnerable

Nazi stronghold in the mountains to the south. Berlin was not an important military target and, therefore, was of little interest to him. When, at the end of March, instead of going through channels as he had done previously, the supreme commander directly informed Stalin of his intention to leave the German capital to the Soviets, Churchill saw it as a blatant effort to shut him up and was outraged. Field Marshal Sir Alan Brooke, the British army commander, noted bitterly in his diary that Eisenhower had "no business to address Stalin directly."

Eisenhower may have wanted to preclude bureaucratic interference in his strategic planning, but his main reason for contacting Stalin was far from devious. It was known that Soviet and German troops had accidentally exchanged gunfire when, after the Nazi–Soviet pact had been signed, they made contact as they went about splitting Poland between them in 1939. As the forces of the western Allies and the Soviet Union were rapidly approaching each other in the middle of Germany in March 1945, it became vital to liaise quickly with Moscow to establish linkup points and contact procedures so that confusion would not lead to tragic incidents when they finally came within shooting distance of each other.

In his controversial message to Stalin Eisenhower informed the Soviet leader that, as they were nearing the climax of the war in Europe, the main thrust of his forces in Germany would be southward toward the region around Leipzig. There, he suggested, the Soviet–American linkup might take place. He did not specifically mention Berlin, but he indicated unmistakably that the Americans would be leaving the city to the disposal of the Soviets.

The Soviet leader promptly replied to Eisenhower that the plan "entirely coincides with the plan of the Soviet High Command. . . . Berlin," he added gratuitously, "has lost its former strategic importance." He told Eisenhower he had assigned only "secondary forces" to move against the German capital. However, Stalin was convinced Eisenhower was trying deceive him. Having for many months considered Berlin his own for the taking, he was both worried and angered by the circumstances that appeared to open a path to the German capital for the western Allies. He was convinced that, despite Eisenhower's assurance to the contrary, the supreme Allied commander was planning a major assault on the city, to claim it before the Red Army could. The Soviet leader did not intend to be so easily bamboozled.

He immediately summoned to the Kremlin Marshal Georgi Zhukov and Marshal Ivan Koniev, his two crack military chieftains, and challenged them with the question, "Well, who will take Berlin, we or the Allies?" Neither had any doubt about the answer. Playing them off against each other, Stalin ordered Zhukov and Koniev to draw up plans for an all-out offensive against the city. They were given little more than two weeks to complete preparations for the assault. Stalin was determined to capture Berlin before the Americans could get there. Though he had told Eisenhower he was assigning only secondary forces to the Berlin front, he was taking no chances. More than one million troops and more than twenty thousand heavy guns were to be earmarked for the job.

Churchill, meanwhile, shared none of Stalin's doubts about Eisenhower's candor. Convinced more than ever that the supreme commander's determination to bypass Berlin would prove to be a historic blunder, and unable to budge him, the British prime minister appealed over Eisenhower's head to Washington. Cabling his concerns directly to Franklin Roosevelt, he tried to impress the president with the consequences of what he believed would be, in effect, needlessly handing the German capital to the Soviets:

> The Russian armies will no doubt overrun all Austria and enter Vienna. If they also take Berlin, will not their impression that they have been the overwhelming contributor to our common victory be unduly imprinted in their minds, and may this not lead them into a mood which will raise grave and formidable difficulties in the future? I therefore consider that from a political standpoint, we should march as far east into Germany as possible, and that should Berlin be in our grasp we should certainly take it.

Churchill's warning and advice earned him nothing. Roosevelt believed that Stalin, though leader of a totalitarian regime, was essentially a reasonable man whose aims were identical with his own— the defeat of Nazi Germany and the establishment of conditions that would guarantee that Germany would never again be a threat to world peace. There was much sympathy in the United States for the Soviet people, whose horrific suffering in the war was extensively reported in newspapers across the country, as were the heroic deeds and accomplishments of the Soviet armed forces and guerrilla fighters.

Suggestions from London that Moscow's designs might be less than honorable were not well received in Washington. Many Americans who knew little or nothing of the Soviet Union referred affectionately to Stalin as "Uncle Joe" (which infuriated Stalin when Roosevelt told him about it at Yalta) and thought of him as a kindly national leader who wanted nothing but peace and freedom for his people. They would have been deeply offended had it been widely known that Churchill thought of the Soviets as potential adversaries and that he was urging Roosevelt to think the same. Misgivings about the Allies, where they existed in Washington, were directed instead primarily against the British who kept talking about their precious Empire. It seemed to some Americans that their British cousins were striving to maintain unjustifiable rights and privileges in far-flung territories that they had ruled through conquest a long time before and in which people were being denied the right to choose their own government.

George Kennan recalled that when the leaders of the victorious nations began parceling out the zones of Germany that they would occupy once the war was over, Roosevelt was far more interested in whether Britain or the United States would gain control of the coveted northwestern industrial zone of the country than in the dimensions of the area designated as the Soviet Zone. Unlike Churchill, Roosevelt was not at all worried that the Soviet Union was gaining its first toehold in Central Europe.

Also, although for operational purposes unity remained firm among the western Allies, British and American generals had been growing disenchanted with each other for some time. The British thought of Eisenhower as a good organizer but indecisive as a supreme commander. They believed that "Ike" tended to be excessively influenced by the last person with whom he conferred, hardly a quality to be desired in a military leader.

Similarly, the American generals were offended by British efforts to complicate the war by injecting nonmilitary considerations. In addition, United States Army Chief of Staff George Marshall, who had nominated Eisenhower as supreme commander, was irritated by criticisms of Eisenhower's performance, conveyed to him privately, and not always tactfully, by some British military leaders. At the same time American generals thought very little of the talents of Field Marshal Montgomery, the senior British officer in the field. They considered him a blowhard and an overly cautious tactician who had missed several important battlefield opportunities in Europe with costly consequences. According to General James Gavin, commander of the American Eighty-second Airborne Division, American troops were tired of the credit Montgomery was claiming "for battles fought and won by the Americans." At one point Eisenhower was so enraged by a self-serving public pronouncement by Montgomery (who told a press conference that he had tidied up for the Americans after the German Ardennes offensive) that he was on the verge of insisting that the British recall him to England. British advice about strategy might have been more effective in swaying Eisenhower—who, as the British rightly believed, was not that hard to sway—had personal friction not been an element in Allied relationships.

There was, in fact, a growing feeling in Washington that Soviet intentions were indeed questionable. Despite carefully spelled out agreements that free elections would be permitted in countries liberated from Nazi rule, the Soviets had already imposed a Communist government on Romania and were in the process of doing the same in Poland. There were other disturbing developments as well. The Soviets reneged on an agreement to let the United States use airfields in Hungary just liberated by the Soviet army and were dragging their feet on cooperation in the setting up of the United Nations, on which Roosevelt pinned his hopes for world peace and security in the postwar world.

But the American president remained reluctant to offend Stalin by challenging Soviet actions, other than to issue mild expressions of concern. He feared that to do so might undermine postwar unity. When it was suggested to him that Stalin could not be counted on to keep agreements, Roosevelt replied, "I just have a hunch that he is not that kind of man." When pressed, he replied confidently, "I can handle Uncle Joe."

He was, however, to be denied the chance to try. No one outside his immediate entourage knew that the president was desperately ill. By the time British objections to Eisenhower's intention to leave Berlin to the Soviets reached him, Roosevelt was dying. Ambassador

Robert Murphy, summoned to discuss the situation in Germany with the president, found him "in no condition . . . to offer balanced judgments upon the great questions of war and peace."

For some time messages to Roosevelt that were related in any way to military operations, like Churchill's about Berlin, had been going instead to the Chief of Staff, General Marshall, who scorned complaints from London about Eisenhower's strategy. Marshall agreed with Eisenhower that political considerations should not interfere with the primary task of winning the war in the quickest possible way with the fewest possible casualties.

If events had occurred as expected, that would have ended the controversy. But the dispute over who should take Berlin had flared and had apparently been settled before the full significance of the German military collapse in the West had been grasped. In its closing days the war had taken on astonishing dimensions. The forces of the western Allies had cut off the Ruhr, trapping a third of a million German troops, whose commander, Field Marshal Walter Model, was soon to commit suicide. A gap 250 miles wide had been opened in German defenses, and Allied forces had stormed through it.

The Allied advance had taken on steamroller proportions. Eisenhower's aide, Captain Harry C. Butcher, recorded in his diary on April 8, "I told the Supreme Commander that I had heard comment from the correspondents, officers and GIs that they wanted to keep going until they got to Berlin. This desire was rampant." Three days later, on the evening of April 11, American troops, having raced a remarkable fifty-seven miles through disintegrating German defenses in the previous twenty-four hours, reached the Elbe River, the last natural obstacle on the road to Berlin and only fifty-three miles from the German capital. Advance United States Army patrols swept into the riverside city of Magdeburg, terrifying after-work shoppers who had no idea the enemy was near and creating a traffic jam. Two days later, the Americans planted a bridgehead on the far side—the Berlin side—of the Elbe.

This was a historic opportunity. The Soviets were closer to the German capital than the Americans. But they still had no orders to advance, and they faced formidable resistance from German defenders who had been reinforced and who had dug in at strongly fortified positions. In contrast, there seemed to be little to block an American spurt forward to seize Hitler's capital and finally bring World War II to a dramatic, irreversible conclusion. Years later, General William ("Big Simp") Simpson, commander of the United States Ninth Army, said,

> The only thing that moved faster than [us] those days was a comparatively few fleeing remnants of the battered and broken German Army. ... [We] had ample supplies to drive on and capture Berlin. There was no question in my mind that we could do it, and do it with little loss.

Nor was Simpson the only one who thought his men would soon be in Berlin. General Walther Wenck, commander of the German forces positioned between the Americans and the city, had little hope of blocking their way. Assigned the task just a few weeks earlier while still recovering from serious injuries suffered in an automobile accident, Wenck examined the situation, despaired at the sight of scratch units that had been stitched together to fashion an "army" for him to command in this endgame, and told his deputy, "If the Americans launch a major attack, they will crack our positions with ease. What is to stop them? There is nothing between here and Berlin."

Eisenhower was faced with a dilemma. Although he had decided to pass up Berlin and had told Stalin of this intention, his men had spurted hell-for-leather to the Elbe and had actually crossed it. The situation had to be reviewed.

If Eisenhower's plans were not going to be altered, Simpson's troops at the Elbe had to be braked hard and braked quickly because neither they nor their commander knew anything about Eisenhower's intention to leave Berlin to the Soviets. There had been no need for them to know. No one could have anticipated the rapidity of their advance or the extent of the German rout in the West. But now, having reinforced their bridgehead on the Berlin side of the Elbe, the Americans were about to storm out of it to claim "the big prize." Patrols had whisked forward, had reported little to worry about, and were already less than fifty miles from Berlin. Simpson had already instructed his staff that they were to go "hell-bent for Berlin" and expected to be there before another full day had passed.

No delay was now possible for Eisenhower. He again had to make a Berlin decision. As Simpson finalized his plans for taking the city by roaring down the *Autobahn* Hitler had built for his Third Reich, the Ninth Army commander was summoned by General Bradley back to army group headquarters at Wiesbaden, where he expected to be asked to outline those plans. Instead he was told by Bradley, "Stop right where you are. You can't go any further."

"Where the hell did this come from?" Simpson demanded.

"From Ike," Bradley said.

Simpson was to clean up his flanks, link up with the Soviets to the south, and deal with remaining German forces there. His forces across the Elbe were not to break out of a bridgehead; they were parked in a dead end. Simpson was baffled and angry. "All I could think of," Simpson recalled later, "was, 'How am I going to tell my staff, my corps commanders and my troops? Above all, how am I going to tell my troops?' "

Eisenhower had been under strong pressure to change his mind about Berlin. Examining the change in battlefield circumstances, he had asked Bradley what it would cost to take the city. Bradley replied it might cost one hundred thousand casualties, "a pretty stiff price to pay for a prestige objective." The cost seemed not only exorbitant but also pointless in view of the Allied agreement that placed postwar Berlin within the Soviet Zone of occupied Germany. Widely criticized later, Eisenhower was to ask, "If I were to seize Berlin at a very great cost in lives, and a day or two later we were ordered to withdraw to comply with the postwar occupation plan, what would the troops think of it and what would the American people think of it?"

General Gavin later said, "Every soldier I know of who has analyzed the fighting during the month of April 1945 is troubled by the fact that Eisenhower's armies stopped on the Elbe." Eisenhower himself later told Willy Brandt that if he had to do it over again, he would have permitted the American troops to roll on to Berlin. But essentially, it was a political decision, and with Roosevelt dying (he died the day after Simpson's men reached the Elbe), American acting political leadership was incapable of making such decisions. It was left to the military, and they were qualified to make only military decisions.

It is impossible to say what casualties the American forces would have sustained had Simpson been given the green light. No doubt there would have been a price to pay. The Soviets suffered three hundred thousand casualties in taking Berlin. But by that time, while resistance to the Soviet forces remained fierce, many Germans prayed to be captured by the Americans rather than by the Soviets, whom they had been led by pathological Nazi bigotry to think of as subhuman Asiatic fiends, bent on rape and plunder. Some German units on the eastern front fought on fiercely against the Soviets in the hope that the Americans would advance fast enough to take their surrender. Without knowing that Simpson had been ordered to halt his forward momentum, General Wenck shifted his makeshift army, originally assigned the task of stopping the Americans, to the East to fight the Soviets instead. In the end-of-war chaos some German officers had been deluded into believing that when the Americans arrived, their own units would join them to go on to fight the Soviets together.

On April 16, three days after Simpson's men had futilely crossed the Elbe, the Soviets, who had been hunkered down on the Oder since January, finally launched their drive to break through to the city. On May 2 they completed their capture of the German capital, effectively ending World War II in Europe.

3

Discord
in the Ruins

LENIN once said that whoever controls Berlin controls Germany and whoever controls Germany controls Europe. The Soviets had now taken possession of that once great city. But they couldn't keep it—not all of it. Though it was located deep inside what was, by agreement of the victorious powers, to be the part of Germany occupied by the Soviet Union, the city itself was to be divided into four sectors. Like the four zones into which vanquished Germany was being split, each sector of Berlin was to be occupied and controlled by one of the four powers—the United States, Britain, France, and the Soviet Union.

At the time Berlin was in ruins. Willy Brandt, later to be mayor of West Berlin, described what he saw when he returned from exile in Scandinavia:

> Craters, caves, mountains of rubble, debris-covered fields, ruins that hardly allowed one to imagine that they had once been houses, cables and water pipes projecting from the ground like the mangled bowels of antediluvian monsters, no fuel, no light, every little garden a graveyard and, above all, like an immoveable cloud, the stink of putrefaction. In this no man's land lived human beings. Their life was a daily struggle for a handful of potatoes, a loaf of bread, a few lumps of coal, some cigarettes.

By carrying out their occupation duties alongside each other in this rubble of humbled Germany, it was expected that the wartime allies would demonstrate and preserve international harmony in a world they had liberated from the horrors of fascism and the ordeal of war. As it turned out, there was trouble practically from the beginning.

Within days of war's end, the Soviets demanded that the United States immediately evacuate Soviet-Zone areas that American troops had overrun in the closing days of the conflict. It had been understood that such a withdrawal would take place once the fighting was over. But the tone and urgency of the Soviet demand seemed unnecessarily severe, amounting almost to a suggestion that the Americans, no matter what they had earlier agreed, intended to make squatters claims to parts of the Soviet Zone.

As always when dealing with the Soviets, Churchill was suspicious of their designs. He advised Harry Truman, who had succeeded the deceased Roosevelt as president of the United States, to delay withdrawing the American troops from the Soviet Zone until details of various agreements with Moscow about postwar Europe could be worked out and, where appropriate, implemented. "It is vital now," the British prime minister warned, "to come to an understanding with Russia and see where we are with her."

Truman was indeed angered by things the Soviets were already up to. He objected to their imposition of Communist rule in parts of liberated East Europe. He was angered by their presumptuous claim that a provisional government they had established in Austria had authority over the entire country, though it had been agreed that Austria was also to be divided into four zones of occupation. Nevertheless, the American president, who at war's end had congratulated Joseph Stalin on his "splendid contribution to the cause of civilization and liberty," maintained that the western Allies were still obliged to fulfill commitments they had made. Despite Churchill's latest call for vigilance in dealing with Moscow, Truman saw no reason during his first weeks as president to make major changes in previously hammered-out plans. Nor did he wish to spurn the advice of his newly acquired military advisers, who couldn't see why American troops, having completed their mission in Europe, should mark time in parts of Germany from which they would have to be evacuated before long.

There was still a war in the Pacific to be won. There was also strong domestic pressure to "bring the boys home" if they weren't being shifted half a world away to take on the Japanese. In addition, Moscow had signaled Washington that concerted Allied occupation arrangements for Germany and for Berlin would not be implemented until American troops withdrew from areas of Germany "they illegally occupy." With these pressures building up, Churchill's forebodings were easily outweighed, and Truman informed the British leader, "Our State Department . . . does not believe that the matter of retirement of our respective troops to our zonal frontiers should be used for . . . bargaining purposes."

Nevertheless, western officials having to deal with their erstwhile Soviet comrades-in-arms found their behavior inexplicably hostile. Colonel Frank Howley, later to be American commandant in Berlin, said, "We went to Berlin in 1945 thinking of the Russians only as big, jolly, balalaika-playing fellows who drank prodigious quantities of vodka and liked to wrestle in the drawing room." But Howley and other American officers were baffled by undisguised Soviet antagonism, particularly in view of the vast quantities of military supplies the United States had sent the Soviet Union during the war, without which the horrendous Soviet casualty rate would have been greater still.

The Americans made allowances, however, for the gallant ally whose people had suffered so horribly at the hands of the enemy. An estimated twenty million Soviets—one in every ten—had been killed. Countless numbers of them had simply been murdered by Nazi execution squads. Another twenty-five million Soviets had been made homeless. The Soviet Union had been ravaged as no country ever had been before. Almost two thousand of its cities and towns had been flattened.

It was understandable that Soviet leaders would now be wary about anything happening in Germany. If their suspicions seemed exaggerated when they were dealing with their friends, that was perhaps understandable too after what they'd been through. Nor was it really strange that individual Soviet officers with whom western officers came in contact were undiplomatic in behavior and speech. If they deviated from conventional standards of courtesy in their dealings with their Allies, they were, after all, a different people. And, as the British observed, Americans themselves were no sticklers for etiquette or conventional courtesies.

Besides, there was very little concern among the Allies about what fate awaited Germany and Germans at the hands of the Soviets. Details of what had transpired in the Nazi concentration camps were for the first time widely publicized. Millions of people had been methodically slaughtered. American and British troops had liberated Bergen-Belsen, Dachau, Buchenwald, and other concentration camps and had seen the stacks of emaciated bodies, the rows of emaciated survivors, the crematoria, the blood trenches, and the gallows. In some cases they had been so enraged by what they had found that they had shot down camp guards on the spot. Surviving inmates, robbed of all vestiges of human dignity in the excruciating struggle to stay alive, told horrific stories of the treatment to which they had been subjected not only by the guards but even by German doctors in the camps, some of whom had engaged in grotesque experiments on humans. Eyewitness testimony and documentary evidence could not be denied.

Germany had become a dirty word, and Germans were thought of as scum. The important thing was not to spar with the Soviets about this or that triviality but to make certain Germans would never again be able to perpetrate crimes against humanity. Allied denazification courts and procedures were established. Nazi officials were arrested, imprisoned, and in some cases executed. American occupation troops who fraternized with German girls were court-martialed. Even antifascist Germans had a hard time persuading Allied personnel that they did not share responsibility for the Nazi crimes. A climate was generated in which people in the West did not care what their long-suffering Soviet allies had in mind for Germany or how they went about it.

The American troops were surprised when, acceding to Soviet insistence that they withdraw from positions they had overrun in the Soviet Zone of Germany, they found themselves shadowed and scrutinized by the Soviets, as if they were thieves absconding with property belonging to the new rightful owners—the Soviets. The western Allies were irritated when, almost as Churchill had forecast, they were told, after the Americans (and the British too, reluctantly) had bowed to the Soviet demand that they withdraw their troops from the Soviet Zone, that it was not yet convenient for them to come to Berlin to assume control of their sectors of the devastated capital. The Americans finally realized that by ignoring Churchill's caveat they had thrown away the only card the West had held for inducing the Soviets to honor their agreements. Nevertheless, it didn't seem to matter much at the time. The war with Germany was mercifully over; the war with Japan was still to be wrapped up. But frustrations in dealing with the Soviets in Germany gradually accumulated, and they centered around Berlin.

On May 8, 1945, the Germans had formally surrendered to the four Allied powers at a ceremony in Berlin. A week later, the Soviets had unilaterally appointed a German civilian governing body for the city, responsible to themselves alone. Two weeks after that, an American advance party commanded by Colonel Howley, en route to Berlin to size up the sector the Americans were to occupy and administer, was halted by the Soviets fifty miles from the city. Howley was told that a Berlin agreement restricted his party to 37 officers, 175 men, and 50 vehicles. Despite Howley's protests that no such agreement existed, the Soviets refused to let his party through until he complied with the Soviet restrictions.

The reduced party was then made to bivouac in a suburb of Potsdam, ten miles from Berlin, and was escorted through the ruins of the capital by a Soviet guard who tried to keep them from districts that the Soviets were methodically stripping of factory machinery and other valuables. Howley was left with the impression that the Soviet officers and men with whom he came in contact "had been briefed that we were their enemy, merely enjoying an armistice, and they regarded us as such." He was startled when an angry young Soviet officer asked him, "Why are you Americans going to fight us?" Gregory Klimov, an officer in the Soviet Military Administration of Germany, recalled,

> Even at [the] first meeting with the Allies, one could not help noticing a great difference between them and us. They welcomed us as joint victors and sincere allies in war and peace. . . . We, on the other hand, regarded the "Allies" as the opposing party, as enemies with whom we had to sit at the one table only for tactical reasons.

Even when the Soviets permitted units of General Simpson's Ninth Army, which had been halted at the Elbe in April, to join them on July 4 in occupying Berlin, the Soviet commandant raised a technicality that he said would unfortunately delay an American take-over of what was to be the American Sector. Thoroughly annoyed by now, Howley—without Soviet permission—sent American officers and troops to seize control of the American Sector at dawn on July 5, taking command of the borough halls in the sector and informing borough officials that they would from then on be responsible only to the American commandant. The Soviets protested angrily when they realized what had transpired, but faced with a fait accompli, they acquiesced. The Americans boasted at the time that they had finally learned how to deal with Soviet intransigence. In fact, they were just beginning to learn what Soviet intransigence was.

Despite this unseemly bickering, western leaders clung to a vision of a Germany and a Berlin that, though divided into different zones and sectors, would be administered as units, overseen by joint commissions on which the occupying powers would be equally represented and where harmony would be the ruling principle. It did not occur to them that their line of contact with Berlin through the Soviet Zone of Germany would present a problem, and they neglected to insist that access be specifically defined by treaty. They assumed that the right to occupy their sectors of the city automatically included the right of access.

Again they were mistaken. It was quickly apparent that the Soviets considered western use of the access routes to Berlin a privilege rather than a right, which they could control and grant or deny. When eyebrows were raised at such an obstructive attitude, the Soviets made it clear that they considered Berlin theirs by right of conquest. They chose to ignore the fact that one third of what was now the Soviet Zone of Germany, overrun by western troops in the closing days of the war and evacuated by them in accordance with agreements, should have been under western rather than Soviet control by the same right of conquest. It was then that the Americans finally came to the conclusion that the Soviet attitude was "What's mine is mine; what's yours is negotiable."

Nevertheless, the Americans and the British (the French, still to be assigned a sector, were not yet deeply involved in the controversy) felt that to avoid complications, they would for the moment accept much more limited access routes to Berlin than they wanted. Changes could be made later after the dust had settled. What they did not realize was that in also agreeing that all decisions of the joint control commissions set up by the victorious powers would have to be unanimous, they had given the Soviets a veto to block any alteration to agreements previously made and procedures previously established. Churchill had warned them, but for the Americans, it was like suddenly finding themselves in a shoot-out when they had expected a sing-along.

The Soviets made no secret of the fact that they considered the German capital their own, regardless of its official four-power status or the proceedings of the *Kommandatura,* on which the commandants of the four occupying powers were supposed to have equal voice in running the city. Communists and others who were prepared to act exclusively on Soviet orders had been deployed in positions to control the workings of the city's civilian administration. Berlin's reconstituted police force had also been put under Communist command. The Berlin radio station was supervised by the Soviet military. Non-Communist newspapers were rigidly censored. A food-rationing system was devised that enabled the Soviets to downgrade the ration card of any Berliner who displeased them. They established a trade union association and kept tight control of it. While the western powers devoted their energies to introducing an elaborate (though hardly immaculate) denazification program in Berlin, the Soviets concentrated on the instruments through which they intended to establish long-term control of the city.

As the months passed, the Allies, and particularly their representatives in Berlin, began to grow exasperated with Soviet presumptions and obstructions. The difficulties they encountered could no longer be shrugged off as products of postwar confusions and dislocations. It was now obvious they were part of deliberate Soviet policy. But Britain, where Churchill was no longer prime minister, and France were caught up in sorting out formidable problems of their own generated by the war and its wake. They were preoccupied with repairing wartime damage, creating jobs for demobilized servicemen, and finding enough food and fuel. Their tables of priorities left little room for rumblings of discord in Hitler's old capital city. They left it to the Americans, with their infinitely greater resources and infinitely fewer hardships, to take the lead in dealing with Soviet shenanigans. But the Americans at that stage were bent on getting along with the Soviets for the greater good of all concerned.

General Lucius Clay, then American deputy military governor in Germany, said, "We were quite willing to start off on their terms." Diplomat George Kennan has written of "dreams of a happy collaboration" with the Soviet Union that he vainly tried to convince others in Washington were "quite unreal." Caught up in the spirit of the budding United Nations, American leaders wanted to believe there was a natural harmony of interests among nations. They weren't going to let a handful of minor frustrations disrupt that harmony.

Accordingly, every effort was exerted to make the joint four-power occupation of Berlin function smoothly. If it meant a few compromises, it seemed a price worth paying—until it became unmistakably clear about a year after war's end that the Soviets saw things and did things very differently. The Soviet military administration in Berlin was, in fact, engaged in a systematic campaign to stifle western-oriented political movements that had begun to re-emerge in the rubble of the city.

The Soviets had reestablished a German Communist party in Berlin within days of the war's end. The Germans who were to be its leaders had been flown in from Moscow where they had spent the war years. But the Communists had been required by the presence of the western garrisons to share the political stage with non-Communist parties. These were led for the most part by men and women who had been interned by the Nazis or who had returned from exile abroad. They, their movements, and their potential popularity posed a serious threat to Soviet plans for Berlin and Germany, far greater it seemed than the threat posed by the western garrisons that Moscow expected would pack up and go home in due course.

Barely had the non-Communist parties surfaced in the city when it became evident that the Communists did not intend to confine themselves to conventional political action to compete with them. Activists were kidnapped and disappeared forever into the Soviet Sector. Others were beaten up. Some withdrew from politics after being warned in the Communist press to cease their "reactionary" activities. Not only political figures were at risk. Three judges who had refused to hand down decisions urged on them by the Communists also disappeared. Students were expelled from the university for commenting unfavorably on the Communist leadership.

In a tactical move the Communists disbanded their own party. In its place they created a new organization, the SED, an acronym in German for Socialist Unity Party. Through a merger, the SED was meant to gobble down the newly established Social Democratic Party, which was seen as a threat to Communist control of Berlin because of its appeal to the working class in what had once been a strongly socialist city. The resulting "merged" political organization was to be kept under strict control of a Communist caucus answerable to the Soviet military authorities. Some Social Democrats were drawn into the SED through dreams of working-class solidarity or because of intimidation. But the party struggled against Soviet-backed pressure in order to retain its independent existence. People were shouted down and roughed up at meetings that were called to discuss the proposed merger. The courage and vigor with which some Social Democratic leaders openly defied Communist bullying persuaded previously skeptical right-wing American army officers in Berlin, who looked on in admiration, that there might after all be a difference between Communists and Socialists.

Their defiance persuaded the Allies to call for citywide elections at the end of 1946 to see exactly how Berliners felt about the pace and direction of events in their city. The results left them in no doubt. Ignoring Soviet warnings and bribes (the Soviets provided the SED with food and coal to distribute in a city desperately short of both), the voters snubbed the Communists. The non-Communist parties took more than 80 percent of the votes. The SED made embarrassingly modest showings even in staunchly working-class districts of the city. A prominent East German Communist who later fled in despair and disgust explained, "To the man in the street, we were known as the 'Russian' party. . . . Our leading officials lived in large country houses hermetically sealed from the rest of the population and guarded by soldiers of the Red Army."

The Soviets saw nothing wrong with that. Scorning the rebuff at the ballot box, they persisted in their efforts to dominate the city so many of their soldiers had given their lives to claim. Through manipulation of municipal personnel under their control, direct intercession by their military officers, intimidation, and stonewalling at the Kommandatura, they were partly successful. But the Allies decided they had been swept along far enough by the tide.

The Kommandatura soon lost its image as a council of common purpose and camaraderie and bogged down in wrangling. The western commandants found ways around Soviet obstructions. They cleaned out remaining vestiges of Soviet control in the police force and municipal administration in their sectors. Radio in the American Sector (RIAS) was set up as a counterforce to the Soviet-controlled radio station in the Soviet Sector. Non-Communist newspapers were supported, as was the Free University set up in the American Sector by students and instructors who could no longer endure Communist ideological rigidity and bullying at the historic Humboldt University in the Soviet Sector. Non-Communist activists were encouraged in their bid to end Communist control of the Berlin trade union organization.

Seeing their plans and expectations increasingly thwarted by these tactics, the Soviets fought back. To frighten non-Communist political activists and media personnel, Communist-run newspapers ran rumors of an impending western withdrawal from the city after which, it was ominously hinted, scores would have to be settled. While reporting western denials, *The New York Times* frightened a lot of Berliners when it reported, "It is a matter of common knowledge that many military government officials openly discuss the probability of a three-power withdrawal."

Soviet officers took to touring parts of western sectors where Allied personnel were billeted, as if preparing to take over their accommodations. In public pronouncements the Soviet commandant in the city repeatedly referred to Berlin as part of the Soviet Zone of Germany, which it was not.

Soviet harassment of Allied traffic between West Germany and West Berlin became habitual. Western airliners flying to the city through the agreed air corridors were buzzed by Soviet fighter planes. Restrictions were imposed on civilian train travel through the Soviet Zone to and from West Berlin. When the Soviets tried to check personnel aboard Berlin-bound American military trains, General Clay, now American military governor in Germany, posted armed guards on those trains to keep the Soviets off. The British did the same. Those actions drew warnings from Moscow that Allied trouble-making over a place the Soviets had paid so steep a price to conquer was testing Soviet patience.

Roosevelt had once told Stalin that he thought American troops were likely to remain in Europe little more than two years after the war ended. But it was already more than three years since the German surrender, and the Americans, the main obstacle to the consolidation and expansion of Soviet influence in Europe, still showed no signs of going home. Indeed, the countries of western Europe, France in particular, were pressing the Americans to join with them in a mutual defense alliance that would guarantee that American forces would remain planted on the continent indefinitely.

The Soviets were also rankled by what was happening in West Germany. The American, British, and French occupation zones were moving toward a merger into one nation. What was more, with substantial American economic aid, West Germany was making a remarkably rapid recovery from the war's devastation. Those developments spawned a specter that haunted the Soviets. The emergence of a strong, hostile, vengeful West Germany was dreaded in Moscow. Wartime memories, hatreds, and fears remained vivid there. That problem had to be dealt with, and Berlin might be the place to deal with it.

Deep within the Soviet Zone of Germany, encased by Soviet military might, Berlin was an ideal place to begin prodding the Americans into their overdue withdrawal from Europe. If Stalin could bring that about, first from Berlin, then from West Germany, the West Germans would have to think again about who their friends should be and to whom they should tip their hats.

As Soviet pressures mounted, the idea of a strategic Allied withdrawal from Berlin was given close consideration in Washington. Realists at the Pentagon, whose job it was to consider military possibilities, pointed out that a city so far behind Soviet lines was indefensible and, in a crunch, unsuppliable. Realists at the State Department pointed out that the Allies were in a no-win situation in Berlin. They were in no position to take any credible diplomatic initiatives there and were forced only to play back Soviet moves.

In Moscow, where such American views were closely monitored, the Soviets debated how much harassment the Americans would endure before throwing up their hands in despair, pulling up stakes, and abandoning the city. The prevailing view was that it was only a matter of time and sustained pressure. However, some in Moscow were not so sure. Still grieving for their country's staggering wartime losses and painfully aware of the nuclear monopoly the United States at that time enjoyed, they believed there were Americans sufficiently hell-bent on destroying communism to welcome a Soviet challenge in Berlin. Such a provocation could be used to justify an American assault on the war-weakened Soviet Union. That was what Hitler, in his last days, had forecast.

There were indeed people in the United States who thought the time was right to destroy communism, but they were neither in positions of influence nor were they to be found in any great numbers. However, there was a group of Americans who had been dealing with the Soviets over Berlin, or had served with the American occupation forces there, or had been connected with the city in some other way, and had grown passionately devoted to guarding its freedom. This Berlin Mafia, as it would later be called in Washington, did what it could to convince the White House as well as the upper echelons of the State Department and the Pentagon that Berlin should not be handed over to the Communists no matter how vulnerable it seemed. It was argued that the American garrison there, though not nearly a match for the Soviet forces deployed around it, was a perfectly credible deterrent, a trip wire the Soviets would not dare to stumble across, no matter how fiery their rhetoric.

The most influential of the Berlin mafiosi was General Clay who had come a very long way since the days when he had amicably agreed to questionable Soviet demands to avoid a confrontation. He had once told State Department Soviet affairs expert Charles Bohlen that the key to getting along with the Soviets was, "You had to give trust to get trust." But as the one who had negotiated with the Soviets about the arrival of American occupation troops in Berlin in 1945, it was Clay who had failed to get written access assurances from them. He had publicly accepted blame for that mistake and was now vengefully mistrusting. In a message to Washington early in 1948 about Soviet pressure on the Allied presence in Berlin, he warned, "If we mean to hold Europe against Communism, we must not budge."

Whether the Allies would budge was soon to be tested. Stalin was determined to force a showdown with the West over the last remaining patch of territory within Communist East Europe in which the Soviet writ did not run and, in the process, show the Americans they no longer had any business being so far from home. In June 1948 the Soviets laid seige to Berlin. Rail, road, and waterway access to the city from the West was severed. "Technical difficulties" was the reason given. But the timing was dictated by a currency reform that the United States, Britain, and France had authorized

for their occupation zones in West Germany, where runaway infla-
tion was threatening trouble.

Blockaded, the western garrisons in Berlin and the people who
lived in the western sectors of the city would be without food and
fuel, all of which was shipped in from West Germany. Denied the
necessities of life, West Berliners would clamor for those garrisons
to pull out and for the Communist East German regime to meet their
needs, as it promised it would. The West would have to beat a
humiliating retreat.

Like the Americans, the British and French condemned this
attempt at geopolitical extortion. But the people of Britain and
France were still suffering the consequences of the war, and most of
them still hated Germans because of it. They themselves had not long
before endured a glacial winter in which food had been scarce and
fuel had been in such short supply that people had succumbed to the
cold at home. They displayed little enthusiasm for risking renewed
war and additional hardship by challenging the Soviets on behalf of
Berliners, no matter how prowestern those Berliners might be.

In Washington too voices were raised questioning the advisabil-
ity of standing fast in a place that was always bound to cause trouble,
that was a lost cause militarily, and that was likely to be more of a
diplomatic liability than it was worth. Fearing the Berlin situation
might easily escalate into war at a time and place of the Soviets'
choosing, several influential figures, including members of President
Truman's cabinet, counseled caution.

But blocking a Communist take-over of Berlin had become as
much of a crusade for General Clay as crushing the German armies
had been for Eisenhower, and Clay wanted action. He proposed
sending an armored column through East Germany to West Berlin
to break the blockade and show the Soviets that Americans could not
be bullied. Clay's idea was quickly quashed by the military chieftains
at the Pentagon because the Americans would have to use force if
the Soviets tried to obstruct the column, and that could mean war.[1]

Denied authorization to bust the Soviet ground blockade, Clay
nevertheless insisted it had to be broken immediately, before the

---

[1]One former State Department official said, "The belief in Europe that American generals are warmongers is way wide of the mark. No one wants peace more
than they do. People get killed in wars. What most of them want to do is merely
get on with their complicated training programs and play with their expensive toys."

Kremlin could build up momentum and before pressure on the Allies to abandon Berlin intensified. He consulted with Ernst Reuter, the mayor-elect of Berlin, who had been barred from office by the Soviets. Officers of the Soviet military administration objected to Reuter for three reasons: He was strong willed, he was a Social Democrat who refused to take orders from them, and he was a former high-ranking Communist who had turned his back on communism twenty-five years earlier.

Reuter told Clay that no matter what the circumstances, Berliners did not want the Allies to leave them to the mercies of the Soviets and their Communist underlings. He said they were prepared to live on reduced rations rather than give in. Clay was impressed. It was what he wanted to hear. Within forty-eight hours of the commencement of the Berlin blockade, acting without clearance from Washington, he began having essential supplies ferried by air into the city from American bases in West Germany.

Clay's presumption and impetuousness ruffled many a feather in Washington, where generals are not expected to make political decisions and are looked upon with suspicion when they do. But when President Truman was advised by senior advisers that abandoning Berlin was an option that had to be seriously considered, Clay or no Clay, he responded without hesitation. "There is no discussion on that point," he said. "We stay in Berlin—period," and he gave his blessings for a full-scale airlift to break the blockade. On the same day, British Royal Air Force transports joined in.

When the full dimensions of what Clay had in mind—a round-the-clock service—were grasped at the Pentagon, Air Chief of Staff General Hoyt Vandenberg began to worry. It would tax America's military transport resources to the limit. Wasn't it a mistake, he asked, to concentrate so much of those resources in one place at a time of international tension? What would he do if the Soviets started trouble elsewhere in the world and some of those aircraft were needed to cope with it? No answer was offered, but soon giant transport planes flown in from the Hawaii, Panama, Alaska, and American bases elsewhere around the globe were shuttling into West Berlin's Tempelhof, Gatow, and Tegel airports (the last built in a hurry during the airlift) right through the day, winging in every pound of food, every ton of coal, clothing, medicine, equipment of all sorts, and everything else needed to keep West Berlin fed, fueled, and functioning, and the Allied garrisons supplied.

Planes were scheduled to fly in at three-minute intervals, but there were times at peak periods over the next eleven months when the planes arrived every ninety seconds. Tempelhof, in the American Sector, was a nightmare for pilots coming in to land in poor visibility, as they often had to do. It was no easy job for them even when weather conditions were satisfactory. The airfield was little more than a grass patch situated right in the middle of the city, in a clearing surrounded by buildings and bombed-out ruins. Pilots brought their heavily loaded, giant Skymasters down low over the tops of apartment buildings, and there they suddenly would be, at Tempelhof, quickly leveling off and hoping not to overrun the runway, which they sometimes did. Years later, landing at Tempelhof was still hardly a relaxing experience for passenger or pilot, even in an airliner not hauling ten tons of coal and even when the pressure was off and the weather was fine.

Soviet fighter planes occasionally buzzed American and British transport planes during the blockade, but though seventy-two lives were lost in ground accidents, no serious Soviet interference was encountered. General Clay had earlier served notice that if such interference did occur, the aircraft would be escorted by armed American jet fighters. Clay took the cautious response of the Soviets to this warning as proof that Moscow was prepared to go only so far and would back off when challenged. It would influence his actions, which in turn caused severe palpitations in the White House later on.

There were moments during the blockade winter of 1948–49 when weather conditions grounded the transport aircraft. Sometimes the planes arrived over Berlin to find they had to turn back because of visibility problems and then, for the same reason, couldn't land at the West German airfields from which they had departed. They would then scout around for fields where they could touch down before their fuel ran out. In one case a Skymaster loaded with coal for freezing Berlin ended up in Marseilles in the sunny south of France.

Essential supplies in the city fell perilously short that winter, and it appeared that the airlift might fail. It was savagely cold. Trees were cut down for firewood. People scavenged for coal dust and other materials they could burn to keep warm. Public transport operated on sharply reduced schedules and came to a dead halt at 6:00 P.M., after which time the city was dark and silent. There was electric power four hours a day, in two two-hour spreads. Dried food products, easier to transport in bulk, became a significant part of the diet of West Berliners.

The Communist press and radio dramatized the hardship and deprivation to which Berliners were subjected, and blamed the United States for it. They confidently asserted that the West would succumb. The Soviets promised immediate relief from the dire conditions if Berliners made clear to the western powers that they no longer required their services. It didn't work. At no time during the blockade did West Berliners call for a western climb-down or a withdrawal of the western garrisons. On the contrary, the hardships generated a stronger spirit of defiance of the Communists. Berliners felt a new sense of purpose and a proud identity, which defeat in the war and the troubles immediately afterward had done much to obliterate.

While the Soviets were trying to lever the West out of Berlin with their blockade, Communist strong-arm mobs were deployed in the city in Soviet-orchestrated bids to regain complete control of the municipal authorities. Council meetings were stormed and outspoken non-Communists were beaten up. Police under Soviet control looked on and did nothing. When such things happened in the Soviet Sector of the city, where the venerable City Hall was located, the Allies—though appalled—could only protest. But elected city councillors could do more, and they did. When the Communists tried to establish a city government that would be their exclusive instrument, non-Communist councillors set up new headquarters for municipal government in the western sectors, where they could operate under Allied protection. The Soviets responded to this challenge by formally incorporating the Soviet Sector of four-power Berlin into the Soviet Zone of Germany. Thus, during the blockade, though the barriers had not yet gone up and people freely crossed back and forth, the city was divided into East and West.

The Berlin blockade was the overture to the Cold War. It marked the moment when the Soviets signaled they were prepared to risk direct confrontation with the West in circumstances that could lead to an outbreak of hostilities, and when the West replied in kind. It was then that nostalgia about the wartime East–West alliance finally fizzled out. It was then that most people in the West began thinking of the Soviets as adversaries. Though wartime hatreds would linger in many places for many years, the Germans, having become participants in a common struggle to preserve western values, ceased being the enemy. The western garrisons in Berlin were no longer occupying forces. They were now the forces of the "protecting powers."

At the same time the response to the blockade dramatically confirmed American leadership of the West. Before the blockade the American government had been thinking of pulling American troops out of Europe by 1952. It believed that the countries of Western Europe would by then be sufficiently recovered from the war and united enough to see to their own security, sparing the United States the expense and responsibility. The blockade changed all that. Not only was it clear to Washington that the Europeans weren't yet anywhere near ready to cope with aggressive Soviet action without the American presence, it was clear to the Europeans as well. The Berlin blockade forged the strategic logic that has kept American troops on European soil ever since.

For Moscow, Allied ability to resist Soviet efforts to drive them out of their rogue enclave in the middle of Communist territory confirmed the unshakable conviction that the West was determined to destroy the Soviet system. There was no longer any doubt in the Kremlin that the Soviet Union would have to become a military superpower to survive. The struggle for Berlin set the stage for the superpower rivalry between the Soviet Union and the United States that was to become the dominant feature in international affairs during the second half of the twentieth century.

For the moment, however, the Soviets realized that they had made a mistake and that the situation in Berlin had to be reassessed. With the onset of spring 1949 bad weather no longer disrupted flights from the West. Soviet expectations that the airlift would fail, and that the city in its entirety would be theirs, crumbled. If anything, it was evident that the western powers were more than ever committed to staying in Berlin.

By the beginning of May the Soviets had accepted the failure of the blockade and realized it had to be called off. The airlift—a staggering total of 276,926 flights, ferrying in more than 2,300,000 tons of supplies—had convinced Soviet leaders that, for the moment at least, they would have to tolerate a western presence in Berlin.

Nothing could disguise the fact that the Soviet Union had suffered an ignominious setback. The Soviets had been forced to concede that they were incapable of doing anything about the capitalist outpost being maintained in mocking style behind Communist lines. It was not a defeat the Kremlin found easy to digest.

Even worse, the Berlin blockade had accelerated the process the Soviet Union feared most, the establishment of a German nation it could not control. In the spring of 1949 the American, British, and French occupation zones of the country merged to form the Federal Republic of Germany—West Germany. Bonn was to be its temporary capital, substituting for Berlin until Germany could be reunited. In October of that year, five months after the blockade had been lifted, the Soviets turned their own zone of the country into the German Democratic Republic—East Germany. Germany was now two rival nations. And Berlin was on its way to becoming two different cities.

East Germany, under Communist rule and with East Berlin as its capital, did not blossom as confidently into existence as West Germany did. How could it when, as everyone in the East knew, life was easier and the rewards greater in the other part of their divided country?

To shield its people from the attractions of West Germany, the East German regime lowered an Iron Curtain along the 858-mile border between the two German states—barbed wire backed up with minefields and other deathstrips, guarded by armed patrols and scanned from manned watchtowers. Western newspapers and journals had long been prohibited in East Germany. To keep people from being led astray by information that still filtered through, the Communist press, radio, and television assured people that life in West Germany was disagreeable, hard, and pockmarked with perils.

Nevertheless, East German officials could not conceal the fact that living and working conditions in East Germany remained backward by comparison. Dislocations of the war were compounded by the postwar Soviet stripping of much of the country's industrial base. Machinery and sometimes whole factories had been dismantled and shipped to the Soviet Union. Misconceived or fumbling attempts to introduce socialist procedures in agriculture, manufacturing industries, housing construction, and the distribution of goods made things worse. The result was endless shortages and recurring bottlenecks. A cloud of discontent settled over East German workers and professionals. The Communist media drew a picture of a harmonious, joyful socialist utopia in the making, but East Germans abandoned their Democratic Republic and trekked to West Germany in great numbers. Virtually all of them decamped through four-power Berlin since the direct route westward had been blocked by the barrier planted between the two German nations.

Stumbling, fumbling its way, East Germany became a burden to the Soviet Union. The wartime hatred for Germans—all Germans[2]—that was still relentlessly harbored by Soviets added to the strain. The Berlin blockade, launched to give the East German Communist leadership a more solid footing, had been a fiasco, which did nothing to enhance that leadership's standing in the Kremlin. The ceaseless flow of East German refugees pouring through Berlin was evidence that the Communist regime in East Berlin was not only unable to cope with the problems it had inherited, but had produced new ones, albeit under Soviet supervision. What was more, the existence of a Communist East German state, whose people were portrayed in the West as practically enslaved, contributed to a fierce anti-Communism in West Germany. That infuriated the Soviets, who equated anti-Communism with fascism. It conjured up for them a picture of an aggressive, menacing West Germany. And that German nemesis was allied to the nuclear-armed United States whose designs and motives the Soviets had suspected even when they were fighting alongside them as allies against the Nazis.

The Kremlin began toying with a daring way of dealing with the problem. Perhaps agreeing to the reunification of Germany and end-

[2]Some Soviets preferred dealing with West Germans, who they did not have to pretend were comrades, to dealing with East Germans whose leaders paraded the myth that they had been liberated from the Nazis rather than vanquished by the Red Army. In East Berlin one day (early in 1961), while walking with a western correspondent, a Soviet diplomat stationed in East Berlin approached a car he had recently acquired for his personal use. When the correspondent admired the vehicle, a Mercedes, the Russian conceded it was not a bad machine. Then he snarled, "There is just one thing wrong with it," and aimed a kick at the East Berlin license plate affixed to its trunk.

ing the occupation of Berlin by all four powers would be the right move to make. The West Germans were clamoring for an end to the division of their country. If properly arranged, with firm guarantees that it would remain strictly neutral, a united Germany could serve a dual purpose. It would relieve Moscow of the East German embarrassment. More important, it would block West German involvement in any organized western military alliance.

Such a plan could provide the Soviets with even greater rewards. Sooner rather than later, it could lead to the promised withdrawal of American troops from the European continent. There would, however, be a price to be paid. East Germany, as a separate Communist state, would have to be jettisoned. Its Communist leaders would have to be abandoned to the rough-and-tumble of bourgeois democratic politics for which, in Berlin at least, they had shown themselves totally unqualified.

Most threatened by this kind of thinking in the Kremlin was Walter Ulbricht, the East German Communist leader. Ulbricht had been living dangerously for a long time. After having fled to France during the 1930s to escape the Nazis, he had gone to live in Moscow. He had managed there to survive Stalin's mindless purges during which a lot of German Communists who had taken refuge in the mecca of world Communism had been hauled away to oblivion for no reason they could understand. Most were billeted at Moscow's huge Hotel Lux where the evening raids by the NKVD (as the KGB was then known) and the unexplained disappearances of residents became terrifying facts of life about which no one dared speak and which no one dared question. People who had devoted their lives to the Communist cause—Hugo Eberlein, a founder of the German Communist party; Hans Kippenberger, head of the German Communist party's military wing; and Willy Leow, head of the German League of Communist War Veterans—were picked up, taken away, and never heard from again. Four members of the Politburo of the German Communist party in exile in Moscow—Hermann Remmele, Heinz Neumann, Fritz Schulte, and Hermann Schubert—and ten members of its central committee were among the victims, suddenly gone for good. Moscow turned out to be a dangerous place for German Communists. During the period of the Nazi–Soviet nonaggression pact, to their bewilderment and anguish, dozens of German Communists were handed over by the Soviets to the Gestapo from which they had fled, as a sign of Soviet goodwill. They were executed or sent to concentration camps, which usually amounted in the end to the same thing.

Ulbricht was spared such a fate. He survived the war years in the Soviet capital, returned to Germany with the Red Army after the war, and was installed as head of the civilian administration operating under Soviet supervision. With Soviet backing, he remained the dominant figure in the East German leadership despite continuing problems in the Soviet Zone and despite grumblings among some of his colleagues about the rigid policies he pursued. There was no reason to replace a man who was so reflexly submissive to Soviet wishes.

After Yugoslavia's Marshal Tito presumed to reject Soviet leadership in 1948, the Kremlin was reluctant to encourage feelings of independence in other Communist leaders. This was especially true in East Germany where some of Ulbricht's independent-minded critics were known to have questioned whether it was right for the Soviets to extract such huge reparations from a country they were supposed to have liberated. There were also some who had suggested at war's end that abortions be permitted for women raped by Soviet soldiers, when the Soviets stonily denied that such misbehavior was taking place. The matter had been raised at a meeting of Communist officials, but Ulbricht, warding off any hint of a suggestion of criticism of the Soviet liberators of East Germany, had quickly and angrily ruled, "There can be no question of it. I regard the discussion closed."

Even among the East German Communists who remained scrupulously submissive to Soviet rule, there were some who urged greater flexibility in policy making than Ulbricht, with his Stalinist training, was prepared to allow. They wanted a softer line to raise worker morale and stimulate economic recovery. Their views were shared by some leading figures in the Kremlin who blamed Ulbricht for the dismal contrast between West Germany's economic vitality and East Germany's difficulties. The Kremlin seriously considered changing the East German leadership and prepared to put the East German Communist leader out to pasture. Ironically, the failure of his policies saved him from being dumped.

In the spring of 1953, three months after Stalin died, East Berlin exploded. It was convulsed by the first major anti-Communist uprising in a country occupied by Soviet troops. On June 17, infuriated by newly promulgated increases in work norms and by the persisting failure of the Communists to improve their standards of living, thousands of East Berliners, led by disgruntled construction workers on the Stalinallee, went on strike and marched through the streets in protest against the regime. Ulbricht and the East German regime were jeered. Demands were made for the resignation of the government, for free elections, and—most daringly of all—for the return of thousands of German prisoners of war still held in the Soviet Union eight years after the war's end. Youths climbed to the top of the Brandenburg Gate, on the border between the Soviet and British sectors, and tore down the Communist flag. The protest was spontaneous, it was devastating, and—because it happened in Berlin—the Communist authorities were unable to conceal this violent spasm of discontent from the world.

The protests began in the Soviet Sector of Berlin, but demonstrations and strikes erupted all over East Germany in almost every major city and town. Hundreds of thousands of workers participated. Local security forces couldn't cope with the situation. In places, Vopos openly sympathized with the demonstrators. The Soviets, to their disgust, had to be called in by the badly shaken East German leaders. Soviet tanks were sent into the streets of East Berlin to teach the demonstrators revolutionary discipline. Before it was over, 246 East Berliners had been killed. All told, some 800 East Germans were reported killed throughout the Soviet Zone before calm was restored. Dozens were sentenced by Soviet military tribunals and East German kangaroo courts to be executed. East German Minister of Justice Max Fechner, who had been unwise enough to concede that the country's constitution guaranteed the right to strike, was arrested and imprisoned.

The Communists publicly maintained that the uprising was inspired by the West to sabotage East Germany's march to socialism and that the effort had failed. But the Kremlin could no longer entertain thoughts of replacing Ulbricht with a more flexible regime. To do so would have been a signal to disgruntled workers in the other Communist-controlled East European lands that public displays of dissatisfaction would not be futile. (Such trouble for the Soviet Union would come in due course anyway in Poland, Hungary, and Czechoslovakia.)

In Moscow the suggestion that East Germany might be abandoned by the Soviet Union so that a neutral united Germany might be created was hastily consigned to the garbage bin. In view of what had occurred, a move in that direction would have been an impermissible confession of Communist failure, with unpredictable consequences.

Though the uprisings were dismissed as having been instigated by western agents, both the Soviets and the Ulbricht regime had to face up to the continuing, indisputable evidence of popular discontent with prevailing conditions. Given no reason to expect changes for the better at home and tantalized by reports from friends and relatives in West Germany of the opportunities available there, a steady stream of refugees continued to flood westward through Berlin—118,000 in 1952; 306,000 in 1953, the year of the abortive East German uprising; 104,000 in 1954; 154,000 in 1955; 156,000 in 1956.

Passage through the four-power city was virtually unrestricted. Tens of thousands of East Berliners had jobs in West Berlin. Family links transcended sector borders; people living in one part of the city had relatives living in the other. People went back and forth all day without delay or difficulty. For people wanting to leave East Germany for good, Berlin was an open door. Departing East Germans who did not already live in East Berlin made their way there by train (a simple commuter trip), slipped into West Berlin, and then either settled there or, with help from the West German government, flew on to West Germany, where they were more than welcome because of the labor shortage.

By 1957 the relentless human leakage had so damagingly compounded an already serious labor shortage in the East that East German leaders listed a new offense in their criminal code—*Republikflucht* ("fleeing the republic"). It was punishable by imprisonment if the flight was foiled. But rarely was it foiled in Berlin. If simple discretion was practiced, departure was as simple as crossing the street or taking a train on the subway *(U-Bahn)* or elevated line *(S-Bahn)* to the next stop.

As the drain away of workers continued unabated, increasingly tough measures were introduced to make good lost production. Workers in mines and factories were urged to emulate heroes of labor who, for the glory of the Socialist Fatherland, were said to have fulfilled their work norms many times over. When this failed to draw the desired response, work discipline was enforced—and still more workers hurried westward through Berlin.

For the Soviets, West Berlin, and the escape route it provided for those who rejected the realities of Communist rule, was an insult and an embarrassment. The corrupting influences—the glitter, the western propaganda, the capitalist enticements—radiating through a city for which their troops had shed so much blood were doubly outrageous because they undermined Soviet plans to build a stable, reliable Communist nation in East Germany. That nation was meant to serve as a buffer for the rest of Communist East Europe against the military and economic threat a revenge-seeking West German state might one day pose. Instead, it was being humbled by the Berlin blot on the socialist landscape. Once more the Soviets decided that blot would have to be soaked up.

4
Ultimatums
and Departures

S OVIET Prime Minister Nikita Khrushchev, a shrewd, articulate man, habitually went far beyond official Kremlin policy in his public pronouncements. This ploy enabled him to seize an advantage if one existed or to back away without damage if it got him nowhere. His device was so well known, however, that not a great deal of attention was paid when, at a Moscow reception on November 10, 1958, Khrushchev took the opening step in the next Soviet campaign to boot the West out of Berlin. He declared that the time had come for the occupation of Germany to be ended. The time had come, he said, for the western powers to deal with the government of East Germany on all questions concerning Berlin, on whose territory the four-power city was situated. That the West did not recognize the East German regime, which claimed sovereignty over West Berlin, and did not intend to recognize it, was not a factor Khrushchev was prepared to take into account.

The statement by the Soviet leader was dismissed by the United States as just another fishing expedition. When questioned at a press conference, Secretary of State John Foster Dulles drawled, "The international Communist movement is disposed periodically to try to probe in different areas of the world to develop, if possible, weak spots." Dulles gave assurances that Moscow would find no weak spot in Berlin, and he forecast that its probing there would then cease.

However, two weeks later the Soviet foreign ministry turned Khrushchev's off-the-cuff remarks into a formal ultimatum. "It should be clear to anyone with common sense," said a message to the governments of the United States, Britain, and France, "that the Soviet Union cannot tolerate a situation in West Berlin that is detrimental to its lawful interests, its security, and the security of other Socialist countries." The Soviet foreign ministry demanded that the western powers remove their garrisons from the city. They were given six months to do so. If they did not get out, the Soviets would unilaterally sign a peace treaty with East Germany, formally bringing World War II to an end. That, they said, would eliminate any need for the continued occupation of Berlin, which would then become a "free city."

Moscow's call for a peace treaty was made repeatedly as the crisis built up. It sounded logical and innocent enough to people persuaded that its only purpose was to bring about an overdue formal conclusion to the war. But such a treaty would have had wider significance. If it had been implemented, it would have put an end to legal justification for the presence of the western garrisons in Berlin. It would have endangered the access routes from West Germany by which those garrisons were supplied and would have left West Berlin open to a Communist take-over. As a "free city" located within East Germany and shorn of Allied protection, West Berlin would not be "free" very long.

The Soviet ultimatum was backed by an implied threat. "Only madmen," it said, "can go to the length of unleashing another world war over the preservation of occupation privileges in West Berlin." But the message also unwittingly implied the converse—only madmen would unleash a world war to end the occupation. No matter how unconventional his behavior from time to time, Khrushchev was no madman. When the West responded to the Soviet ultimatum with firm assurances to West Berliners that they would not be abandoned to the Communists, the Soviets backed off. Harassment of the western access routes through East Germany to Berlin continued sporadically as the Soviets contemplated their next move. But they passed word along that they hadn't really meant to set a six-month deadline; it was only to stimulate four-power talks to find a Berlin solution—and that it did.

At the four-power foreign ministers conference duly held in

Geneva in the summer of 1959, the western powers hoped to defuse the situation before the climate of East–West relations was completely soured. But Soviet Foreign Minister Andrei Gromyko's stony-faced hard line indicated that the Soviets remained determined to terminate the western presence in Berlin. The gathering ended without agreement.

Nevertheless, the Soviets, their eyes focused as always on long-term results, were left with the impression that the West, alarmed by the danger of war, would give ground if Soviet pressure were maintained. If properly prodded, western officials would meet to discuss and debate how to save the world from catastrophe by making concessions. And few world leaders were more skilled than Nikita Khrushchev in sending westerners into a frenzy of hurried conferences and consultations to decipher the significance of his menacing, off-the-cuff pronouncements. Discussing Berlin with veteran American diplomat Averell Harriman, Khrushchev suddenly shouted at him, "If you want war, you can have it. But remember, it will be your war. Our rockets will fly automatically." Did he mean the Soviet Union was already on a war footing? Did he mean he would send those rockets off if he didn't get his way?

Khrushchev's visit to the United States late in the summer of 1959, during which he made repeated references to "peaceful coexistence," left a different impression. He conferred congenially with President Eisenhower at the Camp David presidential retreat in the mountains of Maryland, spoke to the American people on television, was fussed over in Hollywood, and visited a corn field in Iowa. The agreeable tone of his American tour and the cordiality shown by all concerned seemed to signal that peaceful coexistence was indeed possible and that some sort of mutually acceptable Berlin solution could be worked out. It was decided that the situation would be discussed the following spring at a four-power summit in Paris.

Khrushchev made it clear that he expected movement at the summit toward western diplomatic recognition of East Germany and the creation finally of "a normal situation" in Berlin. Eisenhower agreed that the situation in the city was "abnormal." Though it wasn't what the president intended, his comment seemed to imply that the Berlin situation needed changing and confirmed the belief of the Kremlin's America-watchers that the process of attrition was indeed working. It was only a matter of time and persistence before the "abnormality" of West Berlin would be rectified.

The Soviets weren't alone in believing that an American climb-down at the forthcoming summit was a distinct possibility. When, to keep the pot boiling, they resumed their public demands that the Berlin situation be "normalized" without delay, West German Chancellor Konrad Adenauer did not conceal his anxiety. Adenauer warned the White House that the United States would make an irredeemable mistake, with catastrophic consequences, if it permitted itself to be maneuvered by Khrushchev into negotiating over Berlin while ignoring the bigger problem of German reunification, in which the Soviets were no longer interested.[1] West Berlin Mayor Willy Brandt also feared that the West was tiring of the protracted Berlin hassle and might be preparing to succumb to Soviet perseverance.

Though reluctant to engage in a war of words prior to the summit conference, the White House and the State Department came to realize that a lot of people, including the Soviets, were getting the wrong impression. The record had to be set straight. As expressions of concern, both abroad and in the United States, accumulated about how things seemed to be drifting, the American government set about offering assurances that the United States would not be found wanting in defending the cause of freedom. In a speech carefully drafted so that no one would misunderstand, Under Secretary of State Douglas Dillon declared that "No nation could preserve its faith in collective security if we permitted the courageous people of West Berlin to be sold into slavery."

Washington recognized that West Berlin remained a militarily exposed diplomatic trouble spot, the place where the Soviet Union could stir the cauldron of mischief whenever it wished to subject the United States to pressure. Khrushchev knew that West Berlin was "the sore blister" on the American foot in Europe, to be stepped on "anytime we wanted to . . . make them feel pain." But recollections were dusted off in the White House of how Stalin's Berlin blockade had been foiled by American defiance when things had looked grim, and President Eisenhower, who had long been stung by criticism of

---

[1]Yugoslav Ambassador in Moscow Veljko Micunovic recounted a choice bit of Khrushchevian ribaldry on that point: "If you strip Adenauer naked," he quoted Khrushchev as saying, "and look at him from the rear, then you can see clearly that Germany is divided into two parts. But if you look at Adenauer from the front, then it is equally clear that his view of the German question never did stand up, doesn't stand up, and never will stand up."

his failure to capture the city during the war, served notice that the United States would not surrender "the rights we have" in Berlin. As the date for the summit conference in Paris approached and the American position on Berlin publicly hardened, the Soviets realized that their expectations of gaining western concessions there had no chance of being fulfilled.

Khrushchev was now under growing pressure at home. His colleagues in the Kremlin recognized that despite the hullabaloo over his visit to the United States and the forthcoming summit, no progress was being made over Berlin. The western garrisons showed no signs of packing up and pulling out. The only tangible result so far of Khrushchev's ultimatums and threats was a sizable increase in the number of refugees streaming out of East Germany and into West Berlin. East German Communist leaders were whining and moaning about the desperate situation in which they found them- selves and begging the Kremlin to do something about finally driving the West out of the city.

Khrushchev had expected to start that process at the Paris summit in the spring of 1960. But with the United States publicly standing firm over Berlin, the Soviet leader realized that he now had nothing to gain and much to lose from the forthcoming summit conclave. Soviet ambassadors in Washington, London, and Paris reported that the western powers would not be in a generous mood in Paris. Khrushchev would be left with the stark choice of emerging from the conference hall empty-handed or escalating the confronta- tion with the United States, with the danger that it might careen out of control. He had no wish to do either.

For a long time before they could do anything about it, the Soviets knew that high-altitude American reconnaissance planes were overflying Soviet territory. They had made no fuss about them because to do so would have been an embarrassing admission that the Americans possessed far more sophisticated technological wiz- ardry than they did and that they were helpless to do anything about it. But by the spring of 1960 they had developed the means to deal with those spy planes.

Just after dawn on May 1 an American U-2 reconnaissance plane equipped with highly sophisticated ground-scanning cameras took off from a base in Pakistan and entered Soviet air space at a height of more than sixty-five thousand feet. It was to cross the Soviet Union, making a photographic record of security installations, and land at a base in Norway.

But over the city of Sverdlovsk in the Ural Mountains the U-2 was hit by a ground-to-air missile and brought down. Its pilot, American CIA agent Francis Gary Powers, parachuted down and was captured alive. The incident gave Khrushchev the excuse he needed to break up a summit that clearly would earn him nothing but trouble.

Though Soviet espionage operations in the United States were extensive and highly successful, gaining for the Soviets—among other things—important information for the development of nuclear weapons, Khrushchev demanded on arriving in Paris that Eisenhower publicly apologize for the U-2 spy flight. He also insisted that the president dismiss all Americans who had been involved in the spying mission. As Khrushchev knew, the president could not, and would not, comply with those demands. When he did not, the Soviet leader announced that under the circumstances he could not possibly engage in the friendly talks that had been planned and stalked out of the conference.

As Henry Kissinger has said, "The Soviets choose when to be insulted." By seizing that moment to take offense, Khrushchev solved the immediate problem of extricating himself from the summit he no longer wanted. But it left the Berlin situation, which the Soviets still found intolerable, exactly where it had been earlier. It would not stay there very long.

By early 1960, with the crunch still to come, Berlin was already far more conspicuously bisected than any city had ever been before. It remained a single geographical entity, but it was evident even to a newcomer like myself that West Berlin was one place and East Berlin was unmistakably someplace else. And not only the ideological divide, and the Vopos at the Brandenburg Gate checking western cars going in and out of East Berlin for subversive literature and contraband, made them places apart.

West Berlin (the dividing lines between the three western sectors in it were, for all practical purposes, irrelevant) was a bustling place, very much on the move, very much up-to-date, even in its outcroppings of nostalgia here and there. Crossing into East Berlin was a curious experience in contrasts. Notwithstanding huge banners in public places exhorting the populace to work energetically to build socialism, it seemed drowsy and old fashioned, a touch Ruritanian with a big city overlay.

Whatever the overlay, Berlin was a metropolis, a sprawling urban realm with boulevards and backstreets, tenements and trolley tracks, parks and parades, museums and mass-circulation newspapers, with two rivers and a couple of canals meandering through it. A network of subway and elevated train lines covered the city, reaching out almost as far as the thick forests and sleepy lakes on its fringes.

Berlin had a magic that was distinctively its own. In no other city was the contest between two dynamic world philosophies so visibly played out. Berlin also had a fascinating history, part horrific, part seductive. During the hysterical obscenity of Nazi times, here was the heart of a gruesome political organism in which men who loved music and children and toyed with ethical vegetarianism had millions of people systematically tortured and slaughtered.

But before the Nazis had ruled Berlin and ultimately brought it destruction and ruin, the city had been something else altogether. If Paris had been the City of Light in the early part of the twentieth century, Berlin had been the City of Depth and Imagination. It was where Bertolt Brecht had contrived savage caricatures on the stage, where the Bauhaus architectural experimenters had uniquely blended art with craftmanship, where restless movements among artists had created one secession after another from the mainstream, where new ideas had been endlessly in the air, endlessly growing and changing.

In 1960 Berlin was living in the shadow of its past and, most pressingly, in the shadow of the facts that had made it two places instead of one. In the West the rubble of the war had been mostly cleared away or tucked out of sight, though the remains of the tower of the Kaiser Wilhelm Memorial Church was left standing as a bombed out ruin in the heart of the city, a reminder of what Hitler had inflicted on Germany. But consistent with its Bauhaus past, Berlin—at least its western sectors—had again become something of a playground for experimental architects. Some of the buildings that had sprung up where the wreckage of bombing and battle had lain were daring, almost whimsical in concept and design. Not for nothing did Berliners call the new Congress Hall "The Pregnant Oyster."

Whimsy could sometimes also be detected in the vision of a new breed of artists who had turned parts of the Kreuzberg district of West Berlin into a miniature Montparnasse. But they tended to be a serious lot, and their work generally ranged from sensitive artistic perception to deep-seated paranoia, the two not always being mutually exclusive. Variety was very much a part of the city. The grim, glum tenement-lined streets of Kreuzberg and Neukoelln, which had been recreated in many of the weird, surreal pre-Nazi Berlin movies, were, in mood, a world away from the serene atmosphere of the Dahlem district with its tidy single-family homes—as antiseptic a residential quarter as one could expect to find so close to the center of a big city anywhere—and even further remote from the rural tranquillity of Lubars, a country village tacked on to Berlin as if by mistake.

Downtown, the Kurfürstendamm ("Ku'damm"), West Berlin's main thoroughfare, which lit up brightly at night, offered still another aspect of this unique frontier outpost. This broad boulevard, Fifth Avenue (as it once was) and the Champs Élysées rolled into one, had been hewn out of countryside in the sixteenth century to provide local nabobs with a direct path to their hunting haunts in the Grunewald Forest. Now it was flanked part of the way, before its further reaches fizzled into urban ordinariness, by elegant shops flaunting the latest fashions and chic travel goods and by cafés blending old world *Gemütlichkeit* with state-of-the-art ambience. Kempinski's offered the finest ice cream sundaes that side of the Atlantic, though many who lounged in the sun on its Ku'damm patio indulged instead in lush slabs of hazelnut torte capped with outsized dollops of snowy, outrageously rich *Schlagsahne*. Down the street the dignified Kranzler Café had become a meeting place for people of discrimination who preferred to shun the more pedestrian, more up-to-date comforts of one of the first Hilton hotels in Europe, which had risen like a shrine to the American presence in Berlin.

West Berlin—with a population of a little more than two million, twice that of East Berlin—was an intricate complex of moods and images, sensations and experiences, all compounded by politically charged headlines and the presence of foreign soldiers. The troops—five thousand American, four thousand British, and two thousand French—were mostly out of sight except near their quarters. The huge American establishment around Clayallee was practically a village of its own, equipped with a sizable PX, bank, post office, cafeteria, dry cleaning service, movie house, a radio station, bus stops, and "No Littering" signs. The British and the French, with much smaller military, diplomatic, and support contingents, offered their personnel various home-style services as well, though on a more modest scale. Similarly, in the Karlshorst district of East Berlin, where the Soviet garrison and civilian personnel were quartered under tight security, Soviet personnel could buy goods with rubles and see Soviet movies.

There was mystery behind the scenes in both East and West Berlin. Foreign correspondents and their German stringers debated among themselves about which of their colleagues, and others they encountered in the course of the day's work, were "spooks" employed by one espionage organization or another, or perhaps by more than one. The intrigue added to the peculiar magic of the two-part metropolis, as did the Soviet military sedans that cruised daily through West Berlin, counterparts of the American, British, and French "flag-showing" vehicles that, by agreement, did the same in the Soviet Sector.

For a place that was supposed to be a showcase of western lifestyles, cultural life in West Berlin was suitably stimulating. Theater, opera, and concert halls drew large and appreciative audiences hungry especially for cultural imports from abroad. Aside from the aesthetic pleasures that might or might not be involved, these imports lent a cultural solidarity that eased the distinct sense of isolation felt in this frontier outpost of the western world.

It wasn't easy getting a ticket to the German-language rendition of *Kiss Me Kate* or even to the English-language production by a visiting American company of *The Miracle Worker.* To underscore the western presence, the Allies sponsored and ferried in a parade of visiting performers, entertainers, and educators, sometimes to the befuddlement of the Soviets in the East. After a performance by an American troupe of an experimental drama, agonizingly portraying the lives and ways of a group of wretched New York junkies, a Soviet diplomat who had been invited to the premiere confided that he was baffled by the American government's promotion of such a play since "no society in which such things not only happen but are also glorified can long survive." Movie houses, showing American, British,

French, and Italian as well as German films, were full on weekends and didn't do badly during the week either.

As befitted its cosmopolitan aspirations, West Berlin boasted nightclubs—"Charly's," "Cherchez la Femme," "Chez Nous"— that promised programs of entertainment by distinguished *artistes.* Prohibitively expensive by local standards, these tended at the time to be frequented mostly by visitors to the city or resident foreigners. For a convivial night out with friends, native Berliners preferred leisurely dining out, either in the *Gasthaus* around the corner where the *Goulaschsuppe* and *Sauerbraten* could generally be relied on or in such atmospheric city-center hangouts as Hartke's on Meineke-strasse where the house-made *Wursts* were highly commendable (and which served as regular venue for a lunchtime roundtable of American correspondents in Berlin). Generally, only foreigners and well heeled local professionals converged on such up-market estab-lishments as the Ritz, where the wild boar with *Spaetzle* was some-thing unique.

The Stachelschwein ("Porcupine"), a popular downtown caba-ret, had brought clever irreverence back to the Berlin stage, mocking all aspects of politics and society, though it generally found develop-ments in East Germany too easy a target. It was particularly biting about the unstoppable surge of West German consumerism that had swelled into West Berlin. Acquiring a television set and a washing machine had become the prime goal of many of the same people who had dug through the ruins of their city for a potato or a lump of coal a mere fifteen years before. While foreigners and less sophisticated natives might have considered Germany to be the setting of develop-ments affecting the fate of the world, performers at The Porcupine found the country vacuous and boring. Recalling the patriotic slogan "Think of Germany!" they sneered, "We do think of Germany. That's what puts us to sleep at night." And the audience roared with laughter.

West Berliners who could not fall asleep so easily could drop in on any of a handful of creepy all-night dives where the legendary degeneracy of 1920s Berlin was squalidly revived. At one establish-ment a swarthy, unhappy man with sleeked down hair, stripped to the waist, tried and mostly failed to whip a cigarette from the mouth of a worn, vastly bosomed blonde well past her prime, while people sitting at small tables drank an overpriced excuse for *Sekt,* maintained a mask of apathy, and barely managed meager applause when the cigarette was finally whipped to the ground. It was worthy of the scrutiny of scholars at the recently established Free University, which was already turning into one of central Europe's main centers of intellectual probing and controversy.

There were two or three shadowy dancehall pick-up joints, which tended to be packed on weekend nights, and the venerable "Resi" (situated a long time before in what was now East Berlin) where dance or table partners were contacted or mere flirtations conducted through table telephones.

But West Berlin was also very much an out-of-doors city. On weekend afternoons people flocked to the patios of mock rural tea houses in Berlin's leafy suburbs and sat nursing pastries and glasses of tea until they grew weary of defending them from the bees that buzzed around in great but harmless numbers. Sailboats drifted lazily across the Wannsee, and campers, pretending to be miles from civilization, pitched tents in the Grunewald Forest and lived in them for days, sometimes weeks on end. With springtime the fierce Siberian wind, which swept across Berlin in winter and could send thermometers plummeting to below the zero Fahrenheit mark, was forgotten. East Berlin, however, had been living with a Soviet import of a more pervasive kind since the end of World War II.

Someone entering East Berlin for the first time that spring of 1960 by driving from West Berlin through the Brandenburg Gate might easily have felt he was passing through that majestic portal into a realm of enigmatic dreams. Leading up from the gate, which was modeled on the Propylaea in Athens, was the broad avenue of Unter den Linden ("Under the Lime Trees"). Well before Nazi battalions had goosestepped along it, it had been the main thoroughfare of a proud metropolis. Heinrich Heine had lived here. Goethe had stayed here. Still an elegant boulevard, it was flanked part of the way by stately facades of bygone days or the stately remains of them.

But this famous street, once the center of greater Berlin, was virtually deserted. A few Vopos stood outside the new, huge Soviet embassy building, built on the site of the old Russian imperial embassy. Two or three pedestrians were in motion here and there. One or two cars crossed from side streets. But the driver new to the scene might have sensed at first that he was cruising through a void, backed by an imposing but desolate facade.

Further into East Berlin, along Friedrichstrasse and at Alexanderplatz, that desolate sensation was overcome. The stately architectural remains were no longer to be seen, but more people were there, going about their business. There was a different dimension of strangeness here. Unlike West Berlin, there seemed to be no bustle, no sense of time passing, no urgency. The urgent exhortations of the massive Communist street placards—BUILD THE SOCIALIST FA-THERLAND; FOR PEACE AND PROGRESS—were the only visible signs of direction, and they seemed ironic rather than purposeful. The atmosphere seemed very calm, aimless, relaxing.

That feeling was soon overlaid by another. There was a sense of poor-but-honest about the place that evoked sympathy and admiration. Men and women were dowdily attired but not undignified. The men, most clutching well-worn leather briefcases, wore dark-hued, rough woolen trousers and jackets, the jackets often slightly ill-fitting, the trousers usually baggy at the knees. Many of the women were in dresses or blouses and skirts they had apparently tailored themselves with some skill but not always with much flair for design or color sense. At first sight (and last) there was not much to disabuse an outsider of the belief that this was truly a place of straitened circumstances, as indeed it was.

Denied the kind of investment that was pouring into West Berlin from West Germany and western countries (the Soviets had taken out rather than put in), the Soviet Sector of the city was still dotted with countless mementoes of World War II. Even in the center of old Berlin, the precinct that had once been called Mitte ("The Middle"), rusting, twisted girders and rubble marked the spots where buildings had been bombed by American and British aircraft or battered by Soviet artillery more than a decade and a half before. Empty lots that had been cleared of rubble were overrun with weeds.

The East Berlin authorities had made a strenuous effort to deal with the serious housing shortage they had inherited from the war. But the new buildings they had constructed tended to be the humdrum, boxlike edifices with frontages of bathroom-yellow tile. It was the kind of structure that passed for modern housing wherever the Stalinist imagination and a shortage of resources, investment, and labor converged. Prewar edifices that still stood were more substantial in mood and feeling but were invariably pockmarked where bullets or shrapnel had left their mark.

The buildings along the mile-long Karl-Marx-Allee—as Stalin-allee had been renamed after Khrushchev had denounced the Soviet Union's wartime leader—were new, tall, glistening, and largely un-adorned with gimmicks. But they looked like magnified versions of Tinkertoy contrivances, minus the charm, minus the flair. To squeeze in as many accommodation units as possible, planners had decreed that the apartments in the new buildings be basic, often consisting of only one or two rooms with kitchen alcove and toilet. Under the circumstances, in some new buildings, bathtubs were deemed a luxury people could manage without. They could attend clean, accessible neighborhood public bathhouses.

The needs and wishes of East German consumers had to be sacrificed to the greater good. The country was desperate for export markets in which hard currency could be earned. As a consequence, not only bathtubs were hard to come by. Many types of manufac-tured goods were not released onto the domestic market, and those that were available were often made of poor material, shoddily manufactured and, to make matters worse, in short supply.

An East German who could afford a refrigerator had to spend a year working his way up the waiting list before he could buy one. There was a two-year wait for a washing machine. To own a car was a long-term ambition few could realize, no matter how hard they worked. At night, especially on weekends, traffic was sometimes heavy on main streets in Berlin Mitte. But virtually all the cars bore West Berlin license plates. At that stage people could drive in and out of East Berlin with a minimum of formalities.

Restaurants tended to be crowded at night, again mostly on weekends. But again, many of the diners were people from West Berlin—visiting family, taking in the opera or theater, taking advan-tage of the favorable exchange rate, or just slumming. The East Berliners found in the restaurants were generally more highly paid professionals, managers, specialists, and others who had few other places to spend their earnings unless they went over to West Berlin. But in the West their east marks were worth only one fifth of their face value, so spending sprees for East Berliners on the far side of the sector boundary were infrequent. East Berliners who did buy goods in the West had to expect to be confronted at sector crossings by East German customs police who confiscated appliances and other conspicuous items people tried to cart home.

But people with East Berlin identity cards were able to buy cut-rate theater, concert, and movie tickets in West Berlin with their east marks. They were not to be denied all the pleasures of this part of their city simply because they lived in the other part. In 1960, the year before the practice came to a sudden, enforced halt by the building of the Wall, ten million East Berliner admissions to movie houses in West Berlin were subsidized by the West German government. On weekends, while movie houses in East Berlin—strong on propaganda and/or culture—were half full, East Berliners jammed with West Berliners into those on the other side of the border to see the likes of Marilyn Monroe, Marlon Brando, and Brigitte Bardot.

There was, however, no cut rate on food in West Berlin for people from the Soviet Sector. So except for the occasional luxury —coffee or sometimes butter—East Berliners did their food shopping back east, which was usually a dreary experience. The smaller grocery stores were now marked by un-German signs of neglect. The shelves of what had been the proverbial shop-around-the-corner were half empty, and the fresh foods they displayed did not look overly appetizing. Other, newer, state-run stores were scrubbed spotless and displayed neat shelves lined with brightly labeled cans and bottles. But the canned beets from Bulgaria, canned pineapple from Cuba, bottled pickles from Poland, and such stuff seemed largely untouched. People emerged from those stores carrying small string sacks or those omnipresent briefcases into which only one or two purchased items had been squeezed.

There was enough food to go around if people weren't fussy. East Germany had traditionally been the breadbasket of all of Germany and much of the surrounding region. But hearty eating, suspended during the war and immediate postwar years, had not been revived here, except for those who could afford to patronize the Budapest, Warschau, or other upmarket restaurants.

Some foodstuffs were still rationed. The size of the ration depended on where a person lived—200 grams of butter per person per week in Frankfurt am Oder, 150 grams in Leipzig, only 90 grams in Potsdam. East German housewives complained that the different authorized grades of margarine they were offered were exactly the same, except for the different packaging that was supposed to distinguish the higher-price grades from those of inferior quality.

At butcher shops, more often than not, everything but sausage meat was sold out by mid-morning. Coffee, when it was available, cost four times what it cost in West Berlin. Despite all of this, people reflexly lined up outside food stores in the Soviet Sector when crates were unloaded in the odd chance that there might be something to help make a tasty meal. Mary Kellett-Long—a young Englishwoman who, with her husband, Adam Kellett-Long of the Reuters News Agency, lived in East Berlin at the time—vividly described the prevailing circumstances in her diary:

> I walked past the open door of a greengrocer's shop and saw a queue of about 25 people. My already well-trained nose smelt an air of expectancy among the patiently waiting people so I faithfully joined the queue only to find that when my goal was in sight, I had been waiting 20 minutes for nothing other than that, to Western ideas, very ordinary commodity of potatoes! It is incredible I am sure to an English or any other Western housewife to imagine standing in a long queue in the rain in order to be able to give your family potatoes for dinner, but it is not an out of the ordinary occurrence here in East Berlin. . . . Meat is rather limited and the most usually found sorts are pork and beef, although if you are lucky you may have the occasional treat of a piece of rather tough veal or a scraggy chicken or goose. . . . The English habit of having meat twice a day is regarded here with amazement. Butter at the moment is rationed to a half-pound per head per week. . . . East German margarine is, in my opinion, almost uneatable. We are back to the postwar habit of thinking whether we must keep the butter for when we have guests. Often too in the summer months, butter and milk are "off" before you have them home as very few shops have refrigerators. . . . The clothes for women can only be described as shapeless and the majority of East Berlin girls and young women owe their good shoes and short pleated skirts to the West Berlin shops being only too willing to take East Marks at the rate of 5:1 [rather than the artificial 1:1 rate insisted upon by the East German authorities]. Seamless stockings are also unobtainable here and the West Berlin shops must take more money from the East Berliners for stockings than for anything else. When buying shoes in West Berlin, the girls, women too, wear an old pair of shoes to go over in and leave them in the shop and come back wearing the new ones, in this way avoiding the eyes of the Customs men who are apt to pounce on people carrying bulky bags or parcels.

Life in East Berlin was, however, not without its compensations. Although only high-ranking party and government officials, senior managers of industrial enterprises, and some key professional personnel could command spacious, well-appointed accommodations, rents for everyone were very modest. Though there was no great choice or excitement in the variety of foods available in the stores, food prices, except for imported items, were kept very low by government decree.

For those repelled by the more hectic pace of life in the West, East Berlin had distinct attractions. But workers were required to attend regular indoctrination sessions and lectures at their factories and offices. They were also expected to turn out for frequent public demonstrations of support for the government, arranged by the party. Party membership or conspicuous cooperation with party cadre was the path to promotion and to better housing when it became available. But though a person could be jailed for open expressions of dissent from party policy, he could not be fired from his job.

The dismay of the Communists at their inability to control all of Berlin verged at times on hysteria. They called West Berlin a center of slanderous propaganda and psychological warfare against East Germany, which it was, though similar charges could be made about their activities against West Berlin and West Germany. They said that cheap novels and all sorts of militaristic and anti-Communist publications were brought by the planeload into West Berlin and then smuggled into the East. They charged that the movies, the press, television, and radio in the western sectors had been "enlisted for service in the cold war." They said that the authorities in West Berlin had resorted to devious means to damage the East German economy and keep the east mark at a low rate against the west mark. They claimed that more than ninety western espionage and intelligence agencies and organizations in West Berlin were engaged in trying to undermine the German Democratic Republic.[2]

[2]The Soviets were particularly well versed in Allied espionage operations as a result of the activities of George Blake. Blake had been deputy director of technical operations for the British MI-6 intelligence service in West Berlin before being arrested early in 1961 as a Soviet agent. He was convicted and sentenced to forty-two

Whatever its drawbacks as a place to live and work, East Berlin was an exciting place to visit. On various levels the contrast with West Berlin was fascinating. Opera there was superb, particularly at the revived Komishe Oper under the direction of Walter Felsenstein (who preferred to live in West Berlin, and was allowed to). The Berliner Ensemble Theater was still a shrine to the memory of Bertolt Brecht. Under the direction of Brecht's widow, Helene Weigel, it offered regular, entrancing revivals of *Galileo, Arturo Ui,* and Brecht's other dramatic masterpieces. The ancient Greek altar, set out in all its glory at the Pergamon Museum, was (and remains) a breathtaking vision. The outlying regions of East Berlin, endowed even more than those of West Berlin with forests, lakes, and bucolic patches, were excellent for excursions away from the urban swirl.

But East Berlin had no urban swirl. It seemed curiously provincial, an impression reinforced by its newspapers, mostly tiresome publications endlessly glutted with verbatim accounts of documents and speeches emanating from government or party sources in East Germany or other Communist countries. The effect was stultifying.

For a working correspondent from the West, dealing with the East German authorities in East Berlin was generally a frustrating waste of time. Their official spokesmen, usually hard to track down, rarely had anything to say that might make the effort to see them worthwhile. A visit to the House of Ministries could entail an hour's wait in the huge, eerily silent reception hall, and then earned you either regrets that the official you had come to see was unavailable or a paraphrased recital of a speech or document printed that morning in *Neues Deutschland,* the official party daily.

Contacting the Soviets in East Berlin was sometimes more rewarding, though it was startling to observe that a Soviet spokesman at the embassy, Ivan Shishkin by name, appeared to be such a lightweight. Judging from his attitudes and responses, Shishkin understood very little of the Berlin situation. It was remarkable that the Soviets could have put a man like that in so delicate a post. He was, of course, putting it on. He was actually a very high-ranking KGB official, one of the most senior Soviet intelligence officers in that part of the world, and someone who—it later became apparent—was very

---

years in prison because of the damage he had done to British intelligence efforts, but the KGB soon had him spirited from behind bars in England and got him safely to the Soviet Union.

keenly aware of just about everything happening in every corner of that schizophrenic metropolis.

Among other things, Shishkin and his colleagues must have reported back to Moscow that the promise the East German leaders had given five years earlier that East Germany would soon surpass West Germany economically was an absurd fantasy. The two parts of the German nation had been locked in competition for fifteen years and no one—not even dedicated Communists—could pretend that the East was anywhere near catching up with the West. If anything, as a place to live, the West was growing ever more attractive to people in the East. That wasn't merely a matter of opinion. It was a provable fact.

Bertolt Brecht was, of course, being ironic when, after Soviet tanks crushed the 1953 workers uprising, he suggested that if the East German regime could not gain the confidence of the people, it should dissolve the people and elect a new one. However, by the spring of 1961 it looked as though the East Germans were bent on dissolving themselves as a people.

In the period since the end of World War II in 1945, some four million of them had left East Germany, trekking westward. It was the most concentrated mass migration ever in a highly developed industrial society. Between 1949, when the German Democratic Republic was founded, and 1961, when the Wall was built, 2,800,000 people, one in every six, had abandoned East Germany for the West, a total greater than the remaining populations of the dozen largest East German cities.

The Soviet occupation of East Germany was partly responsible. People in that part of the country had long feared and mistrusted their Slavic neighbors to the east. Their folk literature was rich in tales and legends of heroic battles fought against them, even before Charlemagne ("Karl der Grosse") subdued the Slavs in eastern Germany in the eighth century and long before those "barbarians" were pushed back across the Oder River four centuries later. For many Germans the racial rantings of the Nazis, either evoking superstitious fear—Hitler once described them as frogs living in a swamp—or portraying Russians as subhuman creatures who slaughtered indiscriminately, raped, and looted, had turned those prejudices into almost pathological terror as the war ended and the Soviet armies advanced relentlessly. Some outnumbered and outgunned German army units had fought on fiercely to the end in the belief they would be slaughtered even if they surrendered. An epidemic of raping and looting by Soviet troops during the early days of their occupation of the Soviet Zone did nothing to alleviate German fears. Hundreds of thousands of people headed westward, seeking sanctuary from the end-of-war cruelties and from postwar hardships and austerity. Included among them were many who had been driven out of former German provinces that were "cleansed" of Germans and were annexed by Poland as compensation for Nazi atrocities and to make up for the Soviet annexation of a chunk of eastern Poland.

By 1961, though some Germans still pined for the return of the eastern provinces (a few still do), for practical purposes that transaction was past history. However, by then the westward migration across Germany was greater than before, amounting to a ceaseless cascade of refugees streaming away from the Soviets and their East German Communist subordinates. Individuals, married couples, whole families, groups of friends were on the move. Terror was no longer the reason for the continuing exodus, nor was the impetus even essentially political. As the years had passed, more and more people had simply grown fed up with the failure of the Soviet-sponsored government of East Germany to create for the people, or permit them to create for themselves, an acceptable standard of living and way of life.

Some workers were going over merely to sell their labor to a higher bidder. But many had grown weary of endless shortages and rationing, oppressive work conditions, unfulfilled promises by their leaders, police controls, and the snooping of *Obleute* ("party-appointed block wardens"). Workers were fed up with being herded to factory meetings after work hours to be harangued by party activists. They were tired of incessant, sometimes idiotic political hectoring. (Children in the city of Halle, for example, were warned that reading Mickey Mouse comics, available in German, could lead them astray.) They were soured by the general drabness of life in the Soviet Zone and the Soviet Sector of Berlin while their friends and relatives in West Germany and West Berlin were beginning to tap what seemed like the good life—spacious homes, cars, vacations abroad, career advancement. They were angered when threatened by party toughs for complaining that they hadn't seen an orange in weeks and that potatoes were harder to come by than they should have been. Farmers, many of whose families had claimed title to their patches of land for generations, were angry at being forced into agricultural collectives that, they muttered bitterly, were similar to atomic bombs in that they laid waste to the land.

The migrants came from all elements and strata of East German life and society. There were men and women, skilled and unskilled workers, agricultural laborers as well as farmers, scientists, professional people, academics, civil servants, writers, and artists. More than sixteen thousand of those who had fled were trained engineers. In one industrial plant the seventeen key engineers absconded, taking with them the plant's blueprints, either out of spite or to help them find good jobs in West Germany. There were more than five thousand doctors, dentists, and veterinarians among the refugees, including such senior men as the chief physician at Potsdam's St. Joseph's Hospital. The medical director of the surgical clinic at Leipzig University fled. The man appointed to succeed him followed shortly afterward.

Almost one thousand university professors and lecturers (including the entire law faculty of the University of Leipzig) joined the exodus, as did more than fifteen thousand high school and elementary school teachers and some thirty thousand students, many of them waiting to receive their graduation diplomas before departing. A West Berlin television executive says, out of his high school class of twenty-five in a small town outside Erfurt, twenty-two ultimately made their way to the West. More than half the refugees were under twenty-five years of age. Three out of four were younger than forty-five. These were the people the East German Communist leaders were counting on to build the first German socialist state. Older people, on state pensions, generally preferred not to shift to new surroundings so late in life.

The refugees came from all parts of East Germany—from near the new Polish border in the East and from within sight of the West German border in the West, from the countryside in Thuringia and Saxony and the shores of the Baltic Sea in Pomerania. They came from such industrial hubs as Karl Marx Stadt and Cottbus, from historic cultural centers like Dresden and Potsdam, and most of all from East Berlin itself.

A refugee did not have to fear that in abandoning his home in the East, he and his family might be stranded in strange surroundings without help, without resources, and without any way of knowing what awaited them. Refugee halfway houses had been established in West Berlin. Most refugees were accommodated at the huge barracks-like reception center at Marienfelde where people were fed (the United States Army chipped in up to twenty-five hundred field rations daily), processed, and sheltered (the British Army set up tents to house the overflow) before being flown out, if they wished, to West Germany—all at the expense of the West German government. After being interviewed and screened, which could take several days, they were assigned available seats on scheduled Pan American, British European Airways, and Air France flights, and extra flights were chartered when needed. Political refugees who had reason to fear for their personal safety in Berlin and unmarried young men who could be quickly slotted into jobs were flown out without delay. In West Germany the refugees were bussed to any of fifty regional reception centers where they were helped to find homes and suitable jobs.

The process was highly organized and very efficient. For people soured by increased work norms in the factories, the persistence of food rationing, and having to glance over their shoulders whenever uttering unauthorized opinions, it was exceedingly tempting. At the time people joked that the first three words an East German baby learned were "mama," "papa," and "Marienfelde."

At the refugee reception center, lines of refugees waited every day, often in the rain, to file indoors and be processed. Many were surprised at Marienfelde to meet friends, neighbors, or work mates from whom they had carefully concealed their own escape intentions and plans. In one case seven coal miners who worked in the same mine found themselves waiting on the same line, and none had known that any of the others were heading West.

Aside from the obvious general reasons why the refugees had pulled up roots and bolted, there was a variety of specific impulses that had propelled them westward. One man, ambitious for himself and his family, said they saw no future for themselves in East Germany. A woman feared that people would be given identity cards that would confine them to living, working, and traveling in certain restricted areas of the country, which, she understood, was the way the Soviets did things. One man had fled west because he had been instructed by the police to spy on another man who was believed to be contemplating departure.

Some had fled disagreeable work conditions. A car mechanic, for whom there were no cars to repair, had been dispatched to work instead on a collective farm. A farmer who had fled from such a farm spoke with derision of party functionaries put in charge who couldn't tell a hoe from a hockey stick and who were enraged when the farmers took seriously the promise that they would have to work only an eight-hour day once they had given up their private holdings. Some people said they had had enough of shortages, with soap unavailable one day, cheese the next, nails the third, sewing needles, light bulbs, fresh vegetables, sometimes even bread. One young man had left because, considered unreliable by the local police, he had been refused permission to buy a motorcycle with his savings.

But resettlement assistance was extended at Marienfelde only to those who said they were fleeing political persecution in the East. Those believed by the interviewers to have flimsy reasons for fleeing, or merely to be after a better job and higher pay, were not denied permission to stay in the West but were told they would have to fend for themselves. Though work was easy enough to come by in West Berlin and in West Germany, where a half million jobs were going begging, the refugee grapevine quickly spread word of what was required, and soon few people arriving at the reception center claimed to be seeking anything but political asylum.

The effect on the life and economy of East Germany of these mass departures was momentous. There was no telling who would be missing from work, and when. People left their jobs or offices after work one evening and, without offering hint or suggestion, simply did not show up the following morning, having gone west in between. Only the closest of intimates was trusted, and sometimes not even those. To give advance notice would have been an invitation to be hauled in by the police for questioning and worse. So no prior arrangements could be made for the work done by those departing to be taken on by others, even when those others might have been available, which increasingly they were not.

When a clutch of bus drivers employed by the public transport system of an East German city turned up at the Marienfelde center rather than at their depot one day, the city's bus schedule was thrown into chaos. The entire work force of a small rope-making factory went west en masse. People entered stores to find there was no one there to serve them. They went to offices to find that those with whom they had made appointments were no longer to be found.

Plumbers, carpenters, and other skilled workers were becoming vanishing species. A bottleneck caused by a missing assembly-line worker would be resolved with difficulty one morning only to recur the next morning when someone else failed to appear. People often didn't know whether to say good night or goodbye to their work mates and colleagues at the end of each work day.

More and more housewives were drawn into the labor market to fill the gaps left by the refugees. Day nurseries attended by elderly "grandmothers" were established at factories to care for their children during the work day. Shock brigades of women workers were formed to be shunted around where needed. Retired people were urged to return to part-time work. Full-time employees were asked to work longer hours. The five-day work week was dismissed by the East German authorities as a western conspiracy. These were desperate measures by which unskilled people often found themselves expected to handle skilled tasks. But those measures served only to complicate the situation. The long-term economic outlook appeared bleak to East German economic analysts, and totally unpredictable (in a country where everything was done by plan) unless the outflow of workers was halted.

But warnings, threats, and jail sentences handed out to would-be fugitives caught in the act had no noticeable effect on the numbers departing, except sometimes to increase those numbers. Included among the departees were men with criminal tendencies, work-shy individuals, and other antisocial elements. Local authorities welcomed their departure, but it was small compensation for the greater loss East Germany was suffering.

World attention focused on this extraordinary mass procession. Each new headlined departure—a distinguished jurist, a famous doctor, a colorful chimney sweep, a pair of honeymooners—seemed more embarrassing than the last, whether it was the disclosure that among the almost two hundred thousand refugees who had passed through the Marienfelde Reception Center in 1960 were four thousand card-carrying members of Walter Ulbricht's own Socialist Unity Party or the fact that the twenty-one-year-old statuesque blonde beauty who was crowned Miss Universe at Miami Beach in 1961 was an East German refugee.

Aside from the damage done to the country, and the fury of the Soviet Union at this humiliating spectacle, other East European Communist regimes protested that, though not in great numbers, they too were losing people through West Berlin. Communist bloc meetings and conferences held in East Berlin were attended by delegates from Poland, Bulgaria, Czechoslovakia, and the other Communist countries who otherwise rarely had access to the West. Several of those delegates had seized the opportunity to slip away into West Berlin and apply for political asylum. An American military officer, out shopping one afternoon, parked his car, identifiable from its American military-forces license plate, on the Ku'damm. When he returned, he found a high-ranking Hungarian official waiting for him to ask how he could make contact with American intelligence. It became a joke among western intelligence circles in West Berlin that the best way to make contact with would-be defectors from Eastern Europe was to park on the Ku'damm.

Then there were the *Grenzgängers* ("border crossers"). These were people who lived in East Berlin but had regular jobs in West Berlin to which they went every day. Some fifty thousand of these commuters were registered with the West Berlin authorities. Thousands more were unregistered. By choosing to work in West Berlin, the Grenzgängers deprived East Germany of their badly needed services and further contributed to the country's economic shambles. They were also an additional embarrassment to the Communist authorities, disregarding as they so blatantly did the urgings that the good people of the Socialist Fatherland should strive to build a socialist future.

There was, however, nothing ideological in their choice. The simple fact was they were better paid in the West than they would be in the East. They were also able to change some of their west-mark earnings into east marks at black-market rates (change booths were everywhere in downtown West Berlin), which meant that even the lower paid among them ended up with considerably more money at their disposal than their neighbors and friends who stayed at home and worked in the East.

A woman who cleaned offices in West Berlin might earn a standard wage for the job of 200 west marks a month. If she were registered as an East Berlin resident, she would get 40 percent of her wages in west marks, the rest in east marks. Her monthly 80 west marks could be exchanged at a currency exchange booth for 400 east marks, giving her a final salary of 520 east marks. That was a good deal more than even a skilled worker earned in the East. That skilled worker would be, of course, deeply offended and envious of the office cleaner. So would an office cleaner who worked in East Berlin and who had no opportunity of converting her meager earnings into a fat wad of cash.

These Grenzgängers were reviled in the East German media as freeloaders and swindlers and were often harassed by Vopos at the border crossings. Nor were they highly regarded by West Berliners who felt they were exploiting the situation in a not altogether wholesome fashion. Freedom of movement throughout Berlin was guaranteed by treaty, and the Grenzgängers had a legal right to do what they were doing. But, it was widely felt, there was something shabby in the currency exchange advantage that came with their situation and it would have been more appropriate for them to shift over to West Berlin bag and baggage, forsaking the cheaper housing and cheap groceries at their disposal at home in the Soviet Sector.

Nevertheless, these commuters contributed to the economic vigor of West Berlin. The border-crossing office cleaners, hotel housekeeping personnel, and sanitation workers served eminently useful functions. Even more useful were the engineers, mechanics, and other skilled personnel who crossed over each day, infuriating the Communist authorities who saw the border crossers not only as traitors but also as badly needed numbers extracted from East Germany's shrinking labor force. Despite pleas from Ulbricht, the Soviets declined to permit a crackdown on the Grenzgängers. They considered the problem peripheral to the bigger Berlin issues with which they would soon have to cope.

Following the collapse of the Paris summit conference in May 1960 over the U-2 incident Khrushchev was advised by his foreign ministry to play down the Berlin controversy until after the American elections in November of that year. He was told that to challenge the Americans before then would only induce the rival candidates, Richard Nixon and John Fitzgerald Kennedy, to outbid each other in taking vote-winning hard lines on Berlin from which they might not be able to disentangle themselves after the election. It was best to tone things down until a new man, with perhaps a new approach, had moved into the White House.

.   .   .

This waiting game was agonizing for East German leaders. Incapable of stemming the refugee tide themselves, unable to prod Moscow into the promised action of slamming the West Berlin escape hatch closed, they were faced with a collapse of morale in the Socialist Unity Party. Party cadre in the provinces, and in East Berlin itself, questioned how socialism could possibly be built without the people to build it and told of despair permeating party ranks. Party leaders and government officials felt obliged to make repeated public assertions that vigorous steps were about to be taken to guarantee the safety and well-being of the German Democratic Republic. They also tried repeatedly to impress the Soviets with the urgency of the situation.

They were not without advocates in the Soviet hierarchy. Just as there were people in Washington who were certain the Soviets were bluffing in their threats, there were people in Moscow who were convinced the United States would not risk a war over Berlin. And, like Khrushchev, they were outraged at the continued alien presence on what they held to be Communist territory.

In March 1961, as John F. Kennedy was settling in at the White House in Washington, a meeting of Warsaw Pact leaders was convened in Moscow at which the Berlin situation was closely reviewed. Despairing of any immediate Soviet move to give him control of the access routes between West Germany and West Berlin, Ulbricht revived a plan that had been on file since 1958 to end the refugee flow. It involved sealing the border between East Berlin and West Berlin. Barbed wire would be stretched between the Soviet and western sectors. The barrier would be heavily patrolled, and the few border points that remained open for pedestrian or vehicular traffic would be tightly controlled. Thus, Ulbricht said, would the imperialist efforts to destroy the first German workers state be thwarted, pending the signing of a peace treaty to end the occupation of West Berlin.

Ulbricht's plan aroused more anxiety than sympathy from his fellow Communist leaders. Some feared that ending the right of unrestricted passage throughout Berlin, a violation of four-power agreements, would entail a risk of war. Others said that the proposed barbed-wire barrier, in the middle of a big city, would be a poor advertisement for Communism. But they agreed that sooner or later, something had to be done about the refugees and that there would be no harm in preparing to take drastic steps, along the lines Ulbricht suggested, should the situation deteriorate further.

The task of laying the ground work for the building of what was to be the Berlin Wall fell to Erich Honecker, a resourceful Ulbricht protégé and SED Central Committee member (later to be East German leader and party chief himself). In deepest secrecy Honecker set to work gathering the staff and materials needed and making the plans that would be implemented on a hot summer's night five months later.

Khrushchev had raised no objection at the Warsaw Pact meeting to such preparations. But dividing Berlin was not his idea of an acceptable solution. He wanted the West out of the city, not quarantined within it. Arrangements were already in the works for a face-to-face meeting with the new American president, at which the Soviet leader intended to drive that point home and finally get the results he wanted.

5
Collision
in Vienna

THE spring of 1961 should have been a time of jubilation for John Kennedy. He had just become president of the United States, the youngest man and first Catholic ever to attain that office. But his triumph over Richard Nixon in the presidential elections had been very narrow. Of the sixty-nine million votes cast, his victory margin had been a mere one hundred thousand, which meant there were an awful lot of Americans still to be convinced that he was properly qualified to be the nation's leader.

Kennedy's youthfulness, good looks, articulateness, quick wit, and charm did much to persuade many skeptics that he might be worthy of the job. He had stirred patriotic pride when, in his January inauguration address, he had told the world, "Let every nation know . . . that we shall pay any price, bear any burden, meet any hardship, support any friend, oppose any foe to assure the survival and the success of liberty."

That was good old American "can do" talk, and the people loved it. But those brave inaugural words turned hollow and mocking when a mere ninety days later fourteen hundred anti-Castro Cubans, trained and supplied by the Central Intelligence Agency, were left to fend for themselves under withering gunfire on the Bay of Pigs beach in Cuba. Kennedy had been assured by the CIA that this bid to infiltrate men into Cuba to overthrow Castro and his Communist regime would succeed without recognizable direct American military intervention, and that assurance had not been challenged by the joint chiefs of staff. But after the Cuban rebels landed on the beach, it became apparent that the entire adventure, as planned, had been misconceived and doomed to failure from the very start. At that point Kennedy was asked to authorize direct intervention. It would have meant the United States openly joining in an armed invasion of a small country, an act that would have outraged world opinion and much public opinion in the United States as well. Furious, because he had been backed into a corner by his military and intelligence advisers, Kennedy refused. The American government could not be put in such a position. As a result the Cuban rebels were left to die on the beach or be captured by Castro's forces.

Though the operation had been approved and was well into its planning stage before he became president, and though he had relied on the judgment of his military and intelligence experts, Kennedy publicly accepted full responsibility for the fiasco. Privately he muttered to his intimates, "How could I have been so stupid to let them go ahead?" With good reason many people—abroad as well as at home, both hawks and doves—agreed that he had badly botched the first major challenge he had faced as president. Former Secretary of State Dean Acheson, who had been in Europe at the time, reported that America's allies, assessing Kennedy's performance in the Bay of Pigs affair, felt as if they had been "watching a gifted young amateur practice with a boomerang when they saw to their horror that he had knocked himself out." That "gifted young amateur" knew very well what impression he had made. It would color his response to the Berlin crisis that the Kremlin was brewing for him.

As a member of the Senate Foreign Affairs Committee, Kennedy had known even before he was elected president that Berlin meant trouble. He was well aware of the Khrushchev ultimatum and of the harassment of American convoys on the Berlin access routes. Shortly after he moved into the White House he had asked Acheson to undertake an up-to-date analysis of what was happening and likely to happen in the city, and to assess the views of America's allies. At first, however, neither Kennedy nor his chief aides devoted much attention to the subject. Although the Soviets continued to make noises about Berlin, they had blown hot and cold over the fate of the city for more than a decade, ever since the blockade, without posing any tangible threat there. More pressing matters concerned the president as he came to grips with foreign policy problems—Cuba, a Communist take-over bid in Laos, and possibilities for working out an East–West disarmament agreement.

All of these involved establishing an improved line of communications with the Kremlin. Kennedy did not for a moment believe that the Soviet Union's aspirations coincided with those of the United States. But he was convinced that friction between the two countries could be kept within manageable bounds if both better understood what the other was up to. As far as he was concerned, that was the purpose of the forthcoming summit meeting with Khrushchev at which he and the Soviet leader would size each other up and decide how to proceed.

The issue of Berlin undoubtedly would come up at the summit. Khrushchev had only recently sworn to "remove this splinter from the heart of Europe." The Soviet leader had issued such threats before, but Llewellyn Thompson, the American ambassador to Moscow, now believed a showdown over the city was likely later in the year. He thought it probably would come in the autumn after the West German elections, which the Soviets did not want to influence adversely by premature pressure. At least one White House adviser, Henry Owen, believed that "Of all the problems the Administration faces, Berlin seems . . . the most pregnant with disaster."

Accordingly, during the weeks before his departure for Europe, Kennedy had himself thoroughly briefed on Berlin as well as on other issues likely to come up at the summit. Trimming other activities and duties to a minimum, receiving only visitors he felt obliged to see, he pored over scores of intelligence reports. He studied position papers and minutes of previous meetings between Khrushchev and American dignitaries. He was provided with a thorough analysis of Khrushchev's personality and mannerisms. He was warned not to be rattled by the Soviet leader's unpredictability or his often unconventional behavior. He was told that it was not uncommon for Khrushchev to trade pleasantries, laughing and joking one instant, and then to erupt with furious accusations and outrageous demands the next. It could be unnerving and even intimidating for those not prepared for his more spectacular outbursts. Khrushchev was, after all, the man who—to the chagrin of the regular Soviet United Nations delegation—had taken off his shoe at a meeting of the United Nations General Assembly and banged it on the table to signify his disapproval of a speech being made from the rostrum.

Kennedy was advised to stand his ground on matters of policy without responding in kind to Khrushchev's sometimes genuine, sometimes fabricated explosions of anger. Veteran diplomatic trouble shooter Averell Harriman told the president that Khrushchev's style in negotiations was to go on the attack rather than to present his arguments in a reasoned fashion. It was a ploy, a negotiating device. Kennedy was urged by Harriman to rise above such provocations, to take things easy and enjoy himself.

It was easier to say than to do. After the mess that had been made of the Bay of Pigs episode, Kennedy knew well enough without prompting that a gut fighter like Khrushchev would use the summit encounter to test his firmness and resolve. The meeting would be a challenge, but the prospect did not faze him. Instead, he saw the Vienna summit as an opportunity to redeem himself after the Cuba fiasco and establish his credentials as an international statesman.

If the two-day encounter in Vienna at the beginning of June 1961 was to be a moment of truth for the American president, it was meant to be a moment of triumph for Nikita Khrushchev. By then the Soviet premier and chairman of the Communist party of the Soviet Union had been the dominant figure in the Kremlin for the better part of eight years. He was a crafty, intelligent man, profoundly patriotic, with an almost religious belief in the fundamental greatness of Mother Russia. The fact that the Soviet Union lagged far behind the United States in material living standards, technological innovation, and industrial efficiency deeply distressed him. He repeatedly promised that the Soviet Union would soon catch up and surpass the United States ("We will bury you!") and tried to do what he could to make good that promise. The Soviet leader was a devout Communist who believed in the historic inevitability of the collapse of capitalism and the triumph of communism. He was also, as Kennedy had been warned, impulsive, emotional, and mercurial.

Khrushchev's ascendancy had been marked by major achievements by the Soviet Union. It was first in space, having launched the pioneering earth-orbiting satellite in 1957. That same year the Soviets successfully tested an intercontinental ballistic missile and boasted they could now finally match America's ability to dispatch weapons of destruction to any corner of the globe. The Soviet Union's claim to superpower status had thus been authenticated. The Soviets did not, of course, reveal that they had far fewer of those missiles than the United States, but over the years they had so substantially increased their military might that Kennedy's misleading claim during the presidential election campaign that the Soviets had a missile lead over the United States did seem credible at the time.

The Soviet Union was still heavily burdened by economic troubles and travails. But most Soviet citizens, proud of their country's postwar achievements, believed that despite the denial of comforts and conveniences enjoyed by people in the West, their country was marching toward a sublime Communist future. Their access to information and informed opinion carefully controlled by the authorities, few Soviets doubted that Khrushchev was briskly shepherding them along that glory road.

Nevertheless, there were those in Moscow, and even in the Kremlin, who would not have mourned his passing from the scene. The military, ever jealous of its privileges, resented the nonnuclear military budget cuts the Soviet leader had made in order to earmark greater funds to stimulate the country's stagnating civilian economy. Colonel Oleg Penkovsky, a Soviet military intelligence officer spying in Moscow for the West, said, "All officers, especially marshals and generals, were quite unhappy when Khrushchev cut their pay and took away many of the privileges they had enjoyed under Stalin." He also slashed the pensions of retired senior officers.

Some Soviet officials, responsible for implementing government programs, resented Khrushchev's haphazard and unpredictable approach to problem solving. They were increasingly, if quietly, exasperated by not knowing what he was going to do next. In addition, old Bolsheviks, like Molotov and Kaganovich, and other senior figures Khrushchev had elbowed aside in his rise to power retained resentful cronies in the government and party machinery. Aware of these resentments, Khrushchev was continually playing factions off against each other. He strove to prevent his adversaries, who knew enough to keep their heads down, from becoming bolder and grouping together to lever him out of the way (as they finally managed to do three years later).

There was also the Stalin factor. The Soviet people still thought of Joseph Stalin as their wartime leader and hero. Many had been perplexed by Khrushchev's widely publicized exposure of Stalin's crimes against the Soviet people in 1956. That exposure also presented difficulties in Soviet-dominated East Europe where Communist leaders had obediently Stalinized their countries and then had felt obliged to de-Stalinize them.

The pace and direction of events in those countries were not always to Moscow's advantage, and not only in East Germany. The army had been needed to put down antigovernment riots in Poland. Still restive, the Polish people no longer bothered to conceal their anti-Soviet sentiments. Soviet forces had been needed to crush an anti-Communist uprising in Hungary. What was more, the sluggish economies of the East European countries were hardly testimony to the success of the socialist systems those countries had adopted, and unlike the United States, the Soviet Union was in no position to render them meaningful economic assistance.

Khrushchev had experienced setbacks in foreign affairs elsewhere as well. He badly needed a success to balance them off. The drive to spread Soviet influence around the world had bogged down. In the Middle East the United States was unquestionably the dominant big-power influence, with the Soviets reduced to looking on from the sidelines. Relations with Egypt were strained, and Iraq, ostensibly allied to the Soviets, was busily rounding up its Communists and executing them. Patrice Lumumba—the leader the Soviets had counted on to help spread Soviet influence in what had been the Belgian Congo, and in the rest of black Africa—had been murdered, and rivals with closer links to the western powers were in command.

These setbacks were dwarfed by a much more serious Kremlin foreign-policy concern. In the early 1960s the People's Republic of China, previously considered the Soviet Union's junior partner in the international revolutionary movement, featured far more prominently in Moscow's calculations than any of those other countries or regions. Chinese Communist leaders were presuming to challenge the Soviets for ideological leadership of the Communist world. From Peking came accusations that Khrushchev was a paper tiger, making growling noises but actually kowtowing to the evil Americans when the Soviets should be locked with them in a knock-down, drag-out struggle that would truly herald a worldwide Communist future. In East Berlin diplomats from Peking told frustrated East German

F. WILL

in blunder

rmans don't
er because I
e a right to
s wrong
ur powers'
ays later he
iving "an
erroneous

who did not
n't's mistake,
med it.
an unsym-
dy, who
the indis-

movement of people throughout Berlin, told New York
Times columnist James
Reston that East Germans
had had 15 years to flee to
the West. Reston wrote
that Kennedy "has talked
like Churchill but acted
like Chamberlain."

Clearly, there was a
causal connection between
Kennedy's horrible 1961 and
the Cold War's most perilous
moment — Khrushchev's
1962 gamble on putting

The Cold War ended 27
years later when the Iron
Curtain suddenly became
porous and the Wall crum-
bled. Tens of millions of
East Europeans might have
been spared those years of
tyranny, and the West might
have been spared considerable dangers and costs, if
Kennedy had not been com-
plicit in preventing the
unraveling of East Germany.

George F. Will is a columnist for

JIM NEWTON

Like Ike

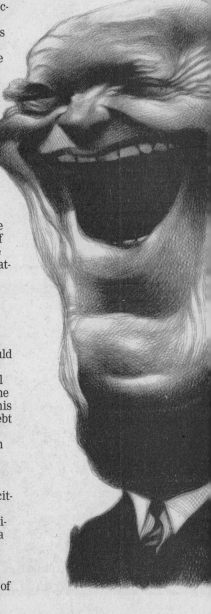

lions of Americans are out of work in part because employers are reluctant to add jobs while the government is so tumultuous. No business can be reassured by congressional leaders who fume and bicker as the government careens toward the precipice.

In fairness, Eisenhower's commitment to reducing tensions and seeking compromise did not always serve him or the country well.

In the area of civil rights, he sought in vain for a center, imagining falsely that those who demanded recognition of their rights were just as "extreme" as those who sought to suppress those rights. Indeed, Eisenhower himself acknowledged that there should be an exception for compromise in matters of moral urgency, though he unfortunately did not place civil rights in that category.

But even there, his legacy is instructive. For congressional Republicans who were willing to jeopardize America's credit, it would be a defense to say that they were taking a stand on a matter of moral principle. If so, however, what is the great principle that undergirded this fiasco? Is it immoral to raise the debt ceiling, as such stalwart conservatives as Ronald Reagan did so often without incident? Or is the moral abomination, perhaps, the willingness to raise taxes, as Obama had hoped to do as part of a larger deficit-reduction package?

The latter is closer to the Republican mark but it, too, falls apart as a moral proposition. John Podesta, who served as chief of staff in the Clinton White House, recently pointed out to the U.S. Conference of Mayors that the entire amount of revenue that Obama was seeking could have been achieved merely by allowing the Bush tax cuts to expire, returning the top marginal tax rate in the U.S. code from 35 percent to 39 percent, where it was when Clinton left office.

As Podesta noted, the country hardly seemed afflicted by the Clinton-era rates; the economy grew, many Americans prospered, and Clinton actually produced budget surpluses.

The Eisenhower prosper
and real, sustained incr
occurred in an era when
paid federal incor

income taxes of 91 percent on all

8/18/11

GEC

JFK's Be

WASHINGTON

Fifty years ago, a metaphor became concrete. Beginning on Aug. 13, 1961, along West Berlin's 27-mile border, the Iron Curtain became tangible in a wall of precast slabs of concrete. It came down 22 years ago. But the story of how it rose, as told in Frederick Kempe's book "Berlin 1961," compels an unflattering assessment of John Kennedy. His serial blunders that year made it the most incompetent first year of any presidency.

In a State of the Union address just 10 days after his inauguration, Kennedy seemed exhilarated by hysteria. He said that "in this brief 10-day period" he had been "staggered" by "the harsh enormity" of the "trials" ahead:

"Each day the crises multiply. Each day their solution grows more difficult. Each day we draw nearer the hour of maximum danger, as ... hostile forces grow stronger. ... Our analyses over the last 10 days make it clear that ... the tide of events has been running out."

Lunging for an equivalence with Lincoln, Kennedy said that during his term Americans would learn whether a nation such as ours "can endure."

Actually, since Election Day he had learned that the "missile gap" he had accused President Eisenhower of allowing to develop was fictitious. And the coming months of danger would begin with the staggering stupidity of the Bay of Pigs invasion. It convinced Nikita Khrushchev, the 67-year-old grandson of a serf and son of a coal miner, that Kennedy, the 43-year-old son of privilege, was too callow to recognize the invasion's risks and too weak to see it through.

Khrushchev knew the steady flow of East German refugees — 2 million in a decade, disproportionately the most educated, produc

Berlin was making that drab nation into a mendicant and revealing socialism's moral bankruptcy. But candidate Kennedy had said "our position in Europe" depends on not being "driven from Berlin" and "is worth a nuclear war."

On May 25, six weeks after Yuri Gagarin became the first man to orbit Earth, Kennedy said "extraordinary times" demanded a *second* State of the Union address. In it he proclaimed "the whole southern half of the globe" a "great battleground," especially emphasizing a place on few Americans' minds: Vietnam.

Then he flew to Vienna to meet Khrushchev — "Little Boy Blue meets Al Capone," a U.S. diplomat said.

Khrushchev treated Kennedy with brutal disdain. In excruciating pain from his ailing back — and pumped full of perhaps disorienting drugs by his disreputable doctor (who would lose his medical license in 1975) — Kennedy said it was the "worst thing in my life. He savaged me."

British Prime Minister Harold Macmillan said, "For the first time in his life, Kennedy met a man who was impervious to his charm." Kempe writes, "From that point forward Khrushchev would act more aggressively in the conviction that there would be little price to pay."

Kempe says that when Robert Kennedy met with his brother back in Washington, "Tears were running down the president's cheeks."

As Khrushchev turned up the temperature on Berlin, Kennedy studied the modalities of conducting a nuclear war. On July 25, he gave a nationally televised address, referring 17 times to the U.S. commitment to *West* Berlin, although the entire city was under four-power (U.S., Soviet, British, French) rule.

On July 30, in a Sunday morning television interview, Sen. William Fulbright

why the East
close their bo
think they h
close it." He
regarding the
rights and fiv
apologized fo
unfortunate a
impression."

But Kenne
dispute Fulb
evidently wel

After Aug.
pathetic Ken
never assert

JOSEPH SABINO MISTICK

The mayor & the guv

It was a small, kind gesture that harked back to more responsible times. When Gov. Tom Corbett announced at the Pittsburgh Zoo & PPG Aquarium that a new baby sea lion would be called Sophie, after former Pittsburgh Mayor Sophie Masloff, the two politicians hugged and smiled, clearly enjoying each other's company.

Not that Sophie would ever let the governor off the hook for any decision that would cut jobs or make it harder for kids to get an education and their families to find health care. She remains true to her beliefs. And Corbett, just as true to his, would never abandon his budget policies in these difficult fiscal times.

But, believe it or not, there was a time when politicians of opposite parties got along personally, disagreed fervently and publicly and compromised on the great issues of the day for the good of their constituents. And Corbett and Masloff have not changed since they met in the early 1990s.

Back then, Corbett was the Republican U.S. attorney and Masloff was the Democrat mayor of Pittsburgh. In a political arena long dominated by Democrats, in which the Republicans were making inroads, there was much political advantage to be gained by strident partisan attacks.

Instead, Corbett and Masloff identified problems on which they could collaborate and went to work. They fought the only war on drugs in this area that was won by the good guys.

McCLATCHY-TRIBUNE

— rapid economic growth ...ses in household income — ...e top bracket of taxpayers ... taxes of 91 percent.

Eisenhower believed in balanced

officials, watching the refugee numbers mount, how different the situation would be if the genuinely revolutionary Chinese rather than the craven Soviets were running the show.

Though infuriated, the Soviets sought to derive advantage from that kind of talk. Before the Sino–Soviet split flared into the open, an East European journalist, based in East Berlin and suspected of KGB links, confided practically in a whisper over lunch that the Americans were really lucky to have a chance to negotiate with the Soviets. The Soviets, he said, were reasonable people, unlike the Chinese who were reckless and who, with their hundreds of millions of people, really didn't care if a nuclear confrontation incinerated ten, twenty, thirty million or so. It soon became apparent that this "confidence" was being entrusted by East European journalists and officials to many western correspondents in Berlin and elsewhere. The Soviet campaign to negotiate the West out of Berlin was beginning in earnest.

Although Khrushchev hoped to benefit from western fears of a nuclear holocaust, he was, in fact, deeply worried that such a catastophe might take place. He fully understood the extent of the devastation that would result from a nuclear exchange. He said, and believed, that "after a nuclear war, the living would envy the dead."

Nevertheless, he had to do something about Berlin. There was great pressure on him to disprove Chinese charges of Soviet revolutionary impotence. More important, the western presence in Berlin, that gaping capitalist hole in Communist East Europe with the glitter, the glamor, and more pedestrian attractions, made a mockery of Soviet boasts about Communist achievements. As he declared repeatedly, dredging up one vivid metaphor after another, Berlin was for the Soviets "a bone stuck in the throat which had to be disgorged," "a splinter that had to be extricated," "a cancer that had to be carved out," "a rotten tooth that had to extracted." No matter what public pronouncements the Americans made about their rights in Berlin, Khrushchev headed for the summit in Vienna with the intention of finally forcing the United States to give way there.

He was confident he would succeed. He needed no position papers to persuade him that Kennedy lacked the determination and daring to face up to the Soviet Union in Soviet-dominated East Europe. He had heard the American president's defiant talk about paying any price and bearing any burden to assure the survival of liberty, but more convincingly, he had seen Kennedy in action at the

Bay of Pigs, and he was not impressed. Khrushchev had dealt with a comparable problem in a different way. Scorning outraged public opinion in the West and ignoring United Nations condemnation, he had, without qualms or hesitation, sent Soviet tanks in to crush the Hungarian anti-Communist uprising.

It seemed obvious to Khrushchev that Kennedy wasn't up to making that sort of decision. It seemed obvious to him that if the American president couldn't cope with trouble at his doorstep, he wasn't likely to be able to handle a showdown thousands of miles from home on territory ringed by twenty Soviet divisions. He had decided that "the time had come to lance the blister of West Berlin. It was no longer possible to avoid using the surgeon's knife, but we wanted to conduct the surgical operation under anesthesia." He was going to the Vienna meeting to administer the anesthetic in his own inimitable fashion.

Both Kennedy and Khrushchev were strong believers in the impact of their personalities. Each was convinced that direct contact between them would serve much more effectively than the efforts of intermediaries to eliminate the possibility of misunderstanding or miscalculation. Khrushchev wanted to terrify Kennedy into abandoning Berlin without too much hassle, something that could not be done by the Soviet ambassador in Washington. Kennedy wanted to make America's determination not to abandon Berlin absolutely clear in this face-to-face encounter, but he was more concerned about prospects for disarmament.

Not all of Kennedy's advisers liked the idea of the summit, which was not to have a carefully prepared agenda. Secretary of State Dean Rusk, a firm believer in low-key diplomacy, tended to be suspicious of top-level free-for-alls. Rusk felt that "though you really can't reach substantial agreement on big issues in just two days, Americans have been conditioned to expect a lot from summit meetings" by the legions of reporters who cover such events. Thirteen hundred newsmen and newswomen converged on Vienna for the Kennedy–Khrushchev encounter. Many were under pressure to justify their expensive presence in the Austrian capital by probing diligently behind bland official press handouts to file exciting headline stories.

The meeting—the first day at the American ambassador's Vienna residence, the second at the Soviet embassy—began satisfactorily enough with an exploratory exchange of views on fundamental differences. To Kennedy's surprise, Khrushchev quickly agreed that greater efforts should be made to arrange a ceasefire in Laos, where a civil war between Communist and non-Communist forces threatened to intensify. They then proceeded to a discussion of a possible nuclear test-ban treaty but found no common ground. However, it wasn't till the second day of the conference, when they turned to the Berlin situation, that it became apparent that Soviet public forecasts of an amicable, fruitful meeting had been decidedly premature. By the time they said their goodbyes, Khrushchev had convinced Kennedy that the world trembled on the brink of catastrophe.

After having kept Berlin quietly simmering on a back burner for so long—more than two years had passed since his 1958 ultimatum—Khrushchev seized the occasion to return to the offensive. It was ultimatum time once more. The Soviet leader told Kennedy that before the year was out, unless the West agreed to a German peace treaty, the Soviet Union would sign a separate peace treaty with East Germany that would "normalize" the situation in Berlin, leaving no reason for Allied garrisons to remain there. Khrushchev said West Berlin would have to be "strictly neutral": "It must not be tolerated . . . that West Berlin be used further as a base for provocative hostile activity against the USSR, the German Democratic Republic or any other state or that it continue to remain a dangerous seat of tension and international conflict."

Berlin would have to become a "free city." The western powers would no longer be able to cross East German territory without the permission of the East Germans. The Soviets would view any violation of East German sovereignty as an act of aggression, and the aggressor would be responsible for the consequences. The United States and the other western powers would have no special legal rights in West Berlin after the peace treaty had been signed.

The Americans, said Khrushchev, would have to realize that the situation was changed. Time had passed. The occupation days were gone forever. The United States would have to face up to realities. There was no going back. To salvage American prestige, Khrushchev allowed that the change in Berlin's status did not have to happen overnight; there could be a delay, but the two-thousand-word declaration of intent he handed Kennedy insisted, "It is necessary to establish deadlines. The Soviet government regards a period not exceeding six months as adequate."

Kennedy was caught completely off guard. His presummit briefings had led him to expect Khrushchev to press for renewed Berlin negotiations, not an American cave-in. But the president refused to be intimidated by the Soviet leader's uncompromising stance. He refused to accept that the Soviet Union could either make the changes it proposed or hand the United States such an ultimatum. He told the Soviet leader that the United States considered its national security directly linked to Berlin. He said that the United States was not in the city by courtesy of the Soviets. Stretching facts a bit, he told Khrushchev, "We fought our way there" and, through international agreement, had established the right to remain there until all parties concerned, including the United States, decided otherwise.

Khrushchev responded with a threat, a warning, and his six-month deadline. Dismissing western rights to the city as obsolete, he said the United States was crazy if it wanted to go to war over a patch of land in the middle of East Germany, and war, he told Kennedy, would result from any interference with the Soviet plan.

Despite his preliminary briefings, despite the warnings that Khrushchev talked tough, Kennedy had never imagined that even before he had properly settled in at the White House he would emerge from the Vienna meeting facing the possibility of a nuclear cataclysm. Never before had an American president been spoken to the way he had been that day. He was badly shaken by it. Khrushchev later recalled, "He looked not only anxious, but deeply upset. . . . I couldn't help feeling a bit sorry and somewhat upset myself. . . . But there was nothing I could do to help him. . . . Politics is a merciless business, but that realization didn't keep me from feeling sorry for Kennedy."

Both men looked somber and weary as they went through the ritual of shaking hands for the press photographers as Kennedy left the Soviet Embassy at the end of their meeting. The handshake was clipped and neither of them smiled. The final communiqué issued jointly by Kennedy's press secretary Pierre Salinger and Khrushchev's press secretary Mikhail Kharlamov revealed nothing of what had transpired between the two leaders. It said little more than that "The president and the chairman have agreed to maintain contact on all questions of interest to the two countries and for the whole world." Correspondents were told that the talks had been "frank [which sounded like trouble], courteous and wide-ranging."

Privately, Soviet spokesmen said that a great deal had been accomplished and the meeting had gone off very well. But correspondents probing for details were advised by White House spokesmen that it might be wise to refrain from optimistic speculation. Word spread that Austrian Foreign Minister Bruno Kreisky had told Khrushchev that Kennedy looked gloomy when seen off from Vienna. Only later was it learned that Kennedy, in a parting remark to Khrushchev, had said it looked like it was going to be a cold winter. As it happened, the political climate was to turn nasty well before winter set in.

John Kennedy returned to Washington from the Vienna meeting badly jolted by his encounter with the Soviet leader. While not wishing to underestimate the seriousness of the situation, American Ambassador to Russia Llewellyn Thompson, who had himself weathered a fair share of threats and scoldings in Moscow, tried to reassure him about Khrushchev's daunting fulminations. "About par for the course," he called them.

Though Kennedy was confident that he had stood up well enough to the demands and threats to which he had been exposed, he had been genuinely shocked by the Soviet leader's attempt to intimidate him. *The New York Times* correspondent James Reston, who saw Kennedy a few minutes after he and Khrushchev had taken leave of each other, described him as "shaken and angry."

British Prime Minister Harold Macmillan, whom the president stopped off to see in London on his way home from Vienna, said he "seemed rather stunned—baffled, would perhaps be fairer." Macmillan said that for Kennedy, meeting Khrushchev had been "rather like somebody meeting Napoleon at the height of his power for the first time."

Chicago Daily News correspondent Peter Lisagor, on the plane that had carried the president to Britain, said, "Kennedy looked kind of tired and a bit used up when we went into London." Columnist Joseph Alsop, who encountered the president on a social occasion during that London stopover, was baffled to hear him say, "I just want you to know, Joe, I don't care what happens. I won't give way,

I won't give up and I'll do whatever's necessary." Not privy to what had transpired at the summit, Alsop wasn't sure what Kennedy meant.

The president was stricken by a sense of foreboding, a fear that even if Khrushchev were bluffing, things could be slipping out of control. To his friend and appointments secretary Kenneth O'Donnell, he said somberly, "If we're going to have to start a nuclear war, we'll have to fix things so it will be started by the president of the United States and nobody else. Not by a trigger-happy sergeant on a truck convoy at a checkpoint in East Germany." In assuming the presidency a few months earlier, Kennedy had promised Americans they would cross a "New Frontier." Could that new frontier turn out to be one of war, death, grief, and destruction?

On his way back to Washington the president pored over notes on his exchanges with Khrushchev to find something he might have missed. Despite his aggressive manner and angry words, the Soviet leader might have dropped a hint that it was really only talk. But Kennedy could find no peg on which to hang that hope. The only relieving aspect of Khrushchev's Vienna warning was the indication that there was still time to prepare for whatever was in store.

Khrushchev had spoken of taking action by the end of the year if his demands were not met. That seemed to confirm Ambassador Thompson's view that Moscow would hold off on Berlin until after the German elections in September and perhaps might even wait until after the Soviet Communist party Congress in Moscow in October.

But October was only four months off. And even if the Soviets held off for the full six months of the deadline period Khrushchev had decreed, preparations for a confrontation could not be delayed. Up to that moment Berlin had not been a high-priority administration consideration. Now it was *the* priority consideration. What were the Pentagon and NATO doing to prepare for all eventualities? What shape was the West Berlin garrison in? What was the State Department's thinking on what would happen next? What about Dean Acheson's Berlin review? What did the American public know, think, and care about the situation?

First of all, Americans had to be prepared for any serious steps the administration would take to meet Khrushchev's challenge. At the same time the country had to be reassured that war was not imminent. The American press, fed only meager bits and pieces of hard fact by the White House and the State Department, was only beginning to appreciate the serious turn the situation had taken.

The Soviet news media were telling a different story. In an apparent bid to hold the United States responsible when things went publicly sour, the Soviets were reporting that the Vienna get-together had been a totally successful affair, "a good beginning," a step on the road to peace and international amity. They were publicly suggesting that the two leaders had not found Berlin a major cause for concern. Kennedy realized that the American public had to be told at once that whatever the Soviets were saying, there was little to cheer about.

His report to the nation on his Vienna encounter was drafted aboard the plane back to Washington and tidied up at the White House for delivery on the night of the president's return home. The report Kennedy gave to the American people did not tell the full story of what had taken place in Vienna, and what it did tell was not completely accurate. But there was no complacency to it:

> I will tell you now that it was a very sober two days. There was no discourtesy, no loss of temper, no threats or ultimatums by either side; no advantage or concession was either gained or given; no major decision was either achieved or pretended. . . . Our views contrasted sharply but at least we knew better at the end where we both stood. . . . At least the channels of communication were opened more fully. . . . I made it clear to Mr. Khrushchev that the security of western Europe, and therefore our own security, are deeply involved in our presence and our access right to West Berlin, that those rights are based on law and not on sufferance, and that we are determined to maintain those rights at any risk.

Kennedy made it clear with both words and tone that the Berlin situation could very well get worse before it got any better. At the same time, in view of war warnings that had emanated from Moscow prior to the summit, he sought to reassure the American public that guns were not about to go off, nor were bombs about to drop.

He did not broadcast the fact that senior personnel at the National Security Council, State Department, the Pentagon, and the CIA had been ordered to immerse themselves immediately in a detailed review of the Berlin situation and American policy with regard to it, and that he himself was about to do the same. The president had no intention of being caught unprepared or ill advised again. One Bay of Pigs was enough for him. He intended to remain on top of this brawl as it slithered inexorably toward a climax.

The strain of dealing with the Berlin situation did the president's health no good. Even before his Vienna excursion he had been troubled by renewed back pain. On a visit to Canada in May he had strained his back while ceremonially shifting three shovelsful of earth to plant a red oak in front of Government House in Ottawa. Despite the steel corset he donned, his back had continued to trouble him. He was in pain before his trip to Vienna. He was in pain during his meeting with Khrushchev. And as he began facing up to the difficult decisions he would have to make, decisions that he believed could affect the lives of millions of people and the security of the United States, that pain became more intense.

Under pressure from the White House press corps and to prepare the public for a planned public appearance of Kennedy on crutches, the president's physician, Dr. Janet Travell, was authorized to give the press details. She said the president's problem was lumbosacral strain, a common cause of low-back pain. It was revealed that he at times used crutches to relieve the pain while moving about when he was out of the public eye. He was also being treated with novocaine injections and hot packs.

To unwind, relax, and rest his back, Kennedy went off to Palm Beach, Florida, to stay at the home of longtime friend Charles Wrightsman. But the intense pain persisted, and a week after his return from Vienna orthopedic specialist Dr. Preston Wade was called in to examine the president and consult with Dr. Travell. Inevitably, stories of the president's earlier back problems were revived and publicized—a football injury while he was at Harvard, followed by the damage done to his back when his PT boat collided with a Japanese destroyer during World War II. It was also publicly revealed for the first time that seven years earlier, he had spent months in the hospital and had undergone a dangerous lumbar fusion operation during which a steel plate had been inserted in his spine. After he had almost died—last rites had, in fact, been administered—he underwent another operation to have it removed. Kennedy also suffered from a form of Addison's disease and lived much of his adult life believing it would kill him by the time he was forty-five. After his assassination in 1963, his brother Robert Kennedy said, "At least one half of the days he spent on this earth were days of intense physical pain."

Though Kennedy was used to pain, the American people weren't used to the image of their president on crutches, particularly one who had charmed so many voters with his youthful sprightliness. To ease his discomfort when he returned from Palm Beach to Washington, Kennedy had to be lifted to the hatch of the plane by a crane, which showed just how much he hurt. One Republican congressman moaned, "Now we've got an invalid for a president." But to the public at large, the Kennedy magic was still effective. When he got back to Washington and appeared in public, the youthful smile was back. So was the old spring in his step once he discarded the crutches.

But Berlin and the Khrushchev threats worried him deeply. Observers, like the Washington correspondent of the London *Times,* noted "a new heaviness of features evident under the outdoor tan." When dealing with other matters, many of them of crucial significance for his new administration, his mind would sometimes wander back to the Berlin conundrum. His repartee, once light and bantering, grew grimmer and sometimes took on a morbid air. When a friend jokingly told him he had decided to build a swimming pool for his home rather than a nuclear fallout shelter, the president told him he had made a mistake.

Having established greater rapport with the Washington press corps than any previous occupant of the White House—he was, in fact, the last president to be protected by the press—Kennedy grew increasingly sensitive to press criticism. He would sometimes telephone newsmen to tell them off because of what their newspapers or broadcast organizations had said about him or the administration, at one time calling a correspondent during dinner with the opening line, "I hear you bastards have done it to me again." No doubt his aching back contributed to his irritability. But the pressure of events as well as conflicting counsel from his advisers and from America's allies didn't make things easier.

Despite Kennedy's vow to remain firm over Berlin, the first public move by the West after the Vienna summit was to give ground. Five days after the president's we-will-stand-fast report to the nation, a meeting planned for Berlin of the upper house of the West German parliament was canceled. It was to have been a symbolic gathering and had been held regularly for years to demonstrate a communion between the people of West Berlin and West Germany.

But the Soviets and East Germans condemned it as a dangerous provocation, and Washington advised the West Germans to call it off.

Kennedy did not want to force the pace of events at this critical moment. He wanted to make certain that whatever was done would, as far as possible, be done under controlled conditions. He did not want to be distracted from the central issues by skirmishes over symbolic gestures. Though there was some grumbling about the cancellation in West Germany, the government in Bonn agreed that under the circumstances, it was probably the wise thing to do. The Soviets saw Kennedy's prudence in a different light. They believed it wasn't a matter of the president having a bad back; it was more a case of his having no backbone.

As summer drew on, the temperature, political as well as climatic, soared in Washington. The American capital was becoming a cauldron of ideas on how to approach the situation. There were hardliners, softliners, and in-betweeners of various persuasions. There were specialists disturbed that others did not grasp the fine points of the situation, and generalists who insisted the specialists were incapable of comprehending the bigger picture. There were some who, in the words of one old Washington hand, "had all the answers and couldn't be told anything" and others who lost themselves trying to tie together all available information. There were people who said, "Let's sit down and talk to the Russians about finding a way out of this mess." There were others who insisted that when the Soviets, as they had done, start giving the United States orders, there is nothing to talk about. And there were those who said, "Yes, let's talk to them, but just to string them along."

There was Kennedy's entourage of bright young advisers who had been through the Bay of Pigs debacle and were determined not to take another drubbing. There were some men in Congress who wanted to know why the United States had gotten into this mess to begin with when, as they believed, it did not touch on America's vital interests. And there were other congressmen who wanted to know who the hell the Soviets thought they were.

The members of the Berlin Mafia in Washington and at the American Mission in Berlin believed that any failure to confront the challenge to the freedom of the city would be disastrous for the

United States and the rest of the non-Communist world. It seemed to them that every time the United States and the Soviet Union had negotiated over Germany since the war, the United States had been outfoxed and had ended up with "less of the salami" than it had before. But there were others who held that the ideological village in which those honorary Berliners dwelled was not the global village and that it was worth surrendering a little piece of "the salami" to safeguard world peace.

Inevitably, one set of views was not always treated with respect or deference by those who espoused others. In addition, the White House contingent was convinced that the State Department was bogged down in bureaucratic hocus-pocus and that it had no idea of how to cope with the developing crisis. State Department people, meanwhile, thought little of the Kennedy entourage. One State Department analyst said, "They had such tremendous self-confidence, such élan, such assuredness and glamor—and then you'd discover they really didn't know the facts."

Some Soviet-affairs specialists in Washington, though believing they had no chance of getting a serious hearing in view of the crisis atmosphere following Kennedy's return from Vienna, were convinced the emergency was artificial. They tried as best they could to examine the situation through Soviet eyes and, sticking to the information provided by the various government intelligence services, believed that the Soviets were nowhere near as strong militarily as Khrushchev's bluster suggested they were. This, they maintained, had been confirmed by the failure of the Soviets to follow through on previous threats.

Even if this view had made its way through the cumbersome machinery by which government departments and agencies reported to the White House, Kennedy would not have been prepared to take heart from such assurances in the nuclear environment that prevailed. Besides, Llewellyn Thompson, America's man in Moscow, an astute and perceptive emissary, continued to pass word along that the Soviets were definitely getting ready to deal with the Berlin situation within the next few months. The president had to prepare for all eventualities.

With war or peace thought to be at stake, weighing the options and deciding on a course of action was a worrying as well as a complicated process. Having to gain agreement on a course of action from America's chief allies made it even more difficult, especially when those allies were represented by such formidable individuals as British Prime Minister Harold Macmillan, French President Charles De Gaulle, and West German Chancellor Konrad Adenauer.

Like Kennedy, all three men made appropriate noises about never abandoning West Berlin. But they were far from agreeing on how to respond to the Soviet challenge. It caused problems and prompted Kennedy to recall that Napoleon had once said that he won his battles because he fought them without allies.

De Gaulle's attitude was, ostensibly, the least complicated. He saw no reason to talk with the Soviets about Berlin. There was, he said, simply nothing to talk about. The Allies were asking nothing of the Soviets in Berlin, so any negotiations could only be based on the assumption that the West would concede something to them there—territory, rights, matters of principle, or all three. De Gaulle wasn't worried by Khrushchev's ultimatums. He had told the Soviet leader that if he signed the threatened separate peace treaty with East Germany, he would, in effect, only be signing the document with himself. It would be meaningless.

The French president believed that when the Soviets were prepared to talk seriously about the overall German problem, disarmament, and other key international issues in which the West had something to gain, there would be time enough to talk with them about Berlin also. But the Soviets had to know that if they interfered with western rights in the city, they risked war.

De Gaulle was, however, interested in more than merely keeping the Soviets at bay. He also objected to negotiations over Berlin because they would inevitably be dominated by the Americans and the Soviets and thus would perpetuate France's secondary status in international dealings. At the same time, with Britain linked in a "special relationship" with the Americans and West Germany not yet sitting at the top table, he saw the situation as offering France an opportunity to provide the distinctive, unsubmissive, "European" voice in the Berlin dispute.

All in all, De Gaulle was not greatly impressed with Kennedy or his policies. He thought of the American president as an attractive, reasonably clever young man but with a great deal still to learn. Kennedy, on the other hand, greatly respected De Gaulle personally, but the Americans were cynical about the French; strong on advice, they were weak on action.

Despite the hard line in Paris, the French Berlin garrison could hardly be considered an impressive example of western defiance. The men who manned it were mostly on rest-and-recuperation after harrowing duty in the French colony of Algeria, where France had been unsuccessfully trying to suppress a bloody, guerrilla-sparked national liberation movement. With the bulk of its army tied down in Algeria and the rest of it braced for an attempted coup by generals who were infuriated by De Gaulle's intention to grant Algeria independence, France could not be counted on to carry its share of the military burden if the Berlin situation turned critical. In the city itself, the French interpretation of western unity of action was so narrow that if the American or British commandants proposed even a ceremonial military display, the French commandant was required to clear it with his superiors in Paris before agreeing.

It was apparent that De Gaulle's dignified stand on principle could not be backed up with French deeds if deeds rather than lofty pronouncements became necessary. But Europe was center stage for this episode, and Kennedy knew he had to establish a strong measure of understanding among the Allies. His national security adviser, McGeorge Bundy, said, "It would not have been to our advantage to be seen to be going it alone. We didn't want to get in a position where an ally would go to the sidelines because we were being unresponsive."

To keep West Germany from just looking on from the sidelines was of particular concern at the White House and the State Department. A West Germany firmly linked to the western alliance was an indispensable element in America's vision of a strong, united Western Europe, capable of containing Soviet influence on the continent. Any suggestion, however fictitious, that the American government was toying with the possibility of making concessions in Berlin sent convulsive shudders through West Germany. Such concessions would have implied de facto recognition of the East German Communist state. They would have signaled American rejection of West German determination to reunify the divided country. The West Germans made sure that Washington, and every American with influential contacts in Washington, understood how strongly they felt about reunification. The message got through, as testified by a letter to Deputy National Security Adviser Walt Rostow from William Griffith of the Massachusetts Institute of Technology Center of International Studies:

> Once the United States is no longer felt by the West German population to be completely committed to reunification, the West Germans will become unreliable allies for us. . . . The stake here is what the Soviets have since 1945 tried to get: Germany. The Germans will be watching us to see if we display *any* sign of weakness, indecision or compromise. If we do, sooner or later, they will begin to look elsewhere.

If American interests were considered in isolation, there was no overriding reason why Washington, if able to extract a suitable quid pro quo, should not have agreed to the peace treaty the Soviets were demanding for Germany, provided West Berlin's special status was absolutely guaranteed and the access routes were kept open (which was not what the Kremlin had in mind). After all, the United States extended diplomatic recognition to such other Communist countries as Czechoslovakia and Hungary, where Soviet forces were also stationed, which were also completely under Soviet control, and whose systems were equally in conflict with western values. No less a cold warrior than the late Secretary of State John Foster Dulles had once suggested that East German guards on the access routes might be acceptable as "agents" of the Soviets.

But East Germany had to be kept in pariah status and denied western recognition. The West German government insisted upon it. It was the only way to keep alive the illusion, fundamental to West German policy at the time, that Germany would not be permanently divided into East and West, that the country would, in the not too distant future, be reunified in freedom and justice, and that the Communist East German state was only a temporary aberration, soon to tumble onto the scrap heap of history. For the United States, Britain, or France to have suggested otherwise, and to have recognized East Germany, might have busted the alliance wide open.

In effect, Adenauer claimed a veto over the western approach to the dispute. The American government could, of course, not concede as much. An acceptable explanation had to be tortuously fabricated and was contained in a National Security Council memorandum:

The fundamental reason why the United States, its allies and the uncommitted nations have refused to recognize the so-called "German Democratic Republic" is that there is in actuality no such country. The area called the "GDR" is in reality only one of the several occupation zones of Germany, the Soviet Zone, and it remains an inseparable part of Germany. According to the criteria of history, culture, language and tradition, according to the desire of the population and according to international agreements, Germany remains a single nation. . . . Recognition of the "GDR" by the United States in the face of the opposition of [West Germany] would jeopardize our entire postwar policy of integrating Germany with the West and utilizing its dynamism and military potential as an essential component of NATO.

That approach had to be ultimately futile, and not a few people in Washington were well aware of it. West Germany was bigger and economically stronger by far than East Germany, firmly in the western camp, and soon to have nuclear weapons based on its soil. It would inevitably dominate any reunified German nation. The threatening reappearance of such a nation in Central Europe would no longer have been tolerated by the Soviets. It would have amounted to a setback of unacceptable proportions, foretelling a collapse of the Soviet East European empire and convincing Soviets still mourning their war dead that their motherland was once more under threat from Germany. Soviet paranoia, acute at the best of times, would have known no limits.

As a Catholic Rhinelander, West German Chancellor Konrad Adenauer personally didn't care all that much for Prussian Protestant Berlin, or for Berliners. Once, when John Foster Dulles, secretary of state in the Eisenhower administration, in an effort to calm West German worries, had told Adenauer, "If the Soviets push us too far, we'll go to nuclear war," Adenauer's shocked response had been, *"Um Gottes willen, nicht über Berlin!"* ("For God's sake, not over Berlin!") Nor had he ever been much enamored of that part of his country that was now East Germany. He was once quoted as saying that when he crossed the Elbe, he felt like he was entering Asia. The chancellor was, nevertheless, committed to stitching his war-splintered country together and removing all parts of it from Soviet and Communist control. And that meant absolutely no concessions in Berlin.

As a shrewd statesman, the West German chancellor made

certain the American commitment to reunification was not only firm but publicly announced at every possible occasion. There had even been times when the American government had felt obliged to pressure the Olympic Committee to bar East German athletes from the Olympic games so as not to give implied recognition to their Communist state. One administration figure in Washington recalled, "if you left a declaration of commitment to the reunification of Germany out of any speech, you could count on the West Germans to come around and ask if you changed your policy." Another moaned at the time, "How many times do you have to tell them you love them?"

As the crisis developed, it apparently wasn't often enough to get the West German government to clarify what turned out to be its confusing attitudes on Berlin. It adopted a hard line on the defense of western rights in the city but recoiled at suggestions that the United States might use force to protect those rights. Having suffered greatly in the war, the West Germans feared their country might again become a battlefield. In addition, despite the absence of diplomatic relations, they had established lucrative trading relations with the East and were reluctant to see them jeopardized by an armed clash. To Washington, this quest after the best of both worlds was exasperating.

Britain's attitude toward Berlin and Germany was no less complicated. To placate the West Germans, the British Foreign Office offered ritual backing for German reunification, but the British would have been appalled if it actually happened. They were already struggling, with limited success, to compete industrially with booming West Germany. The idea of having to match the economic might of a united Germany was too dreadful to entertain.

Still recovering from the damage inflicted by the Germans in the war, the British were in the throes of their sixth serious economic crisis since war's end, while West Germany was on the threshold of its "economic miracle." The man in the street in London or Liverpool needed no persuasion not to want to go to war again for any reason, certainly not to rescue "bloody Germans."

Nevertheless, Britain was deeply committed to the unity of the western alliance, including West Germany. British leaders were not to be outdone in declaring their determination not to be forced out of Berlin. Foreign Secretary Lord Home announced that the West was perfectly content with the status quo and could not see any need for a change. Member of Parliament Desmond Donnelly told the House of Commons that "Britain's frontier was not at Dover but at the Brandenburg Gate."

But the British had no intention of fighting to defend that frontier. They did not think it would ever become necessary. They firmly believed that negotiations could produce a mutually accept- able solution if undertaken with a full appreciation of the horrific alternatives. They did not at all like some of the ideas being batted about in Washington, where Prime Minister Macmillan had sat in on a preliminary assessment of the situation by Dean Acheson earlier in the year. He had been horrified to hear the former secretary of state revive General Clay's old proposal that if necessary to break a Berlin blockade, tanks be sent storming down the autobahn through East Germany to West Berlin. He was apprehensive about what he called "the absurd contingency planning of the Americans." Not long before, he had told De Gaulle that "he could not conceive of himself taking the responsibility for leading his country to appalling destruction simply for the sake of the future . . . of a German city." The defense correspondent of the *Manchester Guardian* suggested that all West Berliners be evacuated to West Germany since their city was indefensible.

Under pressure from the United States, the British indicated they were prepared to agree to specific contingency plans to meet an increasingly likely Soviet squeeze on Berlin. But they wanted final decisions to be taken by the Allies in the light of circumstances prevailing when the crunch came. For American planners that wasn't at all satisfactory. It meant that if the crunch ever did come, there would be delays, hemmings and hawings, and lengthy consulta- tions, by the end of which the moment for effective action would have passed.

While the British thought there were too many trigger-happy people in Washington, the Americans thought that the British were sometimes remarkably naïve in assessing the factors that might influ- ence the Soviets. This view seemed to be confirmed when the London *Times* printed a letter to the editor at the height of the stampede suggesting that Khrushchev might have become so belligerent about West Berlin because he was not really aware of the flood of refugees who preferred not to live in East Germany. Perhaps, it was sug- gested, he might be discreetly informed so that he would better be able to appreciate its significance and revise his views accordingly.

.   .   .

The task of finding common ground for the Allies was intricate. American spokesmen gave assurances that the West would be united in facing the Berlin challenge. But one official conceded that those assurances sounded like the classic alibi of a public relations executive whose client runs into embarrassing trouble: "The situation is entirely normal—and we are doing everything we can to correct it."

6

The Crisis Looms

ON the morning of Monday, June 12, 1961, personnel from the East German government's press office in East Berlin, supplied with rolls of West German ten-*pfennig* coins, were dispatched across the sector border to make telephone calls. Telephonic communications between the two parts of the city having long before been severed by the Communists, they anchored themselves in street phone booths in West Berlin and passed along brief, precise messages to correspondents based there: "Press conference. Chairman of the State Council of the German Democratic Republic Ulbricht. House of Ministries. Thursday. Eleven o'clock. You are invited."

This was indeed to be a special occasion. Though never tongue-tied or hesitant, Ulbricht did not normally expose himself to the probings of people who might raise embarrassing questions. He saw no value in it. But now the East Germans were making a great effort to gain wide attention for what he would have to say. For the first time the West Berlin press corps was being invited to East Berlin practically en masse. On the morning of June 15 Vopos who were inspecting cars entering East Berlin had instructions not to be overly fastidious in checking western newsmen for forbidden newspapers they might happen to have in their possession on their way to Wilhelmstrasse and the press conference. Allowances were being made so as not to detract from the significance of the occasion.

An ornate banqueting hall, once used for special occasions by senior officers of Hermann Goering's *Luftwaffe* and now used largely for East German government receptions, was where Ulbricht was to meet the press. Long tables dotted with little bottles of mineral water and flat orange soda faced a raised rostrum in the hall. Well before the appointed time more than three hundred correspondents, many from the East German and other Communist press but at least half from western media, were in place and speculating among themselves about the momentous announcement Ulbricht would make that had prompted him to grace them with his imminent presence. It was hot in the hall, and the bottled mineral water was tepid.

Ulbricht, when he arrived, was flanked by other East German luminaries. Among them was Gerhard Eisler, the head of the country's broadcasting operations, who some years before had been convicted in the United States—where he had taken refuge during the Nazi years—of spying for the Soviet Union but had jumped bail and had been spirited out of the country aboard a Polish ship. However, Ulbricht, the durable Communist leader of East Germany, was undoubtedly the star attraction that morning. A short, tight-lipped, gray man with rimless glasses and a squeaky voice, he looked like an aging office manager who had nurtured his neatly trimmed goatee to lend his unprepossessing looks greater stature. It was not easy to imagine that this man had had the wit or good luck to survive the Stalin purges in Moscow or that he himself had purged a fair number of colleagues who had dared to take exception to his rigid Stalinist policies.

After an introductory statement that contained no startling revelations, Ulbricht threw the floor open to questions, during which it was presumed those revelations would be forthcoming. It was hard to believe the press conference had been called for no specific purpose. Asked about a suggestion an American senator had made the day before that all Berlin, rather than just the western sectors as the Communists proposed, be turned into a free city, Ulbricht replied that he had no idea who the good senator was. Asked about the future of West Berlin if he and the Soviets had their way, he said its "centers of espionage and subversion" would be put out of business. So would organizations involved in the "slave trade," including, presumably, the refugee reception center at Marienfelde. He said Tempelhof, still West Berlin's main airfield and likely to be used again for airlift purposes if it became necessary to break a land blockade, was a danger and nuisance in the center of a big city and probably would close itself down. He said all access routes to Berlin through East Germany would come under the control of the East German authorities by the end of the year, after the peace treaty was signed with the Soviet Union.

It made a lively story for the assembled correspondents, but there was nothing earth-shakingly new to any of this. Though some of the questions put to him were pointed and designed to draw blood, Ulbricht fielded them without difficulty, sometimes simply by uttering what everyone there knew to be nonsense—like blaming West German restrictions rather than his own decrees for the inability of East Germans to travel legally to the West.

He took two or three questions at a time when he preferred to divert attention from a point a questioner wanted to clarify, thus shrouding the issue in a haze of verbiage. The East German leader had clearly learned a good deal about oratorical ducking and weaving in his long years of ideological shadowboxing in the Communist movement. Not one of the reporters in attendance saw any special significance in his gratuitous declaration that "No one intends to build a Wall" in Berlin to stop the refugee exodus. He said it as if the very idea was absurd, and in fact, it did seem farfetched.

As the proceedings dragged on and the hall grew hotter, some correspondents began to wonder why, after shunning the western press for so long, the East German leader had bothered to make himself available that day. Whatever he had said could just as easily have appeared in that morning's *Neues Deutschland*—indeed, much of it was to be found in past issues of the newspaper. No one was given the opportunity to ask what it was all about. But Ulbricht's purpose later became apparent.

At that stage, despite his ultimatum to Kennedy, Nikita Khrushchev wasn't sure he wanted to risk a showdown by handing control of the western access routes to Berlin over to Ulbricht, with the implied backing of Soviet forces in East Germany. Nor had he yet decided, as an alternative, to let the East Germans take action to stop the refugees. Worried that the Americans might respond forcefully or that they might encourage and support a massive anti-Communist uprising among the disgruntled East German populace, Khrushchev was in no hurry to give Ulbricht, whom he neither liked nor trusted, what he wanted.

Now to the great annoyance of the Soviets, Ulbricht—fearing for the future of his regime, his personal position, and the country's economy—was trying to force the pace and thus preclude another Khrushchevian climb-down. He trusted Khrushchev no more than Khrushchev trusted him. He recalled how the Soviet leader had dodged a Berlin showdown the previous year, after he had walked out of the Paris summit conference, with the words, "We are realists. We shall never follow a reckless course."

Ulbricht could not act against the wishes of the Kremlin. But he could influence events and attitudes. His presence at the press conference and his comments implying that West Berlin would soon be his to do with as he pleased were calculated to raise the level of tension already building in the city, and they did. After his press conference performance was screened on East German television that night and splattered over the front pages of the East German press the following morning, the number of refugees checking in at the Marienfelde reception center rose sharply, as the East German leader must have known it would. And two days later, Willy Brandt, commemorating in West Berlin the anniversary of the 1953 East German uprising, responded to Ulbricht's rhetoric with rhetoric of his own. The West Berlin mayor vowed that the people of Berlin would never abandon the people of East Germany "who had the misfortune to find themselves living at the end of the war" in that part of the country.

A lot of people were getting very nervous. West German officials, fearful that Ulbricht's provocations might stampede the West into making concessions to the Soviet Union to head off an eruption of real trouble, tried to assure Washington that Khrushchev would never let East German hotheads drag him into a shooting war. Fearing that hotheads in the United States Army might perform that task, Senator Mike Mansfield of Montana called on President Kennedy to take steps to prevent such an occurrence:

> We should re-screen all ranking US military officers at home and abroad, connected with possible Berlin operations, to make certain that the men who will give significant commands are persons with the highest sense of professional responsibility, completely disciplined, not given to politics or public relations, and fully cognizant of the significance of subordinating, without question, military action to the dimensions of the diplomatic decisions of the president and the secretary of state.

Lyman Lemnitzer, chairman of the joint chiefs of staff, prepared a report at the request of the president on levels of military supplies for the American garrison in Berlin and stockpiles of essential supplies for the civilian population of West Berlin. The American troops, he reported, had 18-days worth of ammunition and combat rations. For civilians there were 440-days supply of solid fuels; 56-days supply of gasoline; 119-days supply of diesel oil; 180-days supply of dried milk, dehydrated potatoes, and butter fat; and 182-days of medical supplies. Recalling the Berlin blockade, the president told Lemnitzer that improvements should be made "immediately [for] the level reported for gasoline." It was best to be ready. Kennedy aide and speech writer Ted Sorensen came across a gloomy anecdote attributed to a Soviet wise man and found it worth noting down in the presidential-speech-material file: Asked whether there would be peace or war, the sage replied, "There will be no war—but it is doubtful that we shall survive the struggle for peace."

Like people in the West, Russians, virtually all of whom had lost kin in the war, had no wish to find their country pushed into a conflict over Berlin. Talk of such a possibility scared them. They were partially reassured on the day Ulbricht was trying to stir things up when Khrushchev, in a broadcast to the Soviet people, spoke admiringly of Kennedy. The Soviet leader repeated his warning that a peace treaty could no longer be put off and that the Soviet Union would meet force with force. But he assured his people that the American president was no nuclear lunatic. He said he had "formed the impression that [Kennedy] appreciates the great responsibility that rests with the governments of two such mighty states." The Soviet Union, Khrushchev stressed, wanted a peaceful settlement in Germany.

People in the United States weren't so sure. With a few isolated exceptions, defiance rather than caution became the keynote in Congress and in the press. There were calls for an American military buildup to meet the Soviet threat. There were predictions that Soviet bullying, if successful, would not stop at Berlin. A line would have to be drawn somewhere, and Berlin was as good a place as any.

Having failed to elicit the desired response one way, Khrushchev, beginning to flounder, tried another. On June 21, on the twentieth anniversary of the German invasion of the Soviet Union, he made a public appearance in Moscow in the uniform of a Soviet lieutenant general—the rank he had attained as a political commissar attached to the Red Army during the war—to show he was serious about Berlin. Defining western refusal to give way as a threat to the entire Communist world, he declared,

> The might of the Soviet Union and the entire socialist camp has grown to such an extent that if the western powers mobilized all their forces in a senseless attempt to destroy the achievements of the peoples of the socialist countries, this time too, they [like the Nazis] would suffer complete failure.

In case that message wasn't getting through to Washington, he announced that the Soviet Union was prepared to resume its testing of nuclear weapons, suspended three years earlier, if provoked by the West.

The Soviet leader could no longer step back or procrastinate. The pressure on him to act was too great—and not only from the deteriorating situation in East Germany and the relentless Chinese assault on Soviet leadership of the Communist world. Several of his Kremlin colleagues—notably Foreign Minister Andrei Gromyko and Deputy Prime Minister Frol Kozlov—were pressing him to get on with the job if Soviet credibility was not to be damaged. Ulbricht had convinced the leaders of some of the other East European Communist countries that if his regime went under, theirs were likely to be not far behind (Poland's western border was a mere sixty miles from Berlin). Those leaders brought their worries to the Kremlin too, as did the Soviet military, which was fed up with tolerating the presence of western garrisons in the middle of East Germany where, they believed, those garrisons had no right to be. Marshal Vassili Chuikov pressed that point home:

> The historic truth is that during the assault on Berlin there was not a single American, British or French armed soldier around it, except for the prisoners of war, whom we freed. Therefore the claims of the United States, British and French ruling circles to some kind of special rights in Berlin are entirely unfounded. They did not take it. They came there to fulfill the conditions of surrender, and on the basis of the fulfillment of these conditions, the occupation of Berlin should long since have ended.

At the Vienna summit Khrushchev had exploded angrily at Kennedy's concern about possible miscalculation leading to war. "All I ever hear from your people and your news correspondents and your friends in Europe and everyplace else," he said, "is that damned word, miscalculation! You ought to take that word and bury it . . . and never use it again. I am sick of it!"

Sick of it or not, the Soviet leader had to face up to the very real possibility that he had miscalculated. Kremlinologist Robert Slusser has pointed out, "An essential element in Soviet strategy was the calculation that it was an acceptable risk to raise the tension to a point where the West would yield to Soviet demands rather than accept the alternative of war." A Soviet spokesman in Moscow could complain plaintively to western newsmen, "We threaten you with a peace treaty while you threaten us with war." In Washington Soviet Ambassador Mikhail Menshikov could announce that he had reported back to Moscow that "the American people will not fight for Berlin." But Khrushchev's credibility depended on the West's yielding—and that was not happening. Despite Kennedy's warning in Vienna, it looked very much as though the Soviet leader had misjudged the situation and, in the process, had backed himself into a corner.

John Kennedy was in danger of doing the same. The magnitude of Khrushchev's dilemma did not filter through to Washington. The White House was under the impression that though the Soviet leader was subjected to various pressures, he knew pretty much how he intended to deal with them. The fact that Khrushchev had been making the same threat to the Berlin access routes for almost three years without doing anything about them seemed irrelevant.

His aching back still acting up, Kennedy remained immersed in Berlin, brooding over the need to take action that might lead to war and the danger of doing so before all options had been fully explored. At his command everything the Soviets said or did with regard to Berlin was reported to him. He didn't want to miss a thing.

An analysis written later of administration practices during the Berlin crisis stated,

> Washington bureaucrats will long remember John F. Kennedy as a president who stood them on their heads. Quick and impatient, he could not understand how Foggy Bottom and the Pentagon could take so long to answer his questions. . . . [He tried] to force them to adapt the decision-making process to a world in which the president might have only minutes to make up his mind whether to blow up half the northern hemisphere.

Kennedy's sense of urgency and his close scrutiny of Soviet pronouncements made the State Department apprehensive as well as uncomfortable. Officials who had been dealing with the Soviets for years feared that the president might lend exaggerated importance to the blustery utterances emanating from Moscow. It could produce a distorted American response—and some would later say that it did.

But Kennedy was not overly impressed with the views of the State Department, which he called "a bowl of jelly. It's got all those people over there who are constantly smiling." He instructed the department to tighten its procedures so that he would be better able to assess what was going on. He wanted communications with London, Paris, and Bonn streamlined to complement Allied consultations in Washington so that joint decisions could be more quickly reached. He wanted up-to-date assessments on nuances of moods in Moscow. He read all the cables from Berlin on what was happening there and on what people thought was happening.

He asked for reports on how and at what point the West could respond to any objectionable Soviet move with economic measures. He interrogated Treasury Department officials on how the crisis might affect the American domestic economy. He explored ways of seizing the propaganda advantage, so often forfeited by the United States through unimaginative planning. He ordered the Pentagon to report on how the armed forces should and could be beefed up to meet the crisis. He sought the views of foreign leaders who thought they were merely ceremonially calling on him at the White House while passing through Washington.

Secretary of the Interior Stewart Udall, trying in vain to see the president about long-planned domestic campaigns to be initiated under the much-touted New Frontier program, said, "He's imprisoned by Berlin. Ever since his Europe trip, Berlin has occupied him totally." Others who had come with Kennedy to Washington after his election with visions of revitalizing the United States under the new administration found him equally out of reach.

According to Ted Sorensen, for the next weeks and months the president

> saturated himself in the problem. He reviewed and revised the military contingency plans, the conventional force build-up, the diplomatic and propaganda initiatives, the budget changes and the plans for economic warfare. . . . He talked to Allied leaders, to Gromyko, and to the

Germans. He kept track of all the cables; he read transcripts of all the conferences.

On June 29 Dean Acheson, who had been asked to update his preliminary Berlin assessment, was summoned to the White House to present his report on Berlin to members of the National Security Council and key congressional figures. Incisive and unequivocal, Acheson's report and recommendations were sharply controversial. He maintained that Berlin was a problem only because the Soviets wanted to make it a problem, and they wanted to do so for several reasons. They wanted to neutralize Berlin as a first step toward an East German take-over. They wanted to weaken, if not break up, the western alliance. And they wanted to discredit the United States. Acheson said the Soviets believed that if they could force the United States to back down over Berlin, American prestige and influence would be diminished everywhere, giving the Soviet Union greater opportunity to extend their areas of influence and control.

The former secretary of state said the Soviets had to be shown that their assumptions about lack of American firmness and perseverance were dead wrong. He said the United States could threaten to take nuclear action to deter the Soviets but

> this I thought was not a real capability because it would not be believed. . . . It would be perfectly obvious to the Russians we didn't mean it. . . . A second step advocated . . . by some military people was a limited use of nuclear means—that is, to drop one bomb somewhere. I said this I thought was most unwise. If you drop one bomb, it wasn't a threat to drop that bomb—that was a drop—and once it happened, it either indicated that you were going to drop more, or you invited the other side to drop one back. This seemed to me to be irresponsible and not . . . adapted to the problem of Berlin.

But Acheson urged the president to make clear to the Soviets his determination not to be booted out of Berlin by declaring a national emergency and ordering a rapid buildup in American nuclear as well as conventional forces. He said American forces in Germany should immediately be reinforced by two or three divisions and military reserves in the United States should be increased by up to six divisions. Moscow would thus be signaled that if there were any backing down to do in this situation, it was up to the Soviets to do it. The Soviets would see that the American people were irrevocably committed to the freedom of West Berlin.

Acheson dusted off three "essentials," drawn up as far back as 1958 to meet the threat then by Khrushchev, to define American vital interests in Berlin: there must be no threat to the maintenance of the western garrisons; there must be no disruption of western air and surface access; and there must be no interference with the freedom and viability of West Berlin.

If the Soviets or East Germans attempted to interfere with American surface access to Berlin, Acheson said that a 1948-style airlift should be launched. If, as was possible, that airlift proved inadequate this time because of greater supply needs in Berlin and improved disruption methods at the disposal of the Soviets, two American armored divisions should be sent up the autobahn from West Germany to force open the ground access routes. It would show the Kremlin that the United States was prepared go all the way, to nuclear war if necessary, to protect its legal rights in Berlin.

Differences of views in Washington now became more than academic. Kennedy now had to fix on an American response to Khrushchev's challenge, and Acheson's hawkish recommendations served as a point of reference for the debate, which gathered momentum in the weeks ahead. Some people participating in that debate came to be known as hardliners and others as softliners, a development that softliners resented because it seemed to imply they were less determined than the hardliners to defend America's interests.

The hardline view was shared by, among others, Assistant Secretary of State Foy Kohler; the Germany desk at the State Department, Assistant Secretary of Defense Paul Nitze; and the Joint Chiefs of Staff at the Pentagon, Vice President Lyndon Johnson, whose influence in the White House was practically nonexistent, and influential columnist Joseph Alsop, who said that unless there were a strong American military response, the United States would lose the cold war. All agreed that failing to take a demonstratively strong stance on Berlin would undermine the confidence of the Allies in America's protective umbrella and that appearing overly anxious for negotiations would be a mistake.

With Moscow issuing demands, it was a potent argument. But despite their fears of projecting a wimpish image, the softliners who thought Acheson's proposals both excessive and dangerous appeared to outgun those who lined up behind it. They included such formidable personalities as Ambassador Llewellyn Thompson; trusted Kennedy Soviet affairs adviser Charles Bohlen; White House aide

Arthur Schlesinger, Jr.; Senate Foreign Relations Committee Chairman William Fulbright; syndicated columnist Walter Lippmann; and Henry Kissinger, who was at the time a Harvard professor called in as a White House consultant. Bohlen said, "It seemed to us to be too extreme to put the country . . . into full mobilization for a situation like Berlin. This would have created dislocations, repercussions within the country and all over the world. It would have been regarded as proof of American hysteria." Schlesinger called Acheson's proposals "bleak choices."

Thompson, summoned back from Moscow to participate in the debate, maintained that what Acheson suggested would be serious overreaction. He said it was stretching things to believe that the Soviets, in their Berlin probings, were bent on undermining the western alliance or doing damage to American prestige. Rather, he suggested, they were trying to consolidate their position in Eastern Europe. Like the other softliners, he agreed that Moscow's Berlin demands should be resisted and that an American military buildup was advisable. But, like the others, he said that buildup should be far more modest than Acheson had proposed and should be accompanied by an American diplomatic offensive. The object would be to show that America's objectives were peaceful while the Soviet Union's actions were reckless. Kissinger called for a "Kennedy Plan" for Central Europe to deal with an overall European settlement and not just Berlin. He said that if handled properly, an offer to talk with the Soviets would be seen as a sign of strength rather than weakness.

Compared with Acheson's detailed proposals, all of this was vague. Abram Chayes, the State Department's legal adviser, who also took exception to the hard line, recalled, "We didn't have the negotiating alternative very well worked out." He was assigned the task of rectifying that omission. As Chayes set to work on plotting how to approach negotiations with the Soviets on Berlin without damaging the West's position in the city or in Europe generally, Acheson told him, "Abe, you'll see. You try but you will find that it just won't write."

People at the Pentagon had, meantime, been doing some writing of their own, as was revealed in the July 3 issue of *Newsweek,* which appeared a month after the Vienna summit. What the magazine disclosed provoked considerable excitement in all the western capitals and in Moscow as well. It reported that the joint chiefs of staff had drawn up detailed proposals for steps to strengthen America's military capabilities. Included were plans for evacuating a quarter of a million American military dependents in Europe; dispatching forces to West Germany to reinforce the five divisions already there; deploying forces in Europe into combat-ready positions; calling up four National Guard divisions and stepping up the draft; and moving atomic weapons into "ready" positions, resuming atomic weapons tests, or demonstrating in other ways that the United States was ready to use such weapons.

Furious at the publicity it received and the anxiety it provoked at home and abroad, Kennedy immediately ordered the FBI to track down who leaked the report, which he had not yet officially received, much less approved. It turned out that *Newsweek*'s information was not altogether correct. But it was enough to provoke Nikita Khrushchev, who immediately set out to prove that he was as prepared to pick up the American gauntlet as the Americans appeared to be to throw it down. Barely had word reached Moscow when the Soviets began offering their response.

Khrushchev sought out British Ambassador Sir Frank Roberts at a reception and with characteristic vigor informed him that any western attempt to resist Soviet objectives in Berlin would prove futile. As waiters passed around them serving drinks, he told Sir Frank, "Let me tell you, I can destroy your country with six hydrogen bombs." A similar threat was directed at France, and West German Ambassador Hans Kroll was warned that his country could once again be reduced to rubble. In Washington Soviet Ambassador Mikhail Menshikov advised presidential assistant Walt Rostow that the United States shouldn't count on its allies, and certainly not on West Germany. "If the crisis intensified," he told Rostow, "the West Germans would leave West Germany as fast as the East Germans were leaving East Germany."

This calculated bid to frighten the Allies and sow discord among them was the stick segment of a double-pronged Soviet campaign. A carrot was being brandished as well. On July 5 presidential aide Arthur Schlesinger, Jr., known by the Soviets to be a softliner, received a visit from Georgi Kornienko, counsellor at the Soviet Embassy in Washington. Kornienko said he was puzzled by the American attitude on Berlin. He pointed out that Khrushchev had said that the Soviet Union would guarantee the independence of West Berlin after the withdrawal of the western garrisons. He couldn't understand why the United States did not believe the Soviets when they said they "wish to keep things as they are in West Berlin," with only minor changes to the overall context of the situation. When Schlesinger said experience had taught the United States that Soviet guarantees were meaningless, Kornienko said, "Why don't you propose your own guarantees? All we want to do is have a chance to discuss these things."

It appeared to Schlesinger, Kissinger, and others who favored exploratory talks with Moscow, that this might be a genuine Soviet attempt to veer off the collision course to which the two countries were about to commit themselves. They saw it also as an opportunity for the United States to seize the initiative and test Soviet sincerity without losing ground in the process. Fearing that Kennedy was being provoked by Khrushchev's belligerence, Schlesinger urged the president not to overreact or to react prematurely. He advised him to hold hard-line recommendations in reserve, invoking them only if other means failed to deter the Soviets:

> If Khrushchev restrains himself [after a peace treaty with East Germany] from immediate physical violation of West Berlin and keeps saying that he will consider any guarantees for the continued integrity of West Berlin that we wish to propose, we will be very much on the political defensive. We will seem rigid and warlike, while he will seem filled with sweet reason.

Schlesinger touched a raw nerve when he reminded the president that the Bay of Pigs muddle was caused by excessive concentration on operational matters and not enough on political implications. He warned that the hardliners in Washington—by asking, in effect, "Are you chicken or not?"—might be forcing Kennedy into the same position that he had been in at the time of the Bay of Pigs.

But that seemed to be the question Moscow was asking when Khrushchev announced a few days later that a much publicized program for cutting more than a million men from the Soviet armed forces was being scrapped and that the Soviet military budget was being increased by one third. Hardly had that news been digested when West German intelligence sources publicized reports that there were 67,500 Soviet and East German troops and 1,200 tanks in bases circling Berlin, within thirty miles of the city, "the greatest concentration of modern forces in the world." There was nothing new about those forces being there, but the atmosphere of crisis was noticeably thickening.

Time had come for the president to decide what to do. A nation-wide public opinion survey indicated that Americans were prepared to back a hard-line response. An opinion poll commissioned by *U.S. News and World Report* indicated that 71 percent of Americans were prepared to risk war to maintain Allied rights in Berlin; 15 percent wanted to avoid war if possible but wanted the government to remain firm; only 14 percent said they were willing to yield rather than fight for the defense of Berlin.

Kennedy was afraid of letting the situation develop its own momentum. He continued to immerse himself in the implications and consequences of all possible moves. He even asked to be briefed on operational details. On July 10 National Security Adviser McGeorge Bundy told Defense Secretary Robert McNamara that the president wanted to know,

> If we mobilize a million men, what would we do with them—how many would be combat troops, how many would be logistic support units, etc? Would we send the million to Europe, how long would it take to get them over, how many ships if by sea, how many would we plan to send by plane? How many days would it take to get all of them there? Where would they be positioned in Europe when they got there?

After the Bay of Pigs there was very little the president was willing to take on trust.

When he was secretary of state John Foster Dulles had devised a straightforward, uncomplicated system for coping with the threat of Soviet aggression. The United States had a far greater nuclear armory than the Soviet Union. If the Soviets engaged in any aggressive activity contrary to the interests of the United States, it would risk massive nuclear retaliation. If it did not do so, it would have nothing to worry about.

Kennedy realized even before he took office that the Dulles strategy was unrealistic, counterproductive, and restrictive. It was insanity to have a finger poised over the nuclear button in a world where all sorts of disagreeable things happened, or could happen, all the time. It was sheer nonsense to say, as former Joint Chiefs of Staff Chairman Admiral Arthur Radford was reported to have told West German politician Franz Joseph Strauss, that if a single Communist soldier crossed the border into West Germany, the United States would unleash its nuclear weapons against the Communist bloc. Nor, as the Berlin crisis developed, did it seem at all credible to threaten a potentially suicidal nuclear war if the Soviets or East Germans, to test Kennedy's resolve, blocked the autobahn with heavy trucks to stop an American convoy from getting through to Berlin.

Yet, as Robert McNamara had reported, the defense strategy that the administration had inherited required that any military challenge be almost immediately raised to the nuclear level. The United States did not have sufficient nonnuclear forces to cope on any other level. It was the big bang or nothing. More likely, it would be nothing, except the dispatch of diplomatic protests.

It meant that a conventional military buildup of some kind by the United States was inevitable if Kennedy's promise to stand by Berlin was to have any credibility. That presented an additional problem. America's European Allies appreciated the logic of the situation but were deeply suspicious of Washington's shift away from massive-retaliation philosophy. They feared that this shift would mean that Washington would react differently to Soviet military adventures in Europe. Washington might see Soviet probes as purely European affairs. The United States, as leader of the western alliance, would be involved in those affairs, but if they led to a war, it was to be confined to Europe, to be fought in Europe, and won or lost on European soil. The United States would commit troops but would not itself be in danger of being devastated. No longer would America's commitment be total, and in time, though Soviet expansionist objectives would be unchanged, American interest in European defense might fizzle out altogether.

Allied morale was a factor Kennedy had to take into account as he prepared his response to Khrushchev. And that response had to be forthcoming soon because, though the debate in Washington and the nuclear concerns of the Allies were very much offstage, the refugees in Berlin were in the spotlight. They were crossing into West Berlin in ever increasing numbers. East Germany was being drained. It was increasingly evident that whatever decision was finally made on trying to get negotiations going, and no matter how much time was left before Khrushchev's later-in-the-year deadline expired, something was going to happen very soon.

At times it seemed that Kennedy was more outraged by departmental dawdling within his administration than by anything the Soviets might be up to. At one point during the crisis he asked the State Department's Charles Bohlen, a trusted presidential adviser, "Chip, what's wrong with that God-damned department of yours? I can never get a quick answer, no matter what question I put to them."

He was infuriated when it took more than a month for him to receive a State Department draft of a reply to the formal Soviet ultimatum handed to him by Khrushchev in Vienna. That reply was supposed to inform the Soviets officially, for the first time in the current crisis, where the United States stood on Berlin. Not only did Kennedy have to wait so long to see that draft, but when it did finally come, he found nothing in it to reflect the vigor, vigilance, and imagination that he wanted his administration to display to Moscow. It stated the fundamental American position of firmness over Berlin, but Kennedy saw it as merely a dreary recital of old phrases and positions, devoid of spirit or freshness, limp, smothered in officialese. One Kennedy adviser called it "a scissors and paste job" derived from previous documents. The president was described as "totally disgusted with it."

The president considered both the delay and the draft document to be confirmation of his belief that the State Department was a bureaucratic swamp. But State Department people saw the episode differently. According to Martin Hillenbrand, head of the State Department's Germany desk at the time, a draft of a reply to the Soviet note had been sent to the White House fairly promptly. After ten days it was discovered that it had been lost there. The State Department sent over a new draft, and a White House official locked it up in a safe and then went on a two-week leave. The entire exhaustive, time-consuming process of consulting with the Allies over the document's contents was thus held up. State Department personnel who were involved were left with the impression that the people around the president found it more convenient to blame others for the delay than accept responsibility themselves.

As for the criticism of the style of the draft reply to the Soviet note, some people at the State Department thought bitterly that if the president had wanted a public relations presentation rather than a diplomatic *aide-mémoire,* he should have gone to a Madison Avenue public relations firm instead. Some of the president's advisers felt that in view of what they saw as the State Department's sluggish performance, that might not have been a bad idea.

A reply to the Soviet note was eventually patched together and sent off. However, the situation had gone past the stage of an exchange of diplomatic messages and very likely would have done so no matter how soon the president had received a satisfactory draft of the message. The stage was now set for terminal public pronouncements and for action. Both were forthcoming from Kennedy on July 25 in his television report to the nation on what the United States intended to do in response to the Soviet challenge.

Few presidents had ever worked harder to get the right words, establish the right mood, and send the right signals. No president had ever believed more was at stake. After having buried himself so exhaustively in the crisis, Kennedy retired, as usual on weekends, to Hyannis Port for the weekend of July 22 to 23. There he studied the latest position papers, gathered his thoughts, and painstakingly worked over the draft of the television speech. When he returned to Washington on Monday, the speech was chiseled into final shape by his aides for delivery that night.

The president's military adviser General Maxwell Taylor, McGeorge Bundy, Ted Sorensen, Edward R. Murrow, Dean Rusk, and others in the president's entourage went over it word by word. Phrases were altered to add or soften emphasis. Ideas were clarified so there would be no misunderstanding, either in Moscow or Germany. "With all changes and clearances completed and coordinated along the lines of the president's instructions," Sorensen recalled, "I took his reading copy for the 10 PM talk over to [him] around eight o'clock. I found the president sitting up in bed, a hot pad behind his back, scribbling out a personal note with which to close." Then he looked over the speech and got ready to go on nationwide television to tell the American people, the Soviet Union, and the world exactly where the United States stood:

> West Berlin has now become—as never before—the great testing place of Western courage and will. . . . It is as secure . . . as the rest of us —for we cannot separate its safety from our own. I hear it said that

West Berlin is militarily untenable. And so was Bastogne. And so, in
fact, was Stalingrad. Any dangerous spot is tenable if . . . brave men
will make it so. We do not want to fight—but we have fought before.
. . . We cannot and will not permit the Communists to drive us out
of Berlin, either gradually or by force. For the fulfillment of our pledge
to that city is essential to the morale and security of western Germany,
to the unity of western Europe, and to the faith of the entire world.
. . . We will at all times be ready to talk, if talk will help. But we must
also be ready to resist with force, if force is used upon us. . . . We seek
peace, but we shall not surrender.

Nor did Kennedy intend for the United States to be impotent
or unprepared if it was, in fact, to be put to the test. "I must
emphasize," he said, ". . . that the choice is not merely between
resistance and retreat, between atomic holocaust and surrender.
. . . We intend to have a wider choice than humiliation or all-out
nuclear action." He announced that he was asking Congress for an
additional three-and-a-quarter billion dollars for defense, much of it
to be spent on improved conventional weapons. There would be a 15
percent increase in the army's total strength with the draft call
sharply increased and certain reserve and national guard units ac-
tivated. Many ships and aircraft marked for mothballing were to be
retained for active service. Civil defense programs would be expanded and accelerated.

Kennedy had been careful to resist hard-line urgings that he
declare a national emergency or begin shipping troops to West Germany or West Berlin. He wanted to move one step at a time, in the
hope that the next step in the escalation of the crisis would prove
unnecessary. Khrushchev could turn off the heat in Germany just as
easily as he had turned it on, leaving the United States looking
foolish, or he could turn the heat on somewhere else in the world,
making it necessary to move troops sent to Europe around like
baggage.

Kennedy let the Soviets know the United States wasn't looking
for a fight and that he understood their concerns. He announced that
the United States was prepared to sit down and talk about the
situation, to resolve it with words rather than threats. Without speci-
fying, he spoke of his "readiness to remove any actual irritants in
West Berlin," and recognized "the Soviet Union's historical concerns about their security in central and eastern Europe." He was,
in effect, telling Khrushchev that it would be possible to discuss other

matters of great concern to Moscow, like western recognition of disputed postwar borders in East Europe and assurances that no efforts would be made to undermine the stability of East Germany. Rejecting warnings that the Soviets could not be trusted to negotiate in good faith, Kennedy was hoping he could reawaken momentum toward East–West talks both to defuse the immediate crisis and pave the way to more wide-reaching arrangements for peace and security in Europe.

But assurances from American spokesmen that the United States was willing to talk with the Soviets were by then commonplace. Inevitably, to the surprise and regret of White House adviser Arthur Schlesinger, Jr., and other softliners, the "let's talk" elements in the Kennedy speech were totally overshadowed by its defiance of Soviet demands. Kennedy had meant to leave Khrushchev an "out." But it turned out to be unmistakably a tough speech. Boiled down to essentials it said, "We want peace, and you can have it if you want it. But you're trying to push us around, and we're not going to let you do that."

In the closing personal note that Kennedy had added to the speech, he told the American people:

> When I ran for the presidency of the United States, I knew that this country faced serious challenges. But I could not realize, nor could any man realize who does not bear the burdens of this office, how heavy and constant would be those burdens. . . . In these days and weeks I ask for your help and your advice. . . . In meeting my responsibilities in these coming months as president, I need your good will, and your support and, above all, your prayers.

Within minutes telephone lines at the White House were jammed with callers promising all three. The following day, letters and telegrams of support began flooding in. Senators and congressmen of both parties praised the president. Former President Truman offered his congratulations, saying, "The Russians are the greatest bluffers in the history of the world. When their bluff is called, they quit."

Kennedy had touched a chord that warmed and excited the American imagination. Americans felt that the United States could now recover from the Bay of Pigs humiliation. They believed that the freedom of West Berlin was an honorable cause, in the best tradition of American crusades. No doubt the effect of the president's words was strengthened by his stirring delivery, sustained during the length of the speech despite the sweltering heat of the Oval Office, where air conditioning had been turned off to avoid affecting sound quality on television and radio.

Within days, army recruiting stations across the country reported a huge increase in enlistments. First reports from New York, Boston, Detroit, Chicago, and other cities told of an increase of two to three times the number of volunteers coming forward to sign up. Newspapers across the country acclaimed the president, saying he had cleared away any doubts the Soviets may have had about American determination. They pointed out, with many a historical reference, that the price of defending freedom is often steep.

This buoyancy was, however, not without outcroppings of concern and apprehension. Some newspapers urged that any remaining opportunities for negotiations should be carefully examined. Some people were concerned about what the increased defense spending would do to the budget deficit. Young men, parents, wives, and girlfriends jammed the telephone lines of Selective Service offices to find out exactly who would be called to the colors in defense of West Berlin and when the call was likely to come.

The announcement that civil-defense programs were being expanded provoked widespread anxiety. How could it be otherwise when the president had given the dubious assurance, "In the event of an attack, the lives of those families which are not hit in a nuclear blast and fire can still be saved—if they can be warned to take shelter and if that shelter is available. We owe that kind of insurance to our families—and to our country." Much thought had gone into civil defense, as shown in a National Security Council memorandum drawn up shortly before the president's speech:

> The suggested program . . . provided for fifty-four million shelter spaces in existing buildings at the end of four years. To achieve even five or six million of these by January 1, 1962 would require a large effort. . . . It is in order to remind ourselves that while five million shelter spaces are nothing, the lives that they might save in the event of general war represents not the difference between zero and five million casualties but more like the difference between forty million and thirty-five million.

After the Kennedy speech people beseiged local civil defense offices to inquire about measures to protect themselves in case of nuclear war. There was an overnight boom in the sale of prefabricated shelters. Houses up for sale that came equipped with nuclear fallout shelters were gobbled up at prices well above their market value. Stories appeared in newspapers and magazines of how to stock the family nuclear shelter properly with food and other essentials. A California scientist made a name for himself by announcing that his preference in supplies was for beer and encyclopedias. The Department of Agriculture drew up a food storage scheme that involved commandeering grain surpluses for emergency stockpiles to feed nuclear survivors.

Defense Secretary Robert McNamara was quoted as saying he doubted the value of any effort to evacuate Washington in case of a nuclear threat because warning time would be too brief to make a successful evacuation possible. Thinking along the same lines, Washington's Civil Defense Director, George R. Rodericks, announced plans to survey public and commercial buildings in the nation's capital to pinpoint suitable space for fallout shelters. New York's Mayor Robert Wagner commissioned a civil-defense "nuclear survey" of his city. Plans were made by the authorities of other major municipalities to do the same. Air-raid sirens were regularly tested in various places, with radio announcements beforehand so that people would not be alarmed. It was joked that the tricky Soviets would choose the appointed time for the test alert to launch a real attack.

One point of great significance in the Kennedy speech was carefully noted in the Kremlin but virtually overlooked in the American press. The president referred several times to America's commitment not to Berlin but to *West* Berlin. To members of the Berlin Mafia, this amounted to telling the Soviets that contrary to four-power agreements, they could do anything they pleased in the city so long as they left West Berlin alone.

James O'Donnell—who had worked as a newsman in Berlin during the Berlin blockade and after, and who, in 1961, was speech writer for Under Secretary of State George Ball in Washington—was shown a near-final draft of the speech by Ted Sorensen on July 25, prior to its delivery. Kennedy, whom O'Donnell had known for many years, apparently had told Sorensen to let him see it to show him that contrary to rumors circulating among some insiders, the president was not of the SLOB (Soft Line On Berlin) persuasion. A charter member of the Berlin Mafia, O'Donnell immediately spotted the distinction made between Berlin and West Berlin. He told Sorensen, "Ted, if you want to make that speech perfect, take the word West out from in front of Berlin." He pointed out that it was practically an invitation for the Soviets to tighten their control over East Berlin, effectively ending the city's four-power status.

Sorensen flatly dismissed O'Donnell's objection. He told him that the Soviets had exercised control over their sector of the city for many years, no matter what the four-power agreements said. Besides, he said, "this speech has been churned through the mills of six branches of government. We have had copies back and forth for ten days. This is the final version. This is the policy line. This is it."

Karl Mautner, who had been stationed at the American Mission in Berlin some years before and who was now at Intelligence and Research (INR) at the State Department, was among those badly shaken by Kennedy's reference only to West Berlin. "There was," Mautner said, "an 'Oh my God!' feeling. We knew immediately what it meant. But the White House didn't know. Even if we felt our commitment was only to West Berlin, we shouldn't have said so openly. We were undercutting our own position."

National Security Adviser McGeorge Bundy, who was intimately involved in drawing up the final version of the speech, says he cannot recall anyone objecting prior to the speech or saying that the specific reference to *West* Berlin might be construed as Kennedy's announcing he didn't care what happened to *East* Berlin. But, says Bundy, even if someone had said it then, his impression is that the president would have replied, "It's West Berlin I want to talk about."

It was true that all of Berlin came under the four-power agreements. But, as Sorensen had told O'Donnell, the fact was that the Soviets and the East German Communists had long been doing whatever they liked in East Berlin. They had blocked off crossing points whenever they wished, interfered with cross-city traffic, and arrested and imprisoned people—some of whom disappeared forever —without what westerners would consider reasonable cause or due process. The only reaction from the western powers to these violations of four-power agreements was to file routine protests with the Soviet commandant in East Berlin.

The theory of joint control was there. In practice the western powers had less influence over what transpired in East Berlin than the Soviets had in West Berlin. Although the Soviets permitted the East German Communists to designate East Berlin as the capital of East Germany, no one dared arouse Soviet fury by suggesting that West Berlin would, in the foreseeable future, be the capital of West Germany (which was improbable anyway because of the distance between the two). Although troops and military vehicles of the East German army were, in violation of agreements, to be seen in East Berlin by permission of the Soviets, it would have been unthinkable to station West German troops in West Berlin.

These restraints were self-imposed by the western powers. Four-power joint jurisdiction over the entire city had long before lapsed. To think otherwise was dismissed by Prime Minister Macmillan as indulging in "excessive legalism." The president and his advisers, to the extent that they weighed up the matter at all, believed they were being realistic in referring to the freedom of only West Berlin, though it revealed a readiness to give up bargaining points without extracting something in return. That was something of which the Soviets could never be accused. However, aside from the Soviets only a comparative handful of Kremlin-watchers seemed to recognize that.

The Kennedy speech was generally as well received in London and Paris as it had been across the United States, though Macmillan regretted that Kennedy had made so much of a point of civil defense and would have liked him to rattle American sabers less noisily. De Gaulle approved of the tone of the speech, though his spokesmen made it clear that if the matter was to come up again, France still saw no reason why the West should enter into negotiations over Berlin. The West Germans, who seemed to expect to be betrayed, once more displayed their nervousness about American reliability. They were pleased with the president's declared readiness to back up American policy with armed force but were worried that Washington appeared prepared to extend some form of recognition to East Germany if only the Soviets could be persuaded to calm down. They wanted none of that.

For John McCloy, Kennedy's special assistant for arms control, the timing of the president's speech was trouble. McCloy was in the Soviet Union for disarmament talks, with instructions "to explore the widest possible area of agreement." At the moment when

Kennedy was upping the ante over Berlin, McCloy was very much involved in that exploration process as Khrushchev's guest at the Black Sea resort of Sochi. Until word of the Kennedy speech came through, the Soviet leader had been the perfect host—courteous, gracious, friendly, exposing his visitor to none of his customary threats and warnings. But as soon as he learned what the president had said, Khrushchev's mood and attitude darkened.

Questions of arms control and disarmament were abruptly dropped by the wayside. In their place McCloy was subjected to a blistering tirade. He was told that Kennedy's military buildup and his obstinacy over Berlin were virtually equivalent to a declaration of war on the Soviet Union. If the Americans wanted war, Khrushchev roared, they could have it, and if there was a nuclear war over Berlin, John F. Kennedy would be the last president of the United States. He said that there was still time for the Americans to realize how perilous the situation was, that he hoped Kennedy would come to his senses, but that the existing Berlin situation would have to be changed.

The stage was set for the showdown. Both Kennedy and Khrushchev had delivered public presentations of their respective positions, and each had pronounced the other's unacceptable. Not even the softest of the softliners in Washington could assume any longer that the Soviets would wait much longer before doing whatever they intended to do about Berlin. Not even the hardest of the hardliners in Moscow could still insist with total conviction that when snarl came to push and push came to shove, the Americans would prove fainthearted.

Though scheduled to participate in other disarmament talks in Europe, McCloy was immediately summoned back to Washington for a personal report to the president on his meeting with Khrushchev. Kennedy wanted as accurate an account as possible of what had transpired at Sochi. Upon his return McCloy told the press he had been "entertained very hospitably" by the Soviet leader in a "very pleasant" atmosphere. The president was spared such flimflam. McCloy told him that Khrushchev was in no mood for negotiations of any kind; he seemed determined to have his way, no matter what the cost. He demanded that the West give way because he did not intend to.

Time had become a factor for Khrushchev. The Twenty-second Congress of the Communist party of the Soviet Union, scheduled for

October, was already in preparation. He had hoped to sort out the Berlin mess satisfactorily before then so that he would be able to devote his energies exclusively to what he considered the main task at hand—shoring up his position as Soviet leader by neutralizing remaining rivals within the Soviet hierarchy, notably Deputy Prime Minister Frol Kozlov and party theoretician Mikhail Suslov, who had never been happy with his de-Stalinization campaign and generally objected to the style and substance of his leadership. And always nipping at his heels was Ulbricht, who, with the discreet backing of those rivals, continued to press for urgent action on Berlin, offering almost desperate assurances that Kennedy was bluffing: "We simply do not believe and cannot believe that it is the desire, the ambition of the United States to appear before the whole world as an aggressor. . . . We would be pleased if certain people would refrain in the future from answering our peace offers time after time with foolish saber-rattling."

The press in the East kept headlining statements from East German government officials, party functionaries, trade union spokesmen, and ordinary citizens that the long-delayed peace treaty was essential for peace and stability in Europe and that one would soon be forthcoming, courtesy of the Soviet Union, no matter how many sabers the Americans chose to rattle. It issued assurances that the days were numbered for "the espionage activities," "the slave trade," "the kidnapping," and other nefarious practices made possible in Berlin by violation of what should long before have been East German sovereignty over the access routes.

The earlier exchange of fulminations by the superpowers had already accelerated the refugee flow, as had abortive efforts to require East German workers to compensate for production losses resulting from the exodus. Now many East Germans who had been considering going west some time in the future, as well as many who had never before given it much thought, decided it was time to leave and to leave in a hurry. *Torschlusspanik* ("panic to escape before the door slammed closed") set in across the German Democratic Republic and rapidly became contagious.

Longer and longer lines formed at the Marienfelde refugee reception center in West Berlin. More than a thousand persons from all over East Germany were passing through East Berlin en route to West Berlin each day, getting out before it was too late. Barely a subway or elevated train crossed over from the Soviet to the western sectors without its share of passengers seeking directions to Marien-felde and heading there in droves, as if it were a shrine. On the weekend after Kennedy's televised speech, 3,859 refugees registered at the reception center. It was turning into such a torrent that the American Mission reported back to Washington that it was possible that unless something intervened, as many as four million East Germans would flood into and through West Berlin before the end of the year.

Publicly, the Kremlin tried to ignore the stampede. No word of it was mentioned in the Communist press or by Communist officials. Questioned by western newsmen, Soviet diplomats in East Berlin insisted the refugee flood was vastly exaggerated by the newspapers and claimed that most East Germans who went west came back after they had a taste of how corrupt life was under capitalism. But those diplomats knew what was happening, and so did Khrushchev, as he revealed later:

> The drain of workers was creating a simply disastrous situation in the GDR. . . . If things had continued like this much longer, I don't know what would have happened. I spent a great deal of time trying to think of a way out. How could we introduce incentives in the GDR to counteract the force behind the exodus of East German youth to West Germany? . . . How could we create conditions in the GDR which would enable the state to regulate the steady attrition of its working force?

Khrushchev would soon have an answer to those questions. With his approval, the desired "incentives" would soon be intro-duced and the elusive "conditions" would soon be created.

As their workers flooded out, the East German regime struggled to retain some vestige of credibility. Its much trumpeted planning programs, which were to herald future prosperity for the people, were in tatters. House construction, machine building, the chemical industry, and just about every other major component of its detailed economic plan lagged far behind schedule. In an effort to retain some sense of reality factories were sharply reducing planned production levels. In some cases they were closing down altogether. Unable to pretend otherwise, Deputy Prime Minister Willy Stoph had to concede it was proving difficult to supply the population adequately with bread, butter, and meat.

The Communist press carried on as if it existed in another world. It carried photos of happy workers toiling for peace and socialism. It told of tens of thousands of people who had volunteered their free Sundays to work on farms because bringing in the harvest would bring a peace treaty nearer. At a time when refugees transplanted to West Germany were sending back glowing news of the jobs they had found almost immediately upon arrival, it warned that men lured to the West by West Berlin "slave traders" were drummed into the West German Army and trained to be cannon fodder for the Americans and young women tricked into abandoning their homeland were forced to become prostitutes.

Accusations were made that "blood money" was dangled in front of people by West Germany to lure them across the border. West German Minister for All German Affairs Ernst Lemmer, himself a former refugee, denied that his government was doing anything of the kind. Lemmer said, on the contrary, he feared the exodus of East Germans would leave a vacuum that would be filled by migrants from East European countries, thus diluting the German character of the region and diminishing hopes for ultimate reunification of the country. Totally unfounded rumors circulated in Berlin that plans were afoot to import Chinese labor to flesh out the East German work force in the factories and on the land. That anyone could believe such a story was an indication of how thoroughly that work force was being depleted.

In trying to cope with the refugee problem, the East German authorities felt they had no alternative but to compound the labor shortages the refugees created. The security forces and bureaucracy required to cope with the growing crisis were both substantially expanded and given priority in taking on additional personnel. But, as if fleeing a plague, the procession of absconders continued to grow.

7
Bracing for
the Showdown

SHORTLY after he became secretary of state, Dean Rusk learned by accident that a planned American military operation, related to delicate diplomatic maneuverings in Southeast Asia, had been canceled. That he hadn't been consulted before the cancellation offended and appalled him. But he was downright astounded by the fact that though he might have had to engage in discussions or make public statements related to those delicate maneuverings, he hadn't even been notified afterward. It had not been a deliberate attempt to keep the secretary of state in the dark. The frightening fact was that the State Department had no machinery operational at all hours of the day to keep him, or anyone else in the department, automatically informed of things he had to know.

It was different at the Pentagon. A War Room nerve center had been set up there years before, ready to deal with emergencies and keep top brass in the picture around-the-clock. But despite incessant international diplomatic brawls and occasional bouts of much worse ever since the United States had emerged from World War II as a superpower, the State Department—the limb of the American government with responsibility for matters of consequence outside the country—had no central twenty-four-hours-a-day facility to coordinate responses to crises, or even to keep officials posted as they developed.

Each of the many divisions within the department dealt exclusively, on a nine-to-five basis, with any problem that arose in its area of expertise and responsibility. The Office of German Affairs dealt with Germany. The Office of East European Affairs dealt with East Europe. The Office of West European Affairs dealt with West Europe. Communication between those various divisions was usually cumbersome, time consuming, and often obstructed by departmental rivalries or personality clashes.

If a crisis occurred after office hours, a communications clerk, who rarely was finely tuned on international affairs, had to determine if the situation were serious enough to contact a divisional duty officer at home or wherever he might be. If, when contacted, that duty officer thought the development serious enough to drag him away from a dinner party or out of bed, he would drive to Foggy Bottom, size up the situation, and decide whether to contact someone senior enough in the department to make a decision on further action—not something that was encouraged in the middle of the night or on weekends. The dangers built into such a system were glaring.

Shocked by his own experience with the bureaucracy, Rusk set about changing things. He ordered that an operations center be established in the State Department. It was to be a watch bureau and a crisis center, keeping abreast of developments and coordinating intelligence within the State Department so that the department would be equipped to respond to emergencies at any time of the day or night and so that Rusk and his senior subordinates would never again have to rely on luck to learn of developments in world trouble spots.

The Operations Center, nicknamed the "Rumpus Room," was set up on the seventh floor of the State Department building, not far from Rusk's office. Among other things, it was to house and service special task forces whenever one was organized to gather all pertinent facts on a specific problem in foreign affairs and to produce recommendations for action on it.

The center was, however, not equipped to coordinate the State Department's resources with those of other government departments and agencies. Analysts at the State Department, the Pentagon, and the CIA often looked at world problems independently. There were occasional interdepartmental consultations on international problems. But those had never been systematic and had always been plagued by intense rivalries, notably (as is still the case) between the State Department and the Pentagon. Nevertheless, it was obvious that Berlin planning by the various government departments and agencies had to be coordinated. After Kennedy got back from his rough-and-tumble meeting with Khrushchev at the Vienna summit, he issued instructions that a Berlin task force be established for that purpose.

At first, a State Department telegraphic watch center for Berlin was set up. Copies of all cables coming into the department related to Berlin—from Moscow, Bonn, London, Paris, and Berlin itself— were funneled into that center for scrutiny, so that developments in any of those places would not be assessed in isolation. But, as the crisis developed, the actual Berlin Task Force took shape. Its assignment was to acquire information, draw up recommendations, get authority from whatever level of government had to approve the recommendations, and issue instructions for them to be implemented.

Set up in a bank of offices opposite the Operations Center, the Berlin Task Force was basically a joint State Department–Pentagon effort, with Assistant Secretary of State Foy Kohler and Assistant Secretary of Defense Paul Nitze its joint guiding spirits at first. Kohler soon took sole charge, when it was recognized that the State Department was best equipped to coordinate its operations. Personnel, mostly from the State Department's Germany desk but also Colonel Wilbur ("Bur") Showalter from the Pentagon, were detached from other duties and moved full time onto the task force. Gradually, people from other State Department sections—including Intelligence and Research, the Legal Department, and the United Nations desk—and from the Pentagon began participating in informal task force meetings, as did personnel from the CIA, the United States Information Agency, the Treasury Department, and, later, the White House.

Informal sessions of the task force were open to anyone in an official capacity who was instructed or wished to participate in the assessment of what was going on with regard to Berlin and how to deal with it. At times there were as many as sixty people from nine different departments in attendance. There was some confusion as to who was a task-force staff member. At the conclusion of one of those early mass sessions Martin Hillenbrand, director of the Germany desk, who was chairing the session, called on "everyone from the Task Force" to stay on for a staff meeting. "At last," someone said, "we'll find out who's on it and who's not." According to task force member John Ausland, "Those who thought they were on it stayed behind." While various others made important contributions to its workings, the basic task force staff consisted of just a few members: Kohler in charge, Hillenbrand his deputy, Frank Cash, Ausland, Arthur ("Pete") Day, David Klein, and Jerry Holloway, all from the State Department, and Showalter from the Pentagon. Klein remained on the task force when he was recruited onto the White House staff later during the crisis.

In its early stages Kohler, who retained responsibility for the workings of the task force even after Hillenbrand took charge of its day-to-day operations, thought of the open sessions as a place where anyone who thought he had something to contribute could sound off. According to Karl Mautner, a participant sharply critical of the American government's failure to take a stronger line with the Soviets, complainers were made to feel free to continue their verbal sniping. But, said Mautner, "It was made clear we were not to expect to be loved for it."

The Berlin Task Force didn't find its stride until after the July 25 Kennedy television address. Even then it took a while till operational procedures became routine and questions of interdepartmental rivalries, which might have hampered its operations, were resolved. Ausland recalls that the first exchange that he (State) and Showalter (Pentagon) had at the task force was an agreement to be above board with each other. Neither of them thought it remarkable that such an agreement should be necessary between officials of the same government.

One of the task force's jobs was to make arrangements for Washington meetings of the "quadripartite group"—the ambassadors of Britain, France, and West Germany and Foy Kohler—to coordinate Allied responses in the crisis. The arrangement proved not altogether satisfactory. French Ambassador Hervé Alphand, who had never forgiven Kennedy for his condemnation of French policy in Algeria when he had been a senator, was very much on his dignity at all times. He seemed perpetually ready to take offense. The West German ambassador, Wilhelm Grewe, was not at all taken with the bright young problem solvers who ran the American administration. He was an intensely humorless man, much given to delivering longish lectures, which were thought to insult the intelligence of those exposed to them. In due course Bonn was discreetly advised that Grewe was perhaps not the best man to represent West Germany in the United States, and he was replaced.

The Americans had no difficulty with the British ambassador, David Ormsby-Gore, a close personal friend of Kennedy. But in view of the personality problems with Alphand and Grewe the task force took to arranging for lower-level diplomats of the four Allied powers to take over the job of consultations. Allied meetings subsequently flowed more smoothly, though fundamental differences with the French remained unresolved and American and West German attitudes never quite converged.

Well aware of differences within western ranks, the Soviets had embarked on a systematic campaign to engineer a deeper division among the Allies. In Washington and in European capitals Soviet diplomats joined in a coordinated chorus of complaints about the West's failure to respond to Khrushchev's proposal that West Berlin be turned into a "free city," as if Kennedy's rejection of it had been no response at all. Soviet envoys on the black-tie-and-cocktail circuit in London, Paris, Rome, Geneva, and other cities parroted the same line: It was not too late. If the West acted quickly and made serious counterproposals, it would be in a better position—than if it waited until the Soviets acted unilaterally—to extract guarantees from Moscow for West Berlin's independence after the East Germans assumed control of the access routes. The British, with their battered economy, seemed to the Soviets particularly susceptible to the argument that a few changes to remedy the "abnormal" situation in Berlin would bring the world back from the brink of war.

At the Moscow end of the new Soviet maneuver the Soviets reverted to a double-pronged, hard–soft assault on the position Kennedy had spelled out. The Soviet Foreign Ministry declared that when the Soviets spoke of turning West Berlin into a free city, they didn't really mean anything as specific as that. Their message just meant that the Soviet Union was ready "to settle jointly with interested parties" what West Berlin's status would be after the overdue peace treaty was signed. To persuade people that Kennedy was making far too much of the Berlin imbroglio, Khrushchev protested,

"We do not intend to change West Berlin's social and political system."

At the same time the Soviet leader used every opportunity to try to terrify western nations by brandishing his missiles. He told Italian Premier Amantori Fanfani that his country, like others in the western alliance, would be devastated by Soviet nuclear weapons if the Berlin dispute led to armed conflict: "Not only the orange groves of Italy but also the people who created them and who have exalted Italy's culture and arts, people in whose good intentions we believe, may perish." To the Greek ambassador he said, "I will not issue orders that bombs be dropped specifically on the Acropolis. But we will not hesitate to strike a blow at the military bases of the North Atlantic bloc which are located in Greece."

Khrushchev was making history. Never before had nuclear weapons been brandished in a bid to conquer territory.

In early August, as forebodings spread through the West like a nasty rash, Allied military liaison teams based at Potsdam in East Germany stepped up their patrols. They were looking for intimations of Soviet moves against the access routes. Those liaison teams had been stationed in East Germany since the end of the war, just as Soviet military teams had been stationed in West Germany. Though originally designed purely as liaison units to maintain official contact between Soviet and western occupation forces, and though they had primarily fulfilled that function during the brief postwar East–West honeymoon, they had soon also become deeply engaged in spying operations, probing what the other side's military forces were up to. This activity was openly recognized and reciprocally tolerated.

American, British, and French military personnel in uniform and in military vehicles scouted around East Germany, staying clear of restricted areas when under tight surveillance, but keeping an eye on military matters—troop reinforcements, troop deployment, the introduction of new equipment—as best they could. (Soviet liaison missions in West Germany did the same.) They were often on the road for days on end but were rarely without a tail of Communist security personnel, generally believed to be KGB. Colonel Ernest von Pawel, the chief of the American Liaison Mission in East Germany at the time, recognized one of his "shadows" as someone who had tailed him when he had been an American military attaché in

Poland. Once, when von Pawel was out on a reconnaissance mission, they parked across the autobahn from each other in East Germany and the man waved amicably at him.

There were occasions on both sides when liaison officers were chased off or detained for being where they were not supposed to be in their search for military information. But there were no incidents anything near as serious as the one in 1985 when United States Army Major Arthur Nicholson was shot dead by a Soviet sentry when photographing Soviet equipment.

As the Berlin situation grew more inflamed, the Allied liaison teams reported considerable Soviet military activity on the autobahns and roads outside the city. That bit of news was not overly revealing. The Soviets had tens of thousands of troops in the areas. Engaged in training exercises, they were continually moved about to familiarize them with their increasingly sophisticated weapons.

At one point British military intelligence in Berlin received an alarming report about Soviet military movements in East Germany. The report said there were so many Soviet armored vehicles on the autobahn not far from the city that it could only mean a move against West Berlin. A Chipmunk reconnaissance aircraft was dispatched from the British airfield in the West Berlin suburb of Gatow to investigate. It reported back alarmingly that the information was correct—the autobahn was practically jammed with Soviet armored vehicles. A British liaison team vehicle was sent to take a look and discovered that the emphasis of the Chipmunk report had been wrong. The road wasn't *practically* jammed, it was *completely* jammed. Two Soviet divisions on training missions had met face to face and couldn't disentangle themselves.

The liaison missions in East Germany, like western military intelligence organizations based in Berlin itself, did not concern themselves with the activities of civilians in the East—the Communist authorities, the refugees, or anyone else. They were interested exclusively in the Soviet military presence in the area—particularly unusual deployments of troops, the arrival of additional forces, the introduction of new weapons, the construction of additional barracks, anything that might indicate that the military balance in Germany was being altered.

There was a lot of ground to cover. Soviet forces were deployed in great strength near Berlin. The Soviets occupied former German barracks at Oranienburg, Bernau, Potsdam, and Koepenick, all within ten miles of the city. Planes coming in to land at Gatow made their approach over the Soviet barracks at Dallgow, where a division of Soviet troops was based. There was a Soviet military headquarters at Zossen, twenty miles from Berlin. Jüterbog, forty miles from the center of the city, was the headquarters of one of the five Soviet armies in East Germany, with something like two divisions of troops based there.[1] Any of those units, which were always on the move, could have been deployed against the access routes.

Unlike the Allied liaison missions, the Allied commandants in Berlin had more than only military responsibilities. They were in direct supreme command of the city. They were obliged to take into account the well-being of the populace in their sectors and the maintenance of public order as well. As disenchantment with the Communist regime intensified throughout East Germany, the western commandants were faced with the possibility of uprisings in the East, more specifically, in East Berlin from which trouble might spill over into the western sectors.

In Washington the State Department reported that "the Soviets were sitting on top of a volcano." There was no doubt that the Communists would make drastic efforts to control the refugee flood if it continued, that this would magnify discontent in the East, and that a subsequent uprising was a real possibility. It was further believed that if a revolt did break out in the Soviet Zone, the Soviets would deploy whatever military strength was necessary to crush it; therefore, the United States should make no effort to encourage an uprising. That did not rule out gaining as much propaganda mileage as possible out of an anti-Communist insurrection if one occurred.

In addition to worrying that their sectors might be affected by civil disturbances in East Berlin, the western commandants had another concern—the possibility that the Communists, as they had before, might send strong-arm squads into West Berlin to stir up trouble, perhaps using that as a pretext for calling on Soviet forces to restore law and order. To prepare for such a contingency, the western garrisons in Berlin took to practicing riot control. Teams of

[1]Though most western officials appreciated the seriousness of the situation, the lack of understanding of some dignitaries who passed through Berlin was baffling. When, with the aid of a map and a pointer, an official at the American Mission explained the geographical complications and outlined the Soviet military deployment, a visiting congressman asked him in amazement, "Do you mean we're surrounded?"

American soldiers, in civilian clothes and armed with sticks, played at being rioters sent in by the Communists, while other troops, in uniform, were deployed to contain and control them. Officers carefully monitored this training, but the men, enormously enjoying these simulated scrimmages, had trouble taking them seriously.

East German security forces, meantime, were playing a different game. They were attempting more vigorously than ever before to stem the refugee tide. To justify their efforts, they claimed that West Germany was suffering from a polio epidemic from which East Germans had to be shielded. Vopos and transport police scoured all trains from the East German hinterland to East Berlin and from East Berlin into West Berlin. Just about every second passenger was interrogated and had his papers examined. The police ordered a dozen or so people off each train for questioning as a matter of course, so that word would spread of the dangerous gauntlet that had to be run to reach the West. People carrying luggage or packages were automatically searched. Those who were thought to be possibly en route to the West were ordered home, and their local police were informed. Those believed definitely to be on their way out were arrested and charged with attempted *Republikflucht*. Police patrols combed the forests and fields around East Berlin to winkle out people who, to evade detection, had gotten off trains before reaching East Berlin and were trying to make their way westward on foot. Communist vigilante squads, formed by members of the worker brigades and the Free German Youth, roamed downtown districts east of the sector borders in search of refugees to turn over to the police. Vopo strength along the borders was increased, and more and more people were questioned and harassed when crossing into West Berlin.

Fear of arrest and loathing of the authorities grew in intensity. Worry about the future was widespread. A man who fled with his five children said he had been stopped by a Vopo who, while examining his papers, had whispered that he too would be going across if he had children. Throughout East Germany and East Berlin, people resorted to complicated subterfuges to make good their getaway.

A doctor, believing himself watched by his local Vopos, began elaborately decorating his new house, calming suspicions and relaxing the scrutiny paid him, before slipping away one night and making for the West. Families split up and went in different directions, to meet again at Marienfelde with as much relief as if they had escaped from a labor camp.

There was a series of widely publicized show trials in which would-be refugees and those who helped refugees were sentenced to as many as fifteen years in jail for promoting West German war preparations. The logic was simple. If people emigrated to West Germany to work there, and if West Germany was, as the Communists maintained, bent on war, then those people were, ipso facto, accessories. East German Supreme Court Judge Horst Hetzar fled west, charging that "the administration of law has sunk to such a level [in the East] that one is ashamed to be a lawyer."

The crackdown on the Grenzgängers who worked in West Berlin and whom the authorities could more easily control was also intensified. They were ordered to give up their jobs in West Berlin and register for work in the Soviet Sector. Neighborhood party activists went to their homes after they had returned from work in the evening to harangue them. Letters to newspapers asked why East Germany should put up with "free loaders" who creamed off the benefits of socialism without contributing to its construction. People were barred from buying refrigerators, washing machines, and other major manufactured goods in the East unless they could prove they worked there (which was no great punishment because such items were not readily available even to those who could afford them).

When these tactics produced few results, a more effective approach was attempted. The cross-border commuters were ordered by the Communist authorities to pay their rents and utility charges in west marks, which continued to be worth five times the equivalent in east marks. Their children were banned from the state schools. In a joint protest about the harassment of the commuters, the western commandants told Soviet Berlin commandant Colonel E.V. Solovyev that "the principle of freedom of movement is basic to the agreements regarding Berlin which are binding on the four powers responsible for this city." It had no effect whatsoever.

Some Grenzgängers bowed to the pressure and gave up their jobs in West Berlin. Others chose to give up their homes in East Berlin and finally moved west altogether. Weary of being harassed and harangued, a garage mechanic, a wizard with motors (at least he was with my car), was one of those who reluctantly gave up his East Berlin residence to settle in the West. He said he was paid too well for his skills in West Berlin to settle for what an East Berlin garage could offer. Besides, in the East he would be spending all his time trying to scrounge up hard-to-find spare parts rather than tinkering with the insides of cars.

As the hemorrhage of refugees continued unstanched, Ulbricht's pleas to the Kremlin to let him take action to stop the exodus took on a desperate tinge. Knowing that East German newspapers were monitored by the Soviet commandant's office, he permitted them to tuck away on the bottom of inside pages normally censored reports of worrying developments in the Soviet zone.

The Karl-Marx-Stadt *Volkstimme ("Voice of the People")* disclosed that slogans circulating in a local factory dared to call for the reunification of Germany. The *Leipziger Volkszeitung* quoted a worker as demanding unrestricted travel to West Germany. Another newspaper reported that workers were brazenly walking out on lectures given by SED officials. The Soviets might scold the East German Communist leadership for permitting such impermissible slippage in revolutionary discipline; nevertheless, the point, if it still needed making, was made. Command of the situation had to be retrieved before reactionary subversion could contaminate the entire country. The long-simmering pot of trouble was about to boil over.

A countdown to the crunch was also under way on the western side. Allied tanks and troop carriers rumbled through West Berlin for predawn practice alerts during which machine-gun positions were set up at street corners. In Washington on August 1 Congress voted 403 to 2 to grant President Kennedy's request for funds to boost America's conventional military strength. The two opposing votes were by congressmen who believed the United States should, as before, rely on nuclear weapons to deter the Soviets from threatening America's vital interests. On that same day, a curfew was imposed on American forces in Europe. Unless on leave or on an overnight pass, officers and men had to be back in their quarters by midnight—1:00 A.M. on Sundays. No more than 15 percent of personnel were to be off base or off duty at any one time.

Five days later, the biggest maneuvers by American forces since World War II were launched at Fort Bragg, North Carolina. Forty thousand troops were involved, including units of the Strategic Army Corps and the National Guard. Five thousand paratroopers took part in a mass jump. Publicity was provided in the unlikely event that the Soviet Union failed to notice.

By then the foreign ministers of the United States, Britain, France, and West Germany had met in Paris for an urgent review of the situation. They sought once again to firm up a common approach to the Berlin problem. However, agreement remained stubbornly elusive. The Americans, and particularly the British, continued to press for talks with the Soviets, if only to avoid miscalculations by either side. Secretary of State Rusk believed that if the West pushed for negotiations, it would be able to chart the direction those negotiations would take. The West Germans, in the middle of an election campaign and fundamentally wary of negotiations anyway, feared agreeing to talks could be interpreted as paving the way for western concessions to the Soviets on the future of Germany. The French insisted that talks, if they took place at all, should be delayed until after the projected western military buildup. What it all meant was that no accord was reached, except that western rights in Berlin would not be surrendered.

Presidential aide Walt Rostow had already advised Kennedy that as the situation developed, the United States might have to go at least part of the way alone:

> I argued that the somewhat hesitant mood of our Allies, while understandable, did not justify a weakening of the American position. I recalled that Washington, not London or Bonn, had its finger on the atomic trigger. It was one matter to face the possibility of atomic war if your political leaders have their finger on the trigger; it is a quite different matter if someone else's leaders are in that position. . . . The Allies might stay together to the end . . . but . . . we ought to be prepared in our minds for the possibility of a relatively lonely stage; and, recalling *High Noon,* we ought to accept it without throwing our sheriff's badge in the dust when the crisis subsided.

In view of the unrelenting Soviet diplomatic campaign to get the West out of Berlin, it was deemed necessary to make continually certain that everybody concerned understood the whys and wherefores of the situation—that it was right rather than might that justified the Allied presence in the city. Once more, Secretary of State Dean Rusk publicly explained the American position: "We are in West Berlin under the same arrangements which led Allied forces to withdraw from Thuringia and Saxony, large parts of which are now Eastern Germany with a population of some eight million persons." The implication was clear. If the Soviets wanted the West out of

Berlin, they should announce their readiness to withdraw from parts of East Germany in which almost half the population of that country lived. And the Soviets weren't about to do that.

On August 2 rumors circulated in Berlin that Ulbricht had left the city, perhaps for Moscow for consultations in the Kremlin. His presence in the Soviet capital for an important meeting of the leaders of the Warsaw Pact countries was confirmed the following day. Having been less successful in penetrating the Warsaw Pact than the KGB had been in penetrating NATO, western intelligence services had no way of knowing that Khrushchev was about to reveal what he had decided do about Berlin.

All sorts of plans had been drawn up in Washington for responding to a Soviet move against the western presence in the city. As the crisis built up, the Berlin Task Force at the State Department had two file drawers full of plans. When later reduced to a single document for quick reference purposes, those contingency plans still filled more than one hundred pages. Soviet or East European vessels en route to Cuba could be turned back in a counterblockade. The Soviet fleet in the Mediterranean might be harassed. Soviet shipping might be halted at random, as randomly as American convoys were stopped on the autobahn. A unit to oversee such action had been set up, under the code name SEA SPRAY, at United States Naval Headquarters at Norfolk, Virginia. In a study of the possibilities for the Pentagon, the Rand Corporation think tank had advised that the West should not feel constrained to confine its reaction to Berlin or Germany. It said that Soviet leaders could be made "aware of the fact that their broader and more important political interests will suffer if they carry out their threats on any local front where the Soviet Union happens to have superiority."

However, there was a drawback to that approach. The Soviets might well be prepared to accept a reverse elsewhere if it meant they could claim West Berlin, believing that in due course the blockade of Cuba or any other western retaliation would prove pointless and be phased out.

Primary emphasis, therefore, was placed on plans for direct military responses to keep the lifelines to West Berlin open and functioning. These would be under the direction of LIVE OAK, the code name for an Allied military headquarters setup (still in existence) outside Paris under the direction of General Lauris Norstad, the Supreme Allied Commander in Europe. Among LIVE OAK contingency plans was General Clay's old proposal of sending an armored column from West Germany through East Germany to West Berlin to brush aside any Communist obstruction of the ground-access routes.

According to that plan, the armored column was to start its trek across East Germany at Helmstedt, on the border of that part of West Germany in which British NATO forces were based. Accordingly, British troops were to be the vanguard of the column. A Russian-speaking British officer, Captain Michael Burkham, was to be in the lead vehicle. If stopped, he was to say, in effect, "We come in peace. Please, clear the road." No instructions were available (they would be later; they still are—and remain classified) on what to do if the Soviets, or the East Germans, did not remove all obstructions and let the column through.

Burkham was stationed at British military headquarters in West Germany at Rheindahlem. One evening early in August, as he and his wife were getting ready to go to a party thrown by a fellow officer, there was a knock on the door. When Burkham opened it, he found himself face-to-face with a stern-countenanced military police corporal. "This is it," he thought, and prepared to tell his wife to take the children, hop into the car, and head west because he was about to set off in the other direction. As it turned out, the MP had only come to report that the officer throwing the party "sends his compliments but his child has come down with the chicken pox and the party is off."

As things appeared to be approaching a climax, and LIVE OAK and SEA SPRAY reviewed and updated their operational procedures, individuals began looking to their personal contingency plans. Allied military personnel with dependents in West Germany stored jerricans of gas in the trunks of their cars in case a sudden emergency made it advisable for their families, like Burkham's, to scamper to safety without having to join the long lines that would immediately form at gas stations. In West Berlin, where my daughter was born in mid-July, my wife and I decided to get a separate passport for her at the American Mission rather than, as was customary, having the baby put on her mother's passport. It was impossible to forecast what sort of evacuation procedures would have to be followed if the access routes came under threat.

Real-estate values and rents in gentrified districts were plummeting in West Berlin as many propertied West Berliners of a nervous disposition emigrated to West Germany. They included the architect who had built the ranch house not far from the West Berlin border with East Germany in which my family and I lived. He had meant to live in the house himself and take pleasure from its delightful, apple-tree-studded garden, but had felt the danger of a Communist take-over was too great. He had transferred his residence and practice to Düsseldorf. Among those who were joining him in resettling in West Germany were many who had earlier fled to West Berlin from the East and who decided it was time once and for all to put themselves well out of reach of the Communists.

A lot of West Berliners who would eventually stay put debated whether to join them. It wasn't only the incessant threats and warnings from Moscow and East Berlin that made them think of leaving. Nor was it only the sight of the refugees now jamming Marienfelde in headline-making numbers, nor the stepped-up refugee airlift out of Tempelhof. The effect of these images of flight and escape was compounded by the boom of Soviet jet fighters mischievously breaking the sound barrier over West Berlin, as if claiming possession of the sky. The chatter of machine-gun fire coming from the training grounds of the western garrisons did little to convince people that there was nothing to worry about.

There was no panic, no end-of-the-world frenzy, no pervasive gloom, certainly not enough to keep people from their poppy-seed strudel and whipped cream on the patio of Kempinski's or the Kranzler on the Ku'damm—if they were lucky enough to get a seat out in the open—nor to keep the downtown movie houses from filling up. There was, however, a deeply implanted uneasiness, lightly masked by Berlin's big-city sophistication.

People going about their everyday affairs quipped about being the West's expendable frontline troops. Their *Galgenhumor,* their flippancy on the precipice, was contagious. When a garbage truck rumbled past our home in the dark, early hours of the morning, waking us, my wife and I joked about it being a Soviet tank casing the neighborhood. We figured we would learn what had happened during the night by whether we would find the Communist *Neues Deutschland* on our doorstep in the morning rather than the West Berlin newspapers that were normally delivered to our home.

People joked, but the atmosphere was thick with expectation.

It was also so thick with rumor that it was often difficult to distinguish between what was fake and what was not. As countless spy novels and movies have testified, as the only city in the world where western and Soviet influences coexisted, Berlin was a magnet for all sorts of eccentric personalities, situations, and ideas. Rarely was it believed that the truth behind any development had been fully disclosed. There was always more to come. The "real story," in its myriad variations, would invariably follow the rumor, only to be subsequently updated, revised, and sometimes stood on its head.

Rumors were a dime a dozen and, though without substantiation, sometimes blown up into major revelations. The head of the East German intelligence service had fled to West Berlin; no, he hadn't—it was one of his junior subordinates, and it had happened two years earlier; yes, that's the way it was except that he was proved to be a KGB plant. The dependents of American military personnel in Berlin were about to be evacuated to West Germany to get out of harm's way; yes, they would be evacuated, but only if they wanted to be; no, such an evacuation had been contemplated, but it was decided it would be taken by the Soviets as a sign that the Americans weren't as firm over Berlin as they said they were.

Rumors that started in Berlin were often built upon elsewhere. After feeding a broadcast report to New York on the refugee situation one afternoon, I mentioned to the editor on duty at the other end of the line that I had heard an interesting rumor that I wanted to try to substantiate. I told him I had heard that the Soviets would demand that since, as they insisted, East Berlin was the capital of East Germany, West Berlin, rather than all of Berlin, be made a four-power city. According to that rumor, Moscow would propose that a Soviet garrison should move in to take up residence alongside the American, British, and French garrisons in the western sectors of the city.

Returning the next morning by car through the Brandenburg Gate from a fruitless attempt to get a spokesman at the Soviet Embassy to comment on the rumor, I was flagged down by Karl Hartman of the Associated Press, who flashed in front of my windshield an early edition of *Der Abend,* a West Berlin afternoon newspaper. Not only did it headline my rumor on the front page, but it quoted me by name as the source, or rather my "absolutely reliable sources" in the East. Several weeks later, Soviet Deputy Premier Anastas Mikoyan did, in fact, suggest that West Berlin should come under four-power jurisdiction, a theme that soon was to become an official Soviet proposal.

The creeping malaise in West Berlin was due less to a lack of trust in the Allied "protectors" than to a sense of powerlessness about the anticipated Communist move to choke off the refugee flow. No one believed the Allies would simply pull out overnight, leaving West Berlin to Ulbricht's questionable mercies. But the feeling of impotence about the refugees was infectious; there was gut despair that the bigger battle for Berlin might eventually be lost no matter what John F. Kennedy promised. It was a deeply troubling suspicion for those in West Berlin who considered the Ulbricht regime to be a despicable tyranny—and there were few who did not.

No one, neither in West Berlin nor elsewhere, doubted that Ulbricht had the wherewithal ultimately to deal with his refugee problem. *The New York Times* pointed out, "There has never been any East-West agreement that would prevent the Communists from closing the border between East Germany and East Berlin. Why they have not done so in the past is something of a mystery." Senator William Fulbright, chairman of the Senate Foreign Relations Committee, said, "I don't understand why the East Germans don't close the border because I think they have a right to close it." In fact, they did not have that right in Berlin. Fulbright said later that in view of the perils inherent in the situation, he was not overly concerned with legalisms fashioned many years before in different circumstances. He was interested primarily in preventing the dispute from turning into an avoidable armed clash. Whatever his reasons, it was thought by many, and particularly by the ever-suspicious West Germans, that the senator was expressing a view that Kennedy shared but dared not voice for fear of alienating Adenauer.

Kennedy at that stage was, however, giving little thought to whether the Communists did or did not have a legal right to close the border. But without knowing it, Fulbright had been very close to voicing the president's attitude, as Kennedy made clear in a passing remark to Walt Rostow early in August: "Khrushchev is losing East Germany. He cannot let that happen. If East Germany goes, so will Poland and all of Eastern Europe. He will have to do something to stop the flow of refugees—perhaps a wall. And we won't be able to prevent it. I can hold the Alliance together to defend West Berlin but I cannot act to keep East Berlin open."

When asking Washington about contingency plans, Allan Lightner, the minister at the American Berlin Mission, was informed that decisions would depend on "the situation at the time." Lightner was left with the impression he was being told that if the Communists "left West Berlin alone, we would have nothing to worry about," and he was not to "rock the boat."

The Western powers were thus reconciled to the Communists' dealing with the refugees on the eastern side of the border. Not all westerners found that prospect completely disagreeable. Though sympathizing with the refugees, many saw the East German exodus as a potentially perilous phenomenon. They feared that unless halted, it would generate instability and uncertainty in all of East Europe. Confusion would follow in the Kremlin, where a powerful bloc of backseat luminaries had been pressing their belief that Soviet détente with the West was an illusion. It was feared by western pundits who vastly overestimated Soviet military capabilities that if the views of the Moscow hawks prevailed in the Kremlin, peace and security in West Europe could be endangered.

De Gaulle, who thought in more grandiose terms, was troubled by another possibility. He feared that the mass German migration westward would create a vacuum that would draw hordes of Slavs into parts of Central Europe, which had been German since the sixteenth century, altering the ethnic balance of the area.

However, it did not occur to East German leaders that anyone in the West could exhibit such qualms, and if it had, they would have suspected a calculated deception. They were convinced—and drew proof from West German promises of ultimate German reunification —that an insidious plot was afoot to destroy Communist rule and the East German state and that it could very well succeed unless they were vigilant and took drastic steps to foil it. Erich Honecker, a member of the SED Central Committee and the man in operational control of preparations to seal off West Berlin, maintained that "West German monopolies" were planning a step-by-step take-over of the East German economy. The West, he claimed, had engaged in a campaign of slander to promote the refugee outflow and had sent saboteurs into East Berlin to commit arson and create panic among East Germans. Honecker later said, "It became more and more obvious what a danger [the open border] represented to peace."

The belief that the West was bent on destroying the first German workers state was genuine and widespread in Communist ranks. It couldn't be otherwise among people who believed that communism was inevitable and that civilization was reaching the stage where it was due to come about. It followed logically that only conspiracies and plots were holding it back.

Many East German Communists, particularly the older ones, had become cynical puppets of the Soviet Union. The belief in justice that had originally motivated their political involvement had long before been shattered by the tyrannical injustices they had been obliged to excuse and explain away. (Wolfgang Leonhard has described how docilely they had accepted the arrest by the NKVD in Moscow of German Communists who had sought refuge from the Nazis—including, in his case, his mother.)

But not all East German Communists accepted that the panicky police state then existing in East Germany had the makings of a true people's democracy. Many of them believed—and some were imprisoned for presuming to say so—that the day was still to come when they would be able to feel pride in their Socialist Fatherland and could stop trying to explain away its shortcomings. But except for a few who would go west, either physically or spiritually, even those Communists who were pained by the injustices committed in the name of communism subscribed to Robespierre's revolutionary rationalization that "You must break eggs to make an omelette." They believed with a virtually religious passion that any system but communism was wrong and that capitalism was, by definition, criminal and wicked. They hoped to construct a brave new world the inhabitants of which, untrammeled by what they deemed to be the trivializing pseudo-rewards of capitalism, would be able to develop their full potential. If that involved disagreeable tactics, that was regrettable.

It was estimated that if free elections had taken place in East Germany, the Communists, in power for more than fifteen years, would have gained only between 10 and 20 percent of the vote, even after the refugees had gone. But that 10 to 20 percent were prepared to fall into line no matter how many eggs their leaders chose to break in their desperate effort to serve up the Communist omelette.

. . .

On Friday, August 11, as John Kennedy looked forward to going off to Hyannis Port for what had become his regular weekend rest and rehabilitation retreat, as Dean Rusk mulled over how to pin down a concerted Allied policy on dealing with the Soviets over Berlin, and as Nikita Khrushchev sustained his terror campaign with a warning that "hundreds of millions" would die if there were war over the status of the city, the East German *Volkskammer* ("parliament") was summoned into special session in East Berlin to hear from Walter Ulbricht what had transpired at the Warsaw Pact meeting in Moscow the previous week. It received only a sketchy report. Details were not yet to be revealed. There was too great a danger of a leak. But Volkskammer members were told that a moment of crucial decision had arrived and the long-promised effective action against the refugees was about to be taken. They then went through the motions of giving Ulbricht and his Council of Ministers full authority to do whatever was thought necessary to protect the security and interests of the German Democratic Republic.

Khrushchev's decision on what to do about Berlin had been reached a little more than two weeks earlier, when Kennedy's "stand firm" position had been outlined on television. Although he had reacted in fury at the time and had made repeated doomsday threats since, he had realized that it was he, not Kennedy, who would have to back off. He would have to postpone dealing with the access routes. Plans to lever the Allies out of their malignant enclave behind Soviet lines would have to be shelved for the moment.

It wasn't only tough talk from the West that influenced his decision. Reports from Soviet intelligence agents had an important bearing as well. The Soviets were well served by strategically placed spies in Washington and at NATO. Among them were Lieutenant Colonel W. H. Whalen, a United States Army intelligence officer assigned to the joint chiefs of staff and a KGB agent of long standing, who was unmasked and arrested several years later, and Georges Paques, a Frenchman on the NATO staff, who was arrested as a Soviet spy later in the year.[2] Through them, and other Soviet opera-

[2]Secretary of State Rusk told me that, knowing Soviet spies were planted at NATO, he later used the certainty of intelligence leaks there to pass messages he did not want misunderstood to the Soviet government. The Soviets were so security conscious that he believed that route would guarantee those messages more urgent attention in Moscow than if they were delivered by the American ambassador.

tives, Khrushchev had learned a great deal about American nuclear contingency plans, some of which, though frightening, were more ambitious than practicable. He had learned enough to accept that Kennedy was not bluffing. He no longer had reason to doubt that instead of yielding in the face of Soviet war warnings as he believed Kennedy would, the American president actually seemed ready to use his far superior nuclear weaponry to have his way in Berlin.

Ending the Allied presence in West Berlin was high on the Soviet agenda, but it was not as overridingly important to the Soviets as Kennedy insisted remaining in Berlin was to the Americans. Khrushchev's main priority was leading his country along the road to communism. Despite his impulsive nature, he realized he couldn't very well do that by exposing the Soviet Union to nuclear destruction for a prize it could manage very well without, and which would still be there for the taking at a more auspicious moment later on.

But there was still the issue of the refugees. The Kremlin had considered them a serious but subordinate problem, which could wait until the territorial jurisdiction issue was resolved before the year was out. It would then more or less resolve itself. That problem now had to be upgraded and dealt with because, with no overall, satisfactory solution to the Berlin hassle in sight, the population drain posed a serious threat to the future of the East German state. And that *was* a vital Soviet interest.

Nobody in the Soviet hierarchy—neither Khrushchev nor any of his colleagues—liked the idea of letting Ulbricht build a barrier between East Berlin and West Berlin to choke off the exodus. Aside from being a public admission of Communist failure in the open competition between the two systems operating side-by-side in the city, it was a blatant violation of a written agreement to which the Soviet Union was a party. Like all nations, the Soviet Union was not averse to playing fast and loose with treaties that were loosely defined, but the agreements on four-power Berlin were clear and unambiguous. Freedom of movement throughout the entire city was guaranteed. It could be argued that a Vopo crackdown was a police exercise within the purview of the civil authorities. But to build a permanent barrier would be a blatant treaty violation that would invite reprisal and that the Soviets were reluctant to commit unless it was unavoidable.

There was an alternative. With the border between East Germany and West Germany sealed, and with that part of East Germany that bordered directly on West Berlin having also long before been made escape proof, only the sector border in the middle of the four-power city remained open. If people in East Germany were prevented from getting to East Berlin, they would not be able to get close enough to West Berlin to escape. Traffic between the two parts of the city would then be greatly reduced, enabling the Vopos to do a more thorough job of turning back East Berlin residents wanting to head west. The refugee problem would thus be solved. What was more, sealing East Germany off from East Berlin would be under- taken exclusively within what the Allies still regarded as the Soviet Zone, where it would be nobody else's business.

However, the plan had several obvious drawbacks. It would require a tremendous, permanent police operation on all trains and roads to Berlin. Spot checks on travelers in the past had indicated such an operation was not very effective. Besides, a good many East German citizens would be denied right of access to East Berlin, which the Communists insisted, despite western objections, was their capital city. The operation would be cumbersome, difficult to main- tain, expensive, and probably futile in the long run.

To his regret Khrushchev realized that if the refugees were to be stopped, and East Germany saved from collapse, West Berlin would have to be fenced off, no matter how badly such a move would reflect on the qualities of the Communist system. It was the only way to save the good people of the German Democratic Republic from being exposed to siren calls from the capitalist world, to which they had proved so susceptible. The leaders of the Warsaw Pact countries had been called together at the Moscow meeting to be informed of Khrushchev's decision and to agree to it. Like the Americans, the Soviets wanted to make sure all their allies were in accord. Khrush- chev had an easier time persuading them.

The final communiqué of the Warsaw Pact conclave said noth- ing about the Berlin decision. It did, however, again express "the inflexible determination of all its participants to achieve a peace settlement with Germany before the end of the year." Expecting major developments, decisions, and pronouncements, western ana- lysts monitored all public statements and speeches emanating from the meeting. They found nothing new. Waiting anxiously to replay the Soviet Union's Berlin blockade, the West was successfully di- verted from suspecting what the Soviets were really planning. Intelli- gence and Research at the State Department innocently reported,

"Purpose of Moscow 3–5 August meeting was to impress the West with bloc determination to conclude a separate treaty with the East German regime if necessary and to enhance the bloc's bargaining position in negotiations."

Having decided on a plan of action, the Soviets stepped up their stick-and-carrot propaganda campaign to confuse the West into operational paralysis. Two days after the Moscow Warsaw Pact gathering, Khrushchev publicly urged, "Let us sit down honestly at a round conference table. Let us not fan up war psychosis." At the same time he warned that if the United States unleashed a war, its people would taste the horrors of thermonuclear conflict and would face devastation of the kind they had not experienced since the Civil War.

His olive branch was designed to sustain hope in the White House that Moscow would back off before crossing the line Kennedy had drawn. It would thus discourage the president from authorizing precipitous action that might disrupt Soviet plans. The simultaneous nuclear threats were meant to convince Kennedy—as they did—that he might nevertheless finally be forced to order the launching of America's nuclear missiles, with calamitous consequences for Americans as well as Soviets. He would thus be set up to be stunned into a stupor of relief when he realized that the Soviets did not intend to push him that far.

The success of the Soviet campaign in artificially generating an atmosphere of morbid apprehension was demonstrated by the uncharacteristically emotional reaction of veteran diplomat George Kennan, otherwise one of the most perceptive and creative modern American foreign-policy thinkers. As the crisis mushroomed, Kennan told Arthur Schlesinger, "I do not propose to let the future of mankind be settled, or ended, by a group of men operating on the basis of limited perspectives and short-run calculations. I figure that the only thing I have left in life is to do everything I can to stop the war."

It was hard not to worry when Khrushchev boasted that the Soviet Union had developed the capacity to develop a one-hundred-megaton, deliverable nuclear warhead and warned that Soviet missiles "are not for slicing sausages." On August 9, the day he made that statement, 1,926 East German refugees fled west. Also on that day, Soviet intelligence officer and British spy Colonel Oleg Penkovsky learned in Moscow of plans to divide Berlin four days later.

He was, however, in no position to pass word along to his British contact before the event.

On August 10 it was announced that Soviet war hero Marshal Ivan Stepanovich Koniev, former supreme military commander of the Warsaw Pact, had been appointed commander of Soviet troops in East Germany. He normally would have been considered too senior for the position. His appointment was another step in the escalation of threatening Soviet gestures. Koniev had a wartime reputation for capturing enemy-held cities by severing approach roads. He had once said, "A city is like the branch of a tree—cut the roads leading to it and the city will fall." It was an ominous thought in view of the vulnerability of the Berlin access routes.

Koniev's arrival coincided with a flood of rumors that the East German Volkskammer, scheduled to meet the following morning, would soon—possibly within a matter of days—announce measures to restrict travel from East Germany to East Berlin, the plan Khrushchev had rejected. On that day, twenty-four hours after East Berlin Grenzgängers were ordered to give up their West Berlin jobs and report to labor offices in the East to be assigned jobs within the Soviet Sector, 1,709 refugees showed up at Marienfelde. Personnel at the refugee reception center, already bulging at the rafters, were bracing themselves for a record weekend.

8
Something Funny at the Border

As the only western correspondent resident in East Berlin, Reuters correspondent Adam Kellett-Long had an advantage over his colleagues based across the sector border in West Berlin. Hungry for diplomatic recognition by the West to remove any doubts about its legitimacy, the East German regime was gratified that the reputable British Reuters agency had chosen to man an office in East Berlin, rather than having the city covered only from West Berlin. It was a measure of recognition, albeit not yet backed by the British government. Kellett-Long was, therefore, sometimes allowed access to Communist sources that other western newsmen were denied. After the special Volkskammer session, he managed to buttonhole a senior figure in the government to ask what was going on. The man declined to be specific, which was no more than expected, but he mysteriously advised, "If I were you and I had plans to spend this weekend away from Berlin, I wouldn't."

Though pleased to receive what appeared to be an extremely unusual tip-off at a time of great suspense in the city, Kellett-Long found himself in a quandary. Speculation that the Berlin tinderbox was about to ignite had been rampant on a daily basis for the better part of a month. Western newsmen in the city were under pressure from their home offices to stay on top of the story. Some of the major

American broadcast networks had beefed up their Berlin coverage, ferrying in senior correspondents from less tempestuous posts in Bonn, London, and elsewhere to lend appropriate gravity to the story on their news programs. Espying pay dirt, free-lance journalists flowed in from everywhere.

News agency reporters—particularly those at the fiercely competing United Press International, Associated Press, and Reuters— were in a particularly tricky position, being regularly pressed to explain why they had missed (sometimes dubious) stories a rival agency had circulated to its subscribers. Mindful of Reuters' reputation for caution and reliability, Kellett-Long—twenty-six years old and on his first overseas assignment—had tried to stay well clear of far-fetched speculation and rumor, except when reporting the more credible ones and labeling them as such. He had, in fact, been expending much effort and time checking stories that proved to have no basis in fact. His wife, Mary, noted in her diary, "Adam is getting tired of having to keep on throwing down these stories. Of course one day [one of those stories] will be true and then I hope he gets it first."

Now it looked very much like Kellett-Long *would* be getting it first. Exclusive, genuine tip-offs from senior Communist officials on breaking stories of critical importance were few and far between. However, regardless how eminent its source (whom he was bound by the rules of the game not to identify), advice not to go away for the weekend could have meant many things—still tighter police controls, new systems for checking on East German train passengers making for East Berlin, stiffer penalties for apprehended refugees— or nothing at all.

Nevertheless, bright and early Saturday morning, Kellett-Long sat down at the teleprinter in the East Berlin apartment that served as both his office and his home and tapped out a morning lead to London that was to cause him much anguish over the next sixteen hours. "Berlin," it began, "is holding its breath. . . ." Reviewing developments over the past few days, his story strongly suggested that the implementation of drastic measures to halt the flow of refugees to the West was imminent.

Meantime, East Germans who had waited for the weekend to take leave of the German Democratic Republic were descending in great numbers on East Berlin en route to West Berlin and sanctuary. Efforts by Vopos, scouring intercity and suburban trains for refugees among people from the East German hinterlands who had chosen a

Saturday in August for innocent visits to the big city, were hindered by the volume of passenger traffic. The same was true on the sector border and on Berlin subway and elevated trains. The police had trouble distinguishing refugees from people who were simply taking a day trip to West Berlin to visit relatives, window shop, or go to the movies.

Many were turned back. Many were arrested. But by noon it was apparent that the record for the influx of refugees at Marienfelde on a single day would be broken. The lines of new arrivals from the East were growing longer and longer and creating problems. Mayor Willy Brandt's director of staff at Town Hall, Heinrich Albertz, telephoned George Muller, deputy political adviser at the American Mission, to say food supplies on hand at the center were just about exhausted; could the United States Army spare extra field rations? Muller arranged for them to be delivered. Processing procedures were accelerated, and still more planes were chartered to ferry refugees to West Germany.

Meanwhile, in East Berlin, Ulbricht's Council of Ministers, now formally empowered to "implement all measures necessary to safeguard peace," met to put a halt to all of that. Without dissent or question, it formally authorized action by East German security forces to place "under proper control the still open border between socialist and capitalist Europe."

At 4:00 P.M. that Saturday Ulbricht, as chairman of the East German National Defense Council, signed the order formally instructing Erich Honecker to proceed with his task of sealing the border between East and West Berlin. At 11:00 P.M. Honecker's command staff, gathered at East Berlin's central police headquarters, set in motion the operation for which they had been preparing under a blanket of secrecy for weeks. Among those also present were Minister of Defense General Heinz Hoffmann and Minister of State Security Erich Mielke, who were playing key roles in the operation. Without knowing why exactly, security forces under their command had already been put on the alert. It was time to give them their orders.

By nightfall Kellett-Long was worried. His editors at Reuters in London had been asking what he had to back up his morning lead suggesting that the Berlin climax was around the corner, and he had

GEORGE F. WILL

Hitting a wall in Berlin

WASHINGTON — The question of whether Barack Obama's second term will be a failure was answered in the affirmative before his Berlin debacle, which has recast the question, which now is: Will this term be silly, even scary in its detachment from reality?

Before Berlin, Obama set his steep downward trajectory by squandering the most precious post-election months on gun-control futilities and by a subsequent storm of scandals that have made his unvarying project — ever bigger, more expansive, more intrusive and more coercive government — more repulsive. Then came Wednesday's pratfall in Berlin.

There he vowed energetic measures against global warming ("the global threat of our time"). The 16-year pause of this warming was not predicted by, and is not explained by, the climate models for which, in his strange understanding of respect for science, he has forsworn skepticism. Regarding another threat, he

spoke an almost meaningless sentence that is an exquisite example of why his rhetoric cannot withstand close reading: "We may strike blows against terrorist networks, but if we ignore the instability and intolerance that fuels extremism, our own freedom will eventually be endangered." So, "instability and intolerance" are to blame for terrorism? Instability where? Intolerance of what by whom "fuels" terrorists? Terrorism is a tactic of destabilization. Intolerance is, for terrorists, a virtue.

It is axiomatic: Arms control is impossible until it is unimportant. This is because arms control is an arena of competition in which nations negotiate only those limits that advance their interests. Nevertheless, Obama trotted out another golden oldie in Berlin when he vowed to resuscitate the cadaver of nuclear arms control with Russia. As though Russia's arsenal is a pressing problem. And as though there is reason to think President Vladimir Putin, who calls the Soviet Union's collapse "the

greatest geopolitical catastrophe of the century," is interested in reducing the arsenal that is the basis of his otherwise Third World country's claim to great power status.

Shifting his strange focus from Russia's nuclear weapons, Obama said "we can ... reject the nuclear weaponization that North Korea and Iran may be seeking."

Neither the people who wrote those words nor he who spoke them can be taken seriously. North Korea and Iran may be seeking nuclear weapons? North Korea may have such weapons.

Evidently Obama still entertains doubts that Iran is seeking them.

Obama's vanity is a wonder of the world that never loses its power to astonish, but really: Is everyone in his orbit too lost in raptures of admiration to warn him against delivering a speech soggy with banalities and bromides in a city that remembers John Kennedy's "Ich bin ein Berliner" and Ronald Reagan's "Tear down this wall"?

With German Chancellor Angela Merkel sitting nearby, Obama began his Berlin speech: "As I've said, Angela and I don't exactly look like previous German and American leaders." He has indeed said that, too, before, at least about himself. It was mildly amusing in Berlin in 2008, but hardly a Noel Coward-like witticism worth recycling.

His look is just not that interesting. And after being pointless in Berlin, neither is he, other than for the surrealism of his second term.

George F. Will is a columnist for The Washington Post and Newsweek.

LOSS OF TRUST

TRUST · FROM D1

Unless we are willing to risk anarchy or terrorism, the most we can do is set up checks and balances within government — and be a lot more careful in the future than we have been in the past when deciding whom to elect.

Anyone old enough to remember the Cuban Missile Crisis of 1962, when President John F. Kennedy took this country to the brink of nuclear war with the Soviet Union, might remember that there was nothing like the distrust and backlash against later presidents, whose controversial decisions risked nothing approaching the cataclysm that President Kennedy's decision could have led to.

Even those of us who were not John F. Kennedy supporters, and who were not dazzled by the glitter and glamour of the Kennedy aura, nevertheless felt that the president was someone who knew much more than we did about the realities on which all our lives depended.

Whatever happened to that feeling? Lyndon Johnson and Richard Nixon happened — and both were shameless liars. They destroyed not only their own credibility but the credibility of the office.

Even when Johnson told us the truth at a crucial juncture during the Vietnam War — that the Communist offensive of 1968 was a defeat for them, even as the

LETTERS

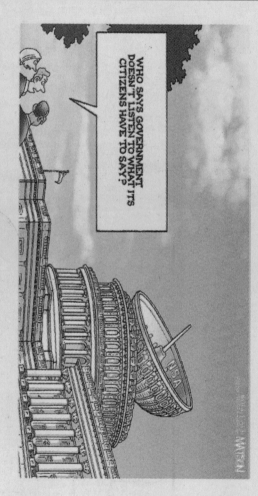

WHO SAYS GOVERNMENT DOESN'T LISTEN TO WHAT ITS CITIZENS HAVE TO SAY?

FREEDOM VS. PRIVACY

We all know that tyranny is a constant in the history of human governance, perhaps even in human nature itself. Any thoughtful person would immediately recognize the danger inherent in putting "government" in control of all written data.

Data can easily be corrupted, altered or taken out of context — misused and abused. The current IRS scandal demonstrates the ease with which politicized government employees can abuse their authority and punish innocent citizens. It is flat-out wrong to provide "government"

with more overwhelming tools to do so.

Like everyone else, Edward Snowden, who leaked details of two National Security Agency surveillance programs, has only his own moral compass to guide him, and I can respect the choice that he made in this case, dangerous though it might be.

Our national anthem ends with the question: "Oh, say does that star-spangled banner yet wave/O'er the land of the free and the home of the brave?" I am concerned that the answer might be "no."

RICHARD J. KRAULAND
O'HARA

· · · · · · · · ·

Regarding the current revelations about government "snooping": Questions are being asked, perhaps late in the game, but better late than never. The NSA and other agencies might have used their powers abusively, perhaps not.

"mouse print," do not mitigate the abusive nature of corporate practices either, notwithstanding the public's seeming willingness to give up valued privacy in pursuit of miniscule rewards offered. Strikes me that the priorities of complainers,

MORE ON CIVIL WAR SITES

In my 2002 book, "Pittsburgh During the American Civil War 1860-1865," I devoted an entire chapter to the fortifications mentioned in Craig Smith's news story "Civil War history hides in, around Pittsburgh" (June 17 and TribLIVE.com).

In the early 1990s, Bill McCarthy and I, at the time both experienced field archaeologists at the University of Pittsburgh, surveyed all the old "fort" locations and determined then that earthen remains existed only for Fort Child, then under a radio tower.

Other so-called remains are the result of construction/housing projects in the late 19th and 20th centuries. Bill later wrote an unpublished master's thesis on the fortifications.

ARTHUR FOX
DORMONT

The writer is professor of world geography at Community College of Allegheny County's Allegheny campus.

POINTLESS 'PRIDE'

Regarding the recent gay Pittsburgh PrideFest: Why not a straight pride fest/parade in Pittsburgh?

The vast majority in this country are heterosexual and as proud and comfortable as the others as to who and what they are.

The celebration would not be to "show off" their gender preference or to defend nothing of substance to offer them. He drove to the Ostbahnhof, East Berlin's main train station, to get a copy of the early edition of *Neues Deutschland*. He hoped it would carry something that might substantiate his forecast. The Communists often broke major stories in the official press rather than through government press offices. But not this time. (At that moment a hand-picked, politically reliable skeleton staff at *Neues Deutschland* was preparing a special second edition of the newspaper that would tell the story for which Kellett-Long was waiting.) The only unusual thing he saw at the train station was a surprisingly large number of black-uniformed railway police coming off trains from out of town. That was curious—but hardly an earth-shattering development in view of the heavy policing to which East Berlin was being subjected.

Feeling like an amateurish blunderer, Kellett-Long drove back to his office to try to figure some way out of the hole he thought he had dug for himself. He sat down at his typewriter and began working on the night lead he was due to file to sum up the day's East Berlin developments. It began, "Contrary to expectations. . . ." And there he stopped. It was limp and transparent. His wife had gone to bed, but though also tired, he decided that before winding up his story and transmitting it, he would wait until the East German news agency, ADN, closed down its wire service for the night, around 1:00 A.M. Though headline-grabbing events were unlikely so late at night, ADN was often used by the East German regime for special announcements.

At midnight exactly, the piercing hoot of a siren sounding through the barracks of the militarized East German border police (*Grenzpolizei,* known as *Grepos),* twenty-five miles from the center of Berlin, shattered the slumber of Grepo Sergeant Rudi Thurow. Thurow thought it was just another practice drill of which there had been an increasing number of late. But he quickly donned his uniform and, to a chorus of curses, went through the barracks prying from their beds men who, despite the siren, were trying to cling to sleep.

At about the same time, in West Berlin, George Muller received another phone call from Heinrich Albertz, not about additional rations for the refugees this time. "Something funny is going on," Albertz told him. "There are more S-Bahn trains going east than are coming west." That was strange, Muller thought, because it was believed that if the East Germans were planning to cause trouble in West Berlin, the movement would be the other way; Communist militia men, posing as workers, would stream west by train and on foot, perhaps to try to seize a West Berlin government building and foment unrest.

There was a contingency plan for that involving the West Berlin police and, if necessary, Allied troops. But clearly that wasn't what was happening. What was taking place instead was a clampdown on train services between the two parts of the city. As would soon become evident, the S-Bahn, one of the most heavily trafficked refugee arteries—also used by tens of thousands of Berliners who traveled back and forth between East and West every day—was being severed. This was confirmed when late night West Berlin travelers and carousers, leaving East Berlin by S-Bahn, began trudging wearily and grumpily on foot up to the sector border. Their trains had been stopped at the last station in the East, where they had been shooed off and made to walk the rest of the way. But though, as Albertz had told Muller, it was "funny," there was as yet no indication that it was any worse than that, perhaps only another one of the games the Communist authorities in East Berlin played now and again to show their dwindling population who was in charge.

At twenty minutes past midnight, Sergeant Rudi Thurow, having pried his men out of bed and gotten them to form up in combat dress on the parade ground outside, was summoned to the office of his company commander, Oberleutnant Witz. When all of the company's officers and NCOs were assembled, Witz announced that this exercise was not just another dry run. The leaders of the German Democratic Republic, he said, had finally been forced to take vigorous steps to block attempts to undermine the Socialist Fatherland. The flesh merchants in West Berlin, who preyed on the citizens of the German Democratic Republic, would be put in their place. The activities of the Grenzgängers, who benefited from living in East Berlin while serving the West, would no longer be tolerated. The espionage and terror centers in the western sectors were about to be dealt a crippling blow. Some upstanding and loyal East Germans might unfortunately be hurt by what was about to happen. But the interests of the people's republic had to come first.

"Is it war?" Sergeant Thurow wondered as Oberleutnant Witz lectured on. There was a sense of foreboding when the company commander, who had himself been briefed only a half hour before, picked up a brown envelope marked "Top Secret," tore it open, took out a document, and started reading from it. "In accordance with the declaration of the member states of the Warsaw Pact . . . ," he began. It was a long declaration, replete with condemnations of West Germany, and stressed the need to take action to preserve peace.

All of that had been heard before. This time, however, it was announced that "To block the hostile activities of the revenge-seeking and militaristic forces in West Germany and West Berlin, controls appropriate for all sovereign states will be established on the borders of the German Democratic Republic, including along the borders of the western sectors of Berlin." There it was! That was how the refugees would be stopped. Contrary to four-power agreements on free movement throughout the city, Berlin was to be split in two.

Silence followed. Then somebody mumbled, "Will the West stand for this?" Through RIAS and other western broadcast media readily picked up in the East, the proclaimed determination of President Kennedy and other western leaders not to be pushed around over Berlin was widely known. But Oberleutnant Witz had been briefed to deal with the concerns of his men. He told them no military response from the West would be forthcoming because the Soviet forces in the area, which greatly outnumbered the Allied Berlin garrisons, had been alerted, as the West well knew. Soviet tanks were already taking positions around Berlin; the men, as they had shaken off the last remnants of sleep and stuffed themselves into their uniforms less than an hour before, had heard them rumbling by their barracks.

At the American military liaison mission in Potsdam the deputy head of mission, Lieutenant Colonel David Morgan, had also heard the tanks. When he drove out to see what was happening, he was stopped by a Vopo just short of the highway and kept there until the tanks, heading to take up positions around Berlin, had passed.

Just before 1:00 A.M., Kellett-Long, still with nothing new of substance to report and despairing of surviving the weekend with his credibility intact, prepared to face the grim necessity of winding up his night lead and dispatching it to London. As he set to it, his telephone rang. A man, speaking German and declining to identify himself, said, "I strongly advise you not to go to bed tonight."[1] Another mysterious tip-off! First not to go away for the weekend, now not to go to sleep. A few minutes later, at 1:11 A.M., the ADN teleprinter in the Reuters office began to chatter. After announcing that an important statement had been issued by the member nations of the Warsaw Pact (the statement drawn up at the Warsaw Pact meeting in Moscow the week before), it began churning out the turgid officialese in which government pronouncements, whether important or trivial, were invariably couched: "The governments of the member nations of the Warsaw Pact have striven for many years to reach a peace settlement with Germany." The statement went on to describe the dangers that were inherent in the prevailing situation and the great patience that the Soviet Union and its Warsaw Pact allies had displayed, patience that now was at an end:

> The present traffic situation on the borders of West Berlin is being used by ruling circles of [West Germany] and intelligence agencies of NATO countries to undermine the economy of the German Democratic Republic. Through deceit, bribery, and blackmail, West German government bodies and military interests induce certain unstable elements in the German Democratic Republic to leave for West Germany. These deceived people are compelled to serve with the *Bundeswehr* [West German Army], and are recruited for the intelligence agencies of different countries to be sent back to the GDR as spies and saboteurs. . . . In the face of the aggressive aspirations of the reactionary forces of West Germany and its NATO allies, the Warsaw Pact member states must take necessary steps to guarantee their security and, primarily, the security of the GDR. . . . The governments of the Warsaw Pact member states [propose to the parliament, government and working people of the GDR that] . . . reliable safeguards and effective control be established around the whole territory of West Berlin.

West Berlin, and its dangerous influences, was to be quarantined. The Warsaw Pact declaration was careful to reassure the Allies that the access routes, on which the Soviets had so skillfully focused the West's attention, would not be touched: "It goes without

---

[1]Kellett-Long thought he recognized the voice as that of someone he knew at ADN. He later thanked the man, who responded with a blank look.

saying that these measures must not affect existing provisions for traffic and control on communications routes between West Berlin and West Germany." The Soviets were, in effect, telling Kennedy, "You told us not to step over the line you drew, and we have not done so. There is to be no interference with the access routes, no encroachment on West Berlin. You have nothing to worry about." Moscow had shaken a threatening finger in one direction, and then, when everyone was looking that way, had moved off in another direction. For all its contingency plans, the West had not been braced for what was happening.

By the time ADN had begun dispatching the text of the Warsaw Pact communiqué, the East German border-bolting operation was already well in hand. Units of the East German army and police were on their way to the sector boundaries. Rolls of barbed wire, concrete posts, wooden horses, picks, shovels, and other construction tools, which had earlier been loaded onto trucks for unspecified "construction projects," were also en route to the border.

At the Reuters East Berlin office, having phoned London as soon as the Warsaw Pact communiqué had come over his ADN teleprinter and having learned that the communiqué was simultaneously being released in Moscow (a more important dateline), Kellett-Long went down into the streets to see what was happening. His immediate impression was that nothing was different. His street, Schönhauser Allee, was dark, silent, and deserted as it always was late at night. He got into his car and drove toward the East–West crossing point at the Brandenburg Gate. Just short of the gate he was stopped by a Vopo brandishing a red-beam flashlight. The Vopo told him he would not be allowed to proceed further. *"Die Grenze ist geschlossen,"* he said ("The border is closed") and motioned him away. When Kellett-Long turned around and drove off to see what was going on elsewhere, his car was again stopped by a Vopo at Karl Marx Platz. This time he was brought to a halt because a column of trucks was passing in the direction of the border. What exactly was taking place wasn't yet clear. But troops and military vehicles were in motion, and the border area was being cordoned off. Vindicated at last, Kellett-Long, the first westerner to know that West Berlin was being closed off from the East, hurried back to his office to report to London. He tapped out a "snap"—"The East–West Berlin border was closed early today"—before filing a longer story on what he had seen.

It was the beginning of a very long night for him and for many others in Berlin. West Berlin taxi drivers, sensitive as always to the winds of change, had begun radioing their dispatchers an hour before not to accept any requests that involved trips into the Soviet Sector. Reports began flooding in to West Berlin police headquarters from police positions and police patrols telling of troop carriers and armored cars arriving at various places along the eastern side of the border. On Bernauer Strasse, where the borderline between the Soviet and French sectors ran down the middle of the road, a line of trucks had rolled up on the east side of the street and parked, their headlights blazing. Reports of truck convoys came in from other locations as well. Soon streets bordering sector crossings resounded with the clatter and clank of bales of barbed wire and concrete posts being unloaded from the trucks and with the shouts of police and army officers as they deployed their men who poured out of armored troop carriers and other vehicles.

When, by 2:00 A.M., it was obvious that a major operation was in progress, West Berlin police headquarters roused Deputy Mayor Franz Amrehn and passed word along also to western duty officers. Awakened at home, officials of the American Mission in Berlin were reluctant to jump to conclusions or send out alarm signals. They recalled that when the Communists had closed the sector border during the Evangelical Church Congress in Berlin the previous month, it had been only a temporary operation. Officers of the mission knew they were regarded in Washington as overly excitable, with a tendency to transform Berlin trivialities into cosmic catastrophes.

In this case not only was it the weekend and nighttime when officials in Washington weren't likely to appreciate being disturbed, but there were no reports of any problems within West Berlin. So far everything seemed to be happening in the Soviet Sector. It had earlier been rumored that the Communists would issue new identity cards to all East Germans as part of the clampdown on refugees and Grenzgängers, a massive operation, which, if it were happening, would account for the hubbub on the border. If that were the case, the western powers would issue the usual formal protest about the East German military presence in Berlin, officially forbidden in the four-power city. There was no reason to get people out of bed for something like that.

After checking with the British military police, Bernard Ledwidge, political adviser at the British Mission, decided somebody should be awakened in London, if only the resident clerk at the Foreign Office whose duties included being roused when needed. Ledwidge put a call through to the Foreign Office. He said there was tumult on the border but that he hadn't much else to report. Patrols were out scouting the terrain, and he would report more when he knew more.

The operation was only just beginning. Ringing all of West Berlin's 103-mile perimeter with an impenetrable barrier was an immense project. It would take time to complete. Men had to be deployed. Materials had to be transported and unloaded. Not all parts of the border could be sealed at once. First to get concentrated treatment was Potsdamer Platz, normally the busiest East–West crossing point in the world, usually almost deserted in the early morning hours, but not now. As hastily reinforced West Berlin police and a gaggle of angry West Berliner night owls looked on, East German soldiers and Vopos went about their business of bisecting the square. With rifle-toting armed guards in front of them facing west, men with pneumatic drills jackhammered out cobblestones and trolley tracks, blasting holes into the ground for posts on which barbed wire could be strung. Others positioned the bales of wire for stringing while other guards, cradling submachine guns in their arms, faced into the Soviet Sector from the border to make certain that no one from east of the border line attempted to interfere with this bizarre, massive construction project, even though night owls had not been much in evidence in that part of the city for a long time.

By 3:30 A.M. the East Germans were installing obstructions on all major streets that had previously been crossing points. Vehicles with East Berlin license plates and East German pedestrians attempting to cross to the West through the obstructions were being turned back, while West Berliners trying to return home from the Soviet Sector were required to show identity papers before being let through. People living near the border were awakened by the clamor in the streets. In tenements nearby, windows were dotted with the faces and shapes of pajamaed people peering anxiously down at the proceedings below. Those on the eastern side who ventured into the street to get a closer look were quickly shooed back indoors by Vopos.

Many East Berliners living further in from the border were also aware that this was no ordinary night. They had been awakened by the sound of trucks and military vehicles rumbling down their normally silent, nighttime streets and, as dawn approached, by the wail of sirens as police cars escorted tanks and more convoys of trucks and armored vehicles to the border line.

Some went down into the streets to see what was causing the commotion. They drifted in the direction of the convoys and toward the din on the border. But when they got there, they were kept well back. Others, having expected the crackdown on the refugees to come at any moment, instinctively realized what was happening. If they did not, they had only to switch on their radios and listen to RIAS, which by 4:00 A.M. was providing the first sketchy reports of the barbed-wire barriers. Already having planned to flee west, several East Berliners grabbed what they could and hurried to and through nearby crossing points or border wasteland patches before guards had taken up positions there and before the barbed wire that would lock them in was properly strung. But most East Berliners, like most West Berliners, would not know till they woke in the morning what had transpired during the night. For them and others living under Communist rule in East Germany, going west at will was becoming a thing of the past.

Senior officials of the Allied missions in West Berlin had been almost continually on the telephone since 2:00 A.M. trying to sort out an accurate account of what was going on and taking calls from others seeking the same information. With the barrage of reports of activity on the sector border pouring in, it was evident that whatever was happening had serious political dimensions. Minister Allan Lightner of the American Mission realized that what was needed was a first-hand report of what was happening. Richard Smyser, one of the junior officers in the mission's Eastern Affairs Section, was roused from deep sleep and told, "There seems to be something going on in East Berlin. Go over there and take a look."

Smyser dressed quickly and, with Frank Trinka, another junior officer at the mission, climbed into Smyser's bluish-gray Mercedes convertible, putting the top down for a better view. They drove to Potsdamer Platz, where the building of the barbed-wire barrier had already been going on for the better part of two hours but where wire was still being rolled out to be strung from the concrete posts. When Smyser drove up to the barrier to cross into the Soviet Sector, Vopos stepped forward to order him to turn around. Motioning toward the official American license plate at the front of his car, Smyser told them, "We are officials of the American forces. You have no right to stop us." The Vopos huddled together for a moment, exchanged some words and then rolled back some of the barbed wire to let them through. They had instructions not to interfere with the movement of Allied officials. Nothing was to be done to complicate the immediate task at hand.

Offstage, the commander of Soviet forces in East Germany kept close watch on the proceedings. He was prepared to move in and take direct charge of operations if things threatened to get out of control. The construction of the barrier was, however, designed to be an exclusively East German affair. Its main objective was to stop the refugees. But it was also meant to demonstrate that, though the Allies could proclaim from here to eternity that Berlin was a four-power city, they had no say or influence whatsoever in East Berlin. The Western powers had been insisting that it remained the Soviet Sector and nothing more, but exclusive sovereignty over East Berlin was herewith being both proclaimed and demonstrated with Moscow's blessings by the East German regime, the same regime that the three western powers and West Germany insisted did not legally exist.

Though put on full alert and threateningly deployed around the city, Soviet forces were keeping clear of Berlin itself, as was reported by the licensed spies of the Allied liaison missions. They had been busily scouting the area without serious interference from the Soviets. The preliminary report of American liaison officers was concise:

> Soviet 19th Motorized Rifle Division, combined with 10th Guards Tank Division and possibly the 6th Motorized Rifle Division moved out early this morning and moved into position around Berlin. Elements of the 1st East German Army Motorized Rifle Division moved out from Potsdam and are presently unlocated. Soviet units deployed

and moved off the autobahn, deploying units into small outposts and roadblocks composed of three or four tanks, an armored personnel carrier and several troops. These outposts were established about 3 or 4 kilometers apart, and appear completely to ring Berlin.

The Soviet commander positioned his forces conspicuously. The Americans were to be discouraged from thinking they might be able to do something about the East German army units that had moved into East Berlin to play a major role in the seal-off operation. Though they had been on display in East Berlin before—at parades and ceremonial occasions— the Allies had the right, on paper, to march into East Berlin and arrest the East German troops for being where they were forbidden. The prospect of that happening was remote, but the Soviet forces ringing the city were telling the Allies that the East German army units would not stand alone if there were trouble. Nor was that all. Soviet rocket forces in East Europe had also been put on the alert. The Allies were to be under no illusions about the strength of the Soviet commitment.

Neither the Soviets nor the East German leaders knew how the men on the front line, those assigned to build and guard the sector barrier, would stand up to the job. No doubt they would obey orders, form up as instructed, drill holes in the pavement, plant the concrete posts, unroll the barbed wire, and string it up. But they had never been tested under pressure. How would they react if, as was possible, American tanks roared up to the border or if American troops moved in on foot to tear apart their handiwork?

Though East German leaders had been pressing the Soviets for permission to slam the border shut, they knew that things could go disastrously wrong. If there was trouble, would the men break ranks? Would they panic? And what would happen then? Indeed, while many of the East German police and soldiers on duty at the border line wore expressions of defiant determination, others seemed glum, nervous, and wishing they were somewhere else.

In previous weeks several Vopos and some East German soldiers had themselves become refugees seeking sanctuary at Marien-felde. Many who did not go west were equally disenchanted with the Communist regime. Vopo officers had reported that some of their men had been less than enthusiastic in carrying out the pre-Wall crackdown on Grenzgängers. Some had been observed on duty treating border crossers with nothing like the severity they deserved. Several had been warned that they had to bring greater enthusiasm and diligence to the job of dealing with enemies of the Socialist Fatherland or they would have to answer for their shortcomings.

It was easy enough for the officials organizing the operation to exude confidence when assuring the Soviets and Ulbricht that everything would work out as planned. But officers on the spot who knew the men and who were responsible for the details of the border closure weren't so sure. They wondered how Vopos and Grepos whose relatives had already fled as refugees would stand up to physically preventing others from doing the same. They wondered how those who happened to be Berliners would react to standing guard while their city was broken in two. Berliners tended to be less submissive to authority than most other Germans. Berlin was where the 1953 anti-Communist uprising began and where it had been carried to its greatest extremes before being bloodily crushed. How would the men react in the days to come when they had to turn back not only Grenzgängers, not only would-be refugees committing the crime of fleeing the republic, but also harmless, ordinary East Berliners merely wishing to visit brothers or cousins in the West or go to a movie there, or simply to cross over to buy a Coca-Cola from a West Berlin border stand? Members of the security forces had all been required to attend regular indoctrination sessions. But the fact that some of them had still chosen to go west left troubling suspicions that others might also be riddled with doubts about which side they were on.

Officials at the Allied missions in Berlin had a problem of a different dimension. Something peculiar was going on in the middle of the city, and they couldn't tell for sure what it was. In addition to trying to piece together a picture of what was happening, they were fielding countless phone calls from others wanting to do the same. George Muller of the American Mission recalled, "The phone kept ringing. The United States establishment in Berlin was huge and practically everybody had something to report or questions to ask. You could hardly sit back and collect your wits."

The American Mission in Berlin made no effort at that stage to file a report to Washington. Officials there realized they could not match the news agencies in quickly transmitting to the United States details of a breaking story. It took from four to six hours to dispatch an official telegram through channels from Berlin to the State Department. Besides, official reports were expected to be more analytical than what-when-where wire service flashes. "We decided," Muller said, "to hold up our reporting till we knew exactly what this was about."

Around 6:00 A.M. Richard Smyser and Frank Trinka returned from their reconnaissance expedition in East Berlin and told of considerable activity there. There was much movement of armored personnel carriers, trucks, and other police and military vehicles in downtown East Berlin, close to the sector border. Judging from what the two men had seen crossing into and out of the East, the activity was part of a very major population-control exercise, the extent of which was still unclear.

Smyser and Trinka had seen victims of this exercise in sharp relief when they had parked near the Friedrichstrasse train station a mile from the American Sector and entered the station hall. With its tired brown walls, the hall—dimly lit and cavernous—seemed like the inside of a huge bunker. People of all ages, including small children, had gathered there. They carried packages and valises. Some sat on them. Their faces were masked by anguish and worry. Some were weeping. These were would-be refugees, their escape route abruptly choked off. Smyser thought the expressions some wore conveyed a feeling of "Oh, my God, if we'd only gone twenty-four hours earlier." For them there was no doubt that the border closure was final, that the escape hatch was closed for good.

Some people in the station hall, uncomprehending, tried to get past the guards onto the platform where westbound trains normally arrived. They were held back, through some of the Vopos seemed not overly happy with the task they had to perform. A few Vopos distributed printed leaflets containing a proclamation explaining, among other things, that citizens of the German Democratic Republic wishing to visit West Berlin would henceforth require special passes, which, it was said, could be obtained at their local police stations. But except for a handful of East German intelligence officers sent west to size up the situation there, no such special passes were available.

It was just after dawn of a bright summer's morning when Smyser and Trinka approached the Brandenburg Gate to drive through to West Berlin again. The gate had not been sealed, but it was heavily policed, and their car was waved to a halt by a Vopo on the East Berlin side. Though informed they were officers of the American forces, he kept them from driving on and consulted a superior in the nearby guardhouse before letting them pass. It was later reported that a senior East German government official had been posted in that guardhouse to make certain no unnecessary difficulties arose at the gate. Everyone was being very careful.

When they gave their report at the American Mission, Smyser and Trinka were pointedly asked whether they had seen any Soviets in East Berlin. They reported that they had not. Regardless of who was sponsoring the border closure, the nuts and bolts of it were being provided by the "nonexistent" East German regime rather than the Soviets, making it a twin challenge to the West.

Among East Berliners who had jobs in West Berlin were restaurant employees, cleaning women, hotel porters, and others who worked on Sundays and who normally got to work early in the morning. Around 6:00 A.M. many of them, unaware of the night's developments, started off for work as usual. They didn't get very far. They found that the gates to the entrances of all twelve East Berlin train stations on crosstown subway lines had been padlocked hours before. Turned away by police, they couldn't at first grasp what was happening and just stood at the entrances bewildered. Some appealed to the Vopos to let them through, not realizing that even if the gates were unlocked and they were let through, they still wouldn't be able to get to West Berlin.

Though the subway system was still operating, trains shuttling under East Berlin from one part of West Berlin to another were not permitted to stop in the Soviet Sector. The only exception was at the Friedrichstrasse station Smyser and Trinka had visited, where people from the West could still enter East Berlin if permitted to pass through the tight security cordon. What was more, Vopos had been posted in the subway stations to keep would-be refugees who managed to slip into the train tunnels from finding their way to freedom on foot. Cross-border commuters who normally went west by elevated S-Bahn also quickly discovered that their way was blocked.

Early morning Grenzgängers were soon joined in their despair by other East Berliners who, unaware, were setting out to visit relatives and friends in West Berlin for the day. Some grew explosively angry when told that was no longer possible. Grepo Sergeant Rudi Thurow heard one man defiantly denounce the government for keeping him from seeing his own mother. Others were equally outspoken. One of Thurow's men, Private Gottfried Herrman, confessed to the sergeant that he was ashamed of himself for what he was required to do. It wasn't long before Herrman vaulted the barbed wire to the West and made his way to Marienfelde. Thurow was to follow him soon afterward.

As the morning drew on, another factor appeared in the equation. Despite the early hour, clusters of angry West Berliners had been gathering at places along the sector borders to look on and hurl catcalls at the Vopos as the barbed-wire barrier was being laid. West Berlin police were getting worried that hotheads among them might try to assault the Vopos. But not only the Communists were the objects of their derision. Voices were raised in mockery of their supposed protectors, the Americans. Though the Communists were already sending men to relieve those who had been on duty since just after midnight, the Americans had not even bothered to send a company of troops to the border in response to this gruesome provocation. The city they had made such moving promises to defend was being ripped apart, and there was no sign of them.

Whatever his own gut reaction to the situation, the American commandant did not feel free to use his own judgment to confront the situation. As tension had built up over the previous weeks, Major General Albert Watson, Jr., had been strongly advised not to be provoked into impetuous action. Watson was careful to observe that admonition. He was in an unenviable position. A tough but even-tempered soldier-soldier rather than a diplomat-soldier—of which the United States Army has many more today than it did then—he had been American commandant in Berlin only three months. But that had been more than enough time for him to realize he was expected to be little more than a messenger boy.

Though the situation might change from day to day and events worthy of immediate response might occur, he was required to tread very carefully in making decisions. He was directly responsible to American Ambassador Walter Dowling in Bonn, an experienced foreign-service officer, who was officially chief of the Berlin Mission, as well as to General Bruce Clarke in Heidelberg, the United States Army commander in Europe, both of whom, in view of the delicacy of the situation, relentlessly peered over his shoulder and made sure he knew it. He was also responsible, through Clarke, to General Lauris Norstad at NATO headquarters in Paris. There were times when Watson's instructions came through both military and diplomatic channels. There were times when both channels were silent. That morning was one of those times, and yet Watson had to make a decision—to do something or to do nothing.

There were no reports of Soviet military activity in Berlin or of East German provocations in the city, so there was no reason in those early hours to disturb people at army headquarters in Heidelberg. The political side of his mission had already begun filing dispatches to Bonn. Later in the morning he would alert his garrison and send a helicopter over the border area to check on developments. But to send troops to the sector border just to watch the East Germans get on with whatever they had in mind might have been deemed a pointless and humiliating overreaction, which Dowling and Clarke—who were both still fast asleep in their respective beds far away—would call on him to explain. As the crisis developed, General Watson was, as one officer put it, "in a hell of a box."

9

"Why Didn't
We Know?"

*Surprise, when it happens to a government, is likely to be a
complicated, diffuse, bureaucratic thing. It includes neglect of
responsibility, but also responsibility so poorly defined or so
ambiguously delegated that action gets lost. It includes gaps in
intelligence that, like a string of pearls too precious to wear, is
too sensitive to give to those who need it. It includes the alarm
that fails to work, but also the alarm that has gone off so often
it has been disconnected. It includes the unalert watchman, but
also the one who knows he'll be chewed out by his superiors if
he gets high authority out of bed. It includes the contingencies
that occur to no one, but also those that everyone assumes
somebody else is taking care of. It includes straight-forward
procrastination, but also decisions protracted by internal dis-
agreement. It includes, in addition, the inability of individual
human beings to rise to the occasion until they are sure it is
the occasion—which is usually too late. . . . Finally . . . surprise
may include some measure of genuine novelty introduced by
the enemy, and possibly some sheer bad luck.*

—THOMAS C. SCHELLING

THERE was a six-hour time difference between Berlin and Washington. Early morning in central Europe was late night of the previous day on the east coast of the United States. If Honecker had deliberately timed his operation for when American leaders would be least prepared to respond quickly, he had chosen shrewdly. There weren't many people in the American capital, or in any of the places they had gone to get away from the oppressive heat of the city, sharply attuned on a Saturday night to the latest developments far away from home.

Washington was to remain very much in the dark about the story unfolding in Berlin for many hours after the bales of barbed wire were first pushed off the trucks on the sector border. A lot of disjointed reporting came in at first, bits and pieces of news being passed along by the wire services—East German troops and police had taken up positions on the sector dividing line; they were tearing up pavement; they were stringing barbed wire. But news-agency reporters in Berlin were not reading too much into what they were at first able to see happening. For one thing, they were too busy covering the story as it developed in the dark of night. For another, like everyone else there, they didn't know exactly what the Communists had in mind. Pedestrian, vehicular, and train traffic between the Soviet and western sectors was being interrupted. The Communists, as always, were making extravagant declarations. It was a good enough story without speculative forecasts on how long the East Germans were prepared to go on with the prodigious effort and expense of manning a barbed-wire, city-center frontier with troops and police.

Having fielded their share of unfounded rumors and exaggerations with various datelines during the previous few weeks, the main bureaus of the news agencies were being cautious. Though he needed no such instruction, Joe Fleming, United Press International bureau chief and newshawk in Berlin, was soon to be advised by New York to be careful not to make it seem that World War III was about to break out.

In Washington, just after midnight (6:00 A.M. Berlin time), John Ausland, Berlin Task Force duty officer for the weekend, was telephoned at home by the State Department's Operations Center and told things were happening along the Berlin sector border though it wasn't yet exactly clear what. There had, as yet, been no report received from the Berlin Mission; just wire service squibs. Ausland, who had gone to bed early, asked to be called back when more specific information was available and went back to sleep. It was almost four hours later before he was awakened again with a more comprehensive report. He got out of bed, dressed, and alerted Berlin Task Force member Frank Cash by telephone before driving to the State Department. Cash said he'd join him there after he took his wife to the airport later that morning.

President Kennedy was still fast asleep at his Hyannis Port retreat and would be for several more hours. Edward Tomkins, head of the Western Department of the British Foreign Office, was alerted by the Foreign Office resident clerk shortly after breakfast and drove immediately from his weekend home in Buckinghamshire to his office in Whitehall. The news was still patchy when he got there. "No one knew what was happening," Tomkins said. Whatever it was, the western commandants in Berlin could not delay a response of some kind, if only for the sake of appearances. They, and the Soviet commandant, were supposed to be in charge of the city. Now they were being shown that they were not in charge.

Armed East German forces—not even Soviet—were presuming to draw a line through the city and deciding who may or may not pass through. A decree by East German Interior Minister Karl Maron, who had no legal status or authority in the eyes of the western commandants, announced that Berlin border-crossing points, all to be controlled by East German security forces, were to be reduced from eighty-eight to thirteen. There would be no new restrictions on foreigners crossing the border, but they would have to show their passports. West Berliners "with peaceful intentions" would be permitted to enter but were required to show their personal identity cards when doing so. "Agents of West German militarism" would be banned from East Berlin. East Berliners were forbidden to enter West Berlin. If any of this was allowed to stand, even the pretense of four-power status for the city would be consigned to the history books and the face of Berlin would be totally transformed.

At 10:00 A.M. the western commandants and their political advisers gathered at the Kommandatura in West Berlin to confer on developments. Some of those attending had not slept at all or had slept very little during the night, and their faces were marked with fatigue. The role of Kommandatura chairman rotated among the commandants, and the job had fallen to Watson for August. It was his job to outline the facts of the situation to his colleagues, as far as they were known. At that point five things were known: (1) the Communists were setting up a barrier that if completed, would effectively seal East Berlin off from West Berlin; (2) in permitting the East Germans to do this, and to issue various decrees, the Soviets were violating four-power agreements; (3) there had so far been no encroachment by the Communists on West Berlin; (4) the western powers were committed to defending their rights in West Berlin and might soon be obliged to live up to that commitment; (5) there was no sign as yet of Soviet military forces being directly involved, though at least two Soviet divisions had been deployed around the city.

Questions were asked for which there were no available answers. Would the access-route lifelines across East Germany to West Berlin be blocked? Would the Soviets continue to stay clear of the operation? Would the East Germans continue to confine their activity to East Berlin, or were they planning a move against West Berlin, about which reports might come in at any moment? It was learned, for example, that not only troops and Vopos were manning the border and laying barbed wire; East German border police (Grepos like Sergeant Thurow), transport police *(Trapos)*, and even East Berlin firemen were also participating. In addition to fresh troops and Vopos to relieve the men who had been on duty through the night, armed units of the Worker Battle Brigades, the paramilitary Communist militia, had just taken up positions at places along the border.[1] The East Germans were deploying every man they had.

The atmosphere at the Kommandatura meeting was grim. The sense of impotence that had overtaken West Berliners in anticipation of a Communist clampdown on the refugees was now shared by the western commandants. They recollected reflexly the blockade thirteen years earlier and asked anxious questions about the level of

[1]The previous Thursday, when Adam Kellett-Long had gone to the Diplomatic Services Bureau in East Berlin to check on the supply of fuel for his office-apartment, he had seen a full field pack in the corner of the office. The man there, a member of a Worker Brigade, had said there was going to be some sort of exercise over the weekend.

essential supplies in the city. Would supplies be adequate until a new airlift could be organized if the ground access routes were again severed? Nor did it escape the imagination of some in attendance that their deliberations might serve no purpose whatsoever, that they might be witnessing the opening act of a major East–West clash in which the comparatively puny western garrisons in Berlin would quickly be overrun.

But such speculation was pointless and distracting. The commandants had to weigh the circumstances prevailing then and there. And further developments could be expected momentarily. No one suggested doing anything about the barbed wire. Nor was there talk of other countermeasures. The possibility that the western Allies could wrest the initiative away from the Communists was not raised. All three commandants and their political advisers awaited instructions from their respective governments. They knew there was nothing else they could do. Their meeting was dominated by foreboding about what might lie ahead.

Realizing that they should at least make a gesture while they waited for their masters to decide on a course of action, Watson suggested that the commandants dispatch a message of protest to their Soviet counterpart in East Berlin. Though reluctant to go along until instructions came from London, the British commandant, Major General Rohan Delacombe, was persuaded to agree. But Major General Jean Lacomme, the French commandant, regretted that not only did he require authorization from Paris to send a note of any kind, but that Paris would insist on reviewing the contents of the note before approval would be given. The way things happened in the French capital during the vacation month of August, that could take days.

However, the French general agreed there was no reason why a public protest, rather than a formal message to the Soviets, could not be made, and the aides of the three commandants were instructed to draft a suitable statement. It was to condemn not only the violation of four-power agreements but the abuse of human rights as well. It would not remove the barbed wire, but it would at least show both West Berliners and the Communists that the western commandants were deeply concerned by developments.

Before the commandants adjourned their meeting, Willy Brandt was invited to join them to give his view of what was happening to his city. Running against Adenauer in elections for West German chancellor the following month, Brandt had arrived back in Berlin from a campaign tour of West Germany only that morning. When the border-sealing operation had begun, he had been asleep on a train heading from one campaign rally to another. At around 5:00 A.M. a railway official knocked on the door of his compartment to tell him what was happening. He and his entourage had left the train at Hannover, its next major stop; had made quickly for the nearby airport; and had taken the first flight back to Berlin. Arriving at Tempelhof, Brandt had gone directly to Potsdamer Platz, where he had been devastated by the sight of the barbed wire and the armed East German troops and police, posted like guards at a prison camp. The full dimensions of the operation weren't yet evident. Trucks were unloading more barbed wire, more concrete posts, and additional loads of rubble to firm up and extend the job begun during the night.

Brandt had been at first profoundly saddened rather than angered by what he saw and by what he heard from West Berlin police about what had been going on. The Communist barrier ran down the middle of streets, dividing neighborhoods and separating neighbors. It was cutting through church yards, cemeteries, and wooded areas and ran along canals, zigzagging through the city, faithfully following the contours of the Soviet Sector. Trolley tracks had been torn up, paving stones had been gouged out, trenches had been dug, trees had been cut down to block off streets. Machine-gun nests had been set up at the Brandenburg Gate—where Brandt had gone next—the guns pointing down the Street of the 17th of June (named to commemorate the East German uprising of 1953) toward West Berliners who had gathered in fury and disgust on their side of that monumental architectural symbol of Berlin. "It was hard," Brandt recalled, "to remain calm and composed."

But when he got to the Kommandatura to confer with the western commandants, he seemed stunned and flabbergasted. Under the circumstances it was not surprising. Brandt was a moody man, a man of deep if generally undemonstrative emotions. Sometimes at meetings, as debate swirled around him, he would say nothing, his long, dark face seemingly clouded in thought. At other times he could be articulate and emotionally engaged. Now he was subdued and somber, the layers of distress that had engulfed him only gradually lifting. It was, remarkably, his first visit to the Kommandatura, and he was surprised to see hanging there, alongside pictures of the western commandants, a picture of General Alexander Kotikov, the last Soviet Berlin commandant to participate in the activities of the Kommandatura before the Soviets walked out thirteen years before. It had not been removed, and a place for the Soviets was reserved at the main Kommandatura conference table, as symbols of continued Allied insistence that Berlin was a four-power city.

Once he rose from the doldrums, Brandt's main concern that morning was that Berliners, both east and west, might be so enraged by the barbed wire drawn across the city that they would erupt uncontrollably in violent protests. By 10:00 A.M. 150 angry West Berliners had gathered at Potsdamer Platz to jeer at the work crews tearing up the pavement and feeding out the wire, and at the armed guards in front of them. By 10:30 the crowd had swelled to 500 and was expanding all the time. By 11:00 there were 2,000 indignant protesters congregated west of the Brandenberg Gate.

Brandt feared that the Soviets would not hesitate to send in their tanks if there were an explosion of popular wrath on the other side of the border. Blood would be shed. People would be killed. But something had to be done. At least, he thought, western patrols should be sent to the border to show West Berliners that whatever was happening in the East, they were not endangered. When informed that the commandants intended to issue a protest to the Soviet commandant, Brandt replied softly, "If all the commandants do is issue protests, people in the East will laugh themselves sick from Pankow all the way to Vladivostok."[2] "Scanning the troubled faces of my American friends," he wrote later, "I could imagine what had happened. They had alerted the Pentagon, the State Department and the White House, only to be told that ungovernable reactions must be avoided at all costs." In fact that had not yet happened.

By midmorning on Sunday the barbed-wire barrier, six feet high in some places, was firmly installed along long stretches of the sector border. Where it wasn't strung up, a beginning had been made. The air was still filled with the chatter of pneumatic drills battering holes into the ground for concrete posts. Bulldozers were ramming mounds of rubble into position along some parts of the border. Armed men—soldiers, Vopos, Grepos, Trapos, Worker Battle Brigadesmen—covered the area.

[2]Pankow is an East Berlin suburb in which there was a district reserved for residences of senior East German Communist officials.

On the eastern side of the wire, but kept back, small knots of East Berliners, stunned more than frightened, bewildered rather than angry, gazed at the proceedings. The full significance of what they were seeing had yet to sink in. They had trouble grasping the fact that streets they had casually crossed day in, day out for years, as readily as people in New York, London, or Paris cross streets, were not only out of bounds but barred to them by uniformed men who were prepared to shoot them.

On the West Berlin side all available police were on duty to control ever larger, ever angrier crowds. Many people, living well away from the border and only now showing up, had learned of developments when called by anxious relatives, elsewhere in West Berlin or in West Germany, who had heard radio news reports. Some people in the city had been telephoned by West Berliners out of town or out of the country on business or vacation, who feared for the safety of their families or who, in the confusion of the moment, worried that they might not be permitted to return home. Some West Berliners had learned what was happening from fellow parishioners at early morning church services. Many who went to join the protesters at Potsdamer Platz and elsewhere along the wire called out pleadingly or bitterly to the East German police and troops, asking them if they had no shame and if they had the nerve to still call themselves Germans.

For a summer Sunday morning on which momentous things were taking place nearby, Karl-Marx-Allee was strangely quiet. No clusters of anxious or curious residents milled about or engaged in public discourse there on the developments of the night. There was no to-ing and fro-ing of people seeking the latest news. The street was virtually deserted. It was as if those living along East Berlin's showcase boulevard, most of them equipped with the untarnished political credentials required to have been allotted accommodations in the new buildings there, had received advance word of a tornado and, not having access to the old, Kansas-style cellar sanctuaries, had closed themselves in their new, model apartments till things blew over.

Nearer the border, however, gatherings of East Berliners continued to expand, swollen by those who realized to their bitterness, grief, or amazement—or all three—that they had been cut off from parents or offspring, brothers and sisters, friends and jobs just a few minutes away. One East Berliner who had been organizing his permanent shift to West Berlin little by little, and had rented an apartment there to which he had been furtively carting his portable possessions one by one, had slept in his West Berlin home-to-be that night to find in the morning that he was separated from his wife, now apparently stuck behind the barbed wire.

Others, though shaken by developments, were not deterred by the newly installed barrier. A middle-aged East Berlin couple, having only learned of the night's developments at 9:00 that morning, went down to see for themselves. Spotting a stretch of wire barrier that was still incomplete and, for the moment, unguarded, the man said to his wife, *"Hop oder top"* ("Now or never"), and across they went to find their way to Marienfelde.

Others did the same, some after carefully reconnoitering the border barrier for weak spots, some on impulse when overcome by the implications of what they saw. A Vopo, the first of several to come through in the following days, came across just before noon on Sunday. A Volkswagen came crashing through, the first of a number of vehicles to make the attempt, some successfully, some not.

Some East Berliners jumped into the Teltow Canal, which marked part of the East–West boundary, and swam to the far side where waiting West Berliners helped them out of the water. Among them was a young couple with their three-year-old son strapped to his father's back. The border guards weren't yet shooting at escapees, but each believed he was risking his life. As the hours passed, as more and more barbed wire was strung, it became increasingly difficult to get through. But during the first few days of Berlin's new era an East German or East Berliner determined enough, daring enough, knowledgeable enough, and capable of making a thorough tour of the border could have found a way through to the West, and not necessarily by swimming a canal. Between dawn and dusk of the first day, eight hundred refugees checked in at Marienfelde.

But most people, and especially those from the East German hinterlands, had no idea they could still get out. The easiest routes, the ones that had earlier been most commonly used for crossing the border, were now sealed. At midday Alexanderplatz, at the heart of East Berlin, began taking on a surrealistic aspect no less nightmarish than the scene Richard Smyser had witnessed in the Friedrichstrasse train station the night before. People, some clutching small suitcases, some with small cardboard cartons tied with string, shuffled back and forth through the square, going nowhere, sometimes stopping to look off in the distance, as if expecting a reprieve or a savior. One man, apparently recognizing that I was not one of their number, approached and started to say something to me but stopped short and turned quickly away, perhaps suspecting I was a police spy.

Some people were trudging around the perimeters of the square as if actually going somewhere. Some just squatted forlornly on their cases or cartons. Like the frustrated travelers at the Friedrichstrasse station, many of these East Germans had learned too late of the border closing—or hadn't believed what they had heard—and had left home for East Berlin in order to cross into West Berlin. Now they had to come to terms with the fact that Marienfelde was as much beyond their reach as Mars. They had no place to go but the homes they had forsaken, perhaps to face the consequences if their attempt to flee the republic had come to the attention of the local police.

The East German authorities were, meantime, relieved that the operation was proceeding as planned, with no sign of either Allied interference or serious repercussions in the streets of East Berlin. But there was a long way still to go before the operation could be deemed a success. The West would certainly be heard from, one way or another. Remaining gaps in the border were still to be closed. There was more barbed wire to string, more embankments of rubble to bulldoze up where such barriers would prove more suitable.

As Sunday wore on, more and more police and troops and Communist militiamen were bussed to the border area, many from outside Berlin, to take part in the operation. No hitches were reported. But it was still to be seen what the workers of East Berlin, people like those who had rioted against the government eight years earlier, would do when they gathered at their jobs the next morning and could coordinate their reactions. An East German army officer who later fled to the West said that though the deployment of Soviet and East German army divisions around Berlin was meant to discourage Allied countermeasures, they were primarily positioned to deal with the greater danger of popular uprisings.

East German radio was now broadcasting regular reports, not about barbed wire being drawn across the middle of Berlin, but about unspecified "measures" being implemented to protect the Socialist Fatherland by blocking off the "slave traders," "kidnappers," and "currency swindlers." A single city, a single people was being monumentally split in two, but radio broadcasts in the East sought to belittle the significance of that aspect of the event by announcing repeatedly that the controls being introduced were of the kind "customary along the border of any sovereign state."

Such announcements, and vivid accounts of the border proceedings by RIAS and the Sender Freies Berlin radio station in West Berlin, attracted still more people to the eastern as well as the western approaches to the border. Some East Berliners complained heatedly when Vopos stopped them from getting within a block of the barbed wire as it was being strung and reinforced. In one case a Vopo beat up a man who insisted the authorities had no right to divide Berlin in that way. Another Vopo, sickened by the sight of such brutality, found a gap in the barbed wire soon afterward and went west.

But for the most part, unless physically provoked, the East Berlin police refrained from assaulting protesters or even arguing with them. They had been instructed to be firm but unprovocative. East German leaders remained haunted by visions of a violent reaction from the people they were fencing in. They had been told by the Soviets that no such reaction would be tolerated, that Soviet forces would move in to deal with riots if necessary, even if it meant that this elaborate display of East German sovereignty in East Berlin would be sacrificed.

Where the situation did threaten to explode into violence, Vopo reinforcements, held in reserve in strategic locations in the city, were rushed in to disperse the crowds, gently if possible, roughly if not. When a group of youths shouted condemnation of the East German regime, demanded their usual access to West Berlin, and refused to back off when ordered, Vopos threw tear gas grenades and smoke bombs to scatter them. In some places the police waded in with nightsticks. But though their presence was an intimidating factor, T-34 and T-54 tanks of the *Volksarmee,* held in reserve on sidestreets near potential trouble spots, were not needed to maintain order. East Berliners vividly recalled how ruthlessly the 1953 uprising had been quashed and how the West had merely looked on as it happened.

Expecting the security forces to come under popular pressure, operation coordinators instructed officers of the Communist youth organization to organize morale-boosting exercises. By early afternoon the guards at the border and the troops and police held in reserve were receiving cheering visits from pink-cheeked, flower-bearing, blue-shirted boys and girls of the Free German Youth, who thanked them and praised the work they were doing on behalf of the peace-loving citizens of the German workers' and farmers' state.

In West Berlin Mayor Brandt was emerging from the numbing shock of what he had seen at the border and the implications of what was happening. Now furious, he called a special session of the West Berlin Chamber of Deputies to condemn the Communist action. He told the deputies, "The cold concrete posts which now split our city have been rammed into . . . the living organism of Berlin." Brandt said the people of Berlin expected the western powers, who had yet to react, to take "energetic steps" in response.

But there was more anguish and desperation than substance to what he was saying. The energetic steps of which he spoke would have been mere gestures—sending Allied patrols to the sector borders as he had urged the commandants to do and vigorously protesting to the Soviets and the Warsaw Pact countries. He later noted bitterly, "Twenty hours elapsed before the military patrols I had requested appeared on the city's internal border. . . . Seventy-two hours elapsed before a protest—couched in terms that were little more than routine—was lodged in Moscow."

But neither Brandt nor the western commandants had any suggestions to offer for action that would produce any significant change in the situation. The barbed wire, the armed East German troops and police, would still be there. Crowds of West Berlin demonstrators, continuing to grow in front of the wire, did, however, offer a few suggestions. "Hang Ulbricht," they shouted. "Open the border." "Ivan go home." They sang the West German national anthem, and then sang it again. They shouted slogans: "There is only one Germany! There is only one Berlin!"

At one point a group of West Berlin youths tore open a gap in the barbed wire and called out to nearby East Berliners who were watching from the other side to hurry through, but the youths were quickly driven back by Vopos who advanced on them, some with fixed bayonets, others with their truncheons drawn. At another place along the border a Vopo was beaten up before others could come to his rescue and before West Berlin police could push back his assaulters.

When a crowd of enraged demonstrators surged toward the

Brandenburg Gate and appeared to be threatening to march through it into East Berlin, East German water-cannon vehicles moved into position, unleashed high-pressure jets on the would-be invaders, and drove them back. When the demonstrators then bombarded the vehicles and the Vopos at the gate with stones, steel-helmeted East German troops clutching their rifles moved forward, and West Berlin police were able to coax the demonstrators back down the street, out of trouble.

The West Berlin police were particularly worried about the two Soviet soldiers ceremonially guarding the Soviet war memorial in the British Sector, a few hundred yards into West Berlin from the Brandenburg Gate. Those soldiers would have been quickly overwhelmed if rushed by the mob, and the demonstrators jeering at them were growing increasingly abusive. The mere sight of Soviet uniforms on West Berlin territory and of the monument's two World War II Soviet tanks—said to be the first to have entered Berlin when the Soviets overran the city in 1945—infuriated the demonstrators. Police reinforcements were hurriedly rushed in to block any move against the monument.

In Washington Berlin Task Force duty officer John Ausland had reached the State Department around 5:00 A.M. (11:00 A.M. Berlin time). Reviewing the available reports from Berlin, he realized that the task force was about to earn its keep. There was work to be done, though acting task force director Martin Hillenbrand was incommunicado on an island off Virginia. Task Force members Pete Day and David Klein were also away. They had arranged vacations when it had been believed that the Berlin crunch was not likely until the fall.

Ausland contacted Colonel Showalter, who rushed to the State Department. When he arrived, he put a call through to American military headquarters in Europe outside Paris, but the duty officer there knew only what was being reported about the Berlin situation by the wire services. This was ten hours after the East German operation had begun! It was later learned that senior American diplomats in Bonn first heard of the situation when, later that day, they returned from an embassy-sponsored Little League baseball game and turned on the radio.

At 6:00 A.M. in Washington things looked serious enough for

a senior State Department official to be alerted. Ausland tried to reach Assistant Secretary of State Foy Kohler by telephone but got no answer. He felt that he didn't yet have enough solid information to rouse Secretary of State Rusk at that time of day. But a White House duty officer, who had been monitoring the news agency reports, telephoned the task force office to find out if Ausland could provide an update on the situation. He said, "We need something for Salinger" (the presidential press officer), in case the president would want to issue a statement after being alerted to developments upon awaking in Hyannis Port. Ausland drafted some points the president might consider. They included the fact that as far as reports indicated, what the Communists were doing was confined to East Berlin. The Warsaw Pact declaration had given assurances that the access routes would not be affected. Much as what was happening might be deplored, it was not something over which, according to declared policy, the United States was prepared to take military action.

Shortly after 7:00 A.M. having delivered his wife to the airport, Frank Cash got in. Ausland had been trying without success to find the file with a contingency plan for dealing with the latest Berlin developments. Cash was able to locate the file, but it contained nothing relevant to the situation that had arisen. All the planning in Washington had been directed toward coping with other contingencies—a Communist move against the access routes and an East German uprising in the event of a refugee clampdown. Despite weeks of gradually escalating tension, despite streamlined procedures for consultations between government departments and between the Allies, the Berlin Task Force hadn't yet gotten around to contemplating more far-fetched possibilities—like the lowering of the Iron Curtain in the middle of Berlin. Kennedy later complained to a task force officer, "Why, with all those plans, do you never have one for what happens?"

At the time offical communications between Washington and the American Mission in Berlin took forever. Officers were required to use only secure telephone lines. The process was absurdly complicated, involving specialized equipment that was not readily accessible. As a result no direct voice contact with Berlin had been made. With reporters in the divided city still out covering their story, press accounts of what was going on were sketchy and inconclusive. Embarrassingly, the most detailed early-morning report on developments in Berlin reached the State Department through an unofficial channel—Lothar Loewe, a West Berlin correspondent based in Washington. A diligent and personable reporter, Loewe had established close personal contacts with some State Department officials. When he heard a radio report of trouble on the sector borders, he checked with the State Department crisis center but was told they didn't know much. He then did what State Department officials were not authorized to do. He telephoned West Berlin on an ordinary commercial line and reached Albert Hemsing, the press officer at the American Mission, who gave him a rundown on the situation as far as he knew it. Loewe also telephoned journalist colleagues in Berlin and got a detailed report from them as well. He then went to the State Department to pass on his information to people at the task force.

"Where did you get your facts?" they asked suspiciously.

"It was simple," he replied. "I called Al Hemsing. Why didn't you?"

"We have to go through channels," they explained limply.

As more information became available, Ausland again tried to contact Foy Kohler by telephone and was finally able to reach him. Though he had also heard radio news reports of the Berlin developments, Kohler was not overly alarmed. Apprised of the task force's efforts to gather information, Kohler said that Cash and Ausland appeared to have the situation well in hand and that he, therefore, would not be coming in.

But after subsequently conferring with Rusk on the telephone, Kohler did show up, just before 10:00 A.M. Rusk also arrived to take charge. Kohler was first brought up to date on developments by Cash and Ausland and then went to Rusk's office to discuss the situation. It was decided that it was time finally to contact Kennedy, who presumably had not yet been alerted since there had been no calls from Hyannis Port requesting information and no further contact with the White House duty officer since 6:00 A.M. Before calling the president, Rusk wanted to confer with the American Mission in Berlin. Not to waste time, he had Kohler disregard the rule on security and had him put through a call on an open line. There wasn't much that would be said that could be of use to the Communists, who were presumed to be tapping the telephone line as it ran through East Germany.

Allan Lightner in Berlin took the call from Kohler and filled him in on the latest developments at the border and on the proceedings at the commandants' meeting. He reported that the commandants had decided to issue an open protest to the Soviets. After conferring with Rusk, Kohler vetoed the idea. Though the Americans in Berlin had worked hard to persuade their reluctant British and French counterparts to agree to issue the protest, they were ordered to make no statement whatsoever. The situation was deemed too serious to be left to the diplomats and generals in the field. Whatever official comment was to be made would come in due course from Washington. Having long been irritated by insinuations from their American colleagues in Berlin that they were too weak-kneed to face up to the Soviets, personnel at the British Mission were not overly distressed seeing them stamped on from above.

Barred from issuing a protest on the spot, officials at the American Mission waited with great anticipation for the protest to come from Washington. As they waited, a sense of frustration set in, nourished by the conviction that Washington could not grasp what was at stake. Howard Trivers, political officer at the Berlin Mission at the time, complained, "It was exceedingly difficult to make the Kennedy Administration see beyond its abstract preconceptions and come to understand the actual situation in West Berlin." His deputy, George Muller, said, "Washington, the president, the Administration didn't know or didn't want to know that there were many residual threads that wove all Berlin together." Richard Smyser said that Washington "didn't understand that what was happening in East Berlin would affect the vitality of West Berlin."

The White House, on the other hand, remained convinced that personnel at the mission were afflicted by a disorienting disease known as Berlinitis, the prime symptom of which was an unshakable belief that Berlin was the center of the universe and that each incident there, no matter how commonplace in the greater scheme of things, was earthshaking. Even the American Embassy in Bonn, to which the mission was responsible in the chain of command, didn't completely trust the judgment of mission officers who were thought to be supersensitive to every move the Soviets made. Martin Hillenbrand, who had himself earlier been an official at the Berlin Mission, later observed, "We always noted that when we sent people to Berlin, they became Berliners by adoption and adopted the psychological atmosphere of Berlin. They did not have the view that Washington had in a nuclear age."

Members of the Berlin Mafia in Washington shared the disquiet of the Berlin Mission. But those in the higher councils of state, notably Rusk, displayed no urgency about responding to the reports from Berlin. Upon taking office in January, John Kennedy had named the low-keyed Rusk to be his secretary of state because he really wanted to do the job himself. Kennedy and the bright, young advisers he had brought with him to the White House were confident that they knew pretty well how to deal with international questions in such a way as to protect America's basic interests while keeping the world at peace. Unlike Dean Acheson and John Foster Dulles, his forceful, policy-pushing predecessors at the State Department, Rusk had been made to understand that his job was merely to run the State Department bureaucracy efficiently and carry out White House instructions on policy.

As the Berlin crisis developed, Kennedy regularly consulted Rusk, who had wide experience in international affairs and whose judgment he valued. But hungry for fresh ideas that might point the way out of the crisis, he sometimes also conferred with lower-level experts at the State Department, telephoning them out of the blue without Rusk's knowledge and failing to tell Rusk of the conclusions drawn from such exchanges. Whatever his feelings about Kennedy's modus operandi, Rusk—a mild-mannered, unassuming professional with a keen understanding of both how to administer foreign policy and keep his advice to himself when it wasn't wanted—had been content to work according to the Kennedy ground rules.

But thus hamstrung, the secretary of state could only wait for instructions from the president in Hyannis Port on the course to follow as the Berlin signals began flashing that Sunday morning. With those signals indicating that western interests were not under threat, Kennedy had been shielded by his solicitous aides from unnecessary bother when he awoke that morning. As much as possible, the president's weekends away from Washington were meant to be brief escapes from presidential pressures. Kennedy had gone off with his family to 10:00 A.M. mass at the Church of St. Francis Xavier in Hyannis Port. (It was already 4:00 in the afternoon in divided Berlin.) He then returned home to change his clothes for a relaxing cruise on Nantucket Sound aboard *The Marlin,* his father's yacht.

Armed guards in a watchtower on the border between East Germany and West Berlin prior to the erection of the Wall, posted to prevent the escape of refugees to the West. The only route still open at the time was within the four-power city.

As the barbed wire barrier dividing Berlin is strung, East German soldiers, their backs to West Berlin, face a crowd of sullen East Berliners.

Members of an East Berlin worker brigade on duty at the barbed wire.

The Wall goes up.

Hastily erected, the Wall, made of concrete blocks, at first collapsed in places under its own weight.

The Brandenburg Gate, once the symbol of Berlin and once astride Berlin's major Unter den Linden thoroughfare, was sealed off from the East in 1961.

The same scene in 1985, with the Brandenburg Gate still sealed off.

As the East Germans build the Wall with Soviet approval, British troops string wire around the Soviet war memorial in West Berlin, ostensibly to protect it from enraged West Berliners.

West Berliners wave over the Wall toward East Berlin, hoping to be spotted by relatives there.

Separated from their relatives by the Wall, West Berlin parents hoist their children for grand-parents in East Berlin to see.

A West Berlin bride and groom come to the Wall in the hope of being seen by relatives and other guests in East Berlin prevented by the Wall from attending their wedding.

East German soldiers armed with automatic weapons patrol a section of the sector border where concrete is replacing the original barbed wire barrier.

As the Wall goes up, East Berlin refugees flee West through ground-floor windows of buildings on the sector border.

Windows of an East Berlin border building are bricked up to prevent further escapes through them by refugees. Later this and all other buildings on the border were leveled to make a no-man's-land easier to guard against East Berliners hoping to commit the crime of "Fleeing the Republic."

Vopos guard a hole in the Wall made by a heavy truck in which two young East Berliners crashed through to West Berlin.

Makeshift memorial in West Berlin to "The Unknown Refugee," one of the many who died trying to flee through the Wall.

West Berliners jam the square in front of their Town Hall in August 1961 to protest the splitting of the city four days earlier and to demand a more forceful western response.

British troops escort a boy to school from one part of West Berlin to another through Vopo lines in the rural outskirts of the city.

Token American reinforcements arrive in West Berlin to raise morale.

General Lucius Clay, sent to Berlin as President Kennedy's personal representative to calm the fears of West Berliners after the Wall went up. He believed his mission was to stop the Russians from encroaching further on western rights in the city, and acted accordingly.

The Wall runs down the middle of the street in parts of the city. The buildings on the left are in the West Berlin borough of Kreuzberg.

Jeeps with armed American soldiers escort a civilian vehicle through the Communist barrier at Checkpoint Charlie in October 1961 on the eve of the tank confrontation there.

American tanks roll up to the Wall to back the right of unrestricted access to East Berlin by Allied officials.

A tense moment at Checkpoint Charlie in the winter of 1961.

American tanks move into position during the Checkpoint Charlie confrontation with the Russians, kindling fears around the world that an armed clash between the superpowers could be imminent.

Rapturous reception in West Berlin for President John Kennedy in 1963. With him are Mayor Willy Brandt (*middle*) and Chancellor Konrad Adenauer.

View from observation platform overlooking the Wall on the West Berlin side. The watchtower and lightpost rise over the no-man's-land between the Wall and a secondary concrete barrier that East Berliners are not permitted to approach.

Checkpoint Charlie today, manned by British, French and American military police. In the background is East Berlin with the East German checkpoint, manned by Vopos, and slalom barriers to prevent refugees from crashing through into the West in vehicles.

On Unter den Linden in East Berlin, less than a mile from the wall, East German soldiers goose-step in 1985 during a changing of the guard at the Memorial to the Victims of Fascism. Onlookers are mostly West German tourists with one-day visas.

At about the time *The Marlin* was setting off from shore, details of the trouble in Berlin were finally being relayed from Washington to the presidential message center set up by the Signal Corps in the basement of Hyannis Port's Yachtsman Hotel. When the report was received, a messenger was dispatched to deliver it to the president's military aide, Brigadier General Chester Clifton, who was acting as presidential on-shore duty officer while the president was at sea.

Clifton opened the sealed envelope in which the report came, read the contents, and contacted the Secret Service agent aboard *The Marlin* by walkie-talkie. The president, Clifton said, had to return to shore at once. A message had been received from Washington that required his immediate attention. Kennedy was informed and ordered *The Marlin* to turn back to shore.[3]

The news from Berlin infuriated Kennedy—but not because of the action the Communists were taking. That struck him as ugly and despicable, but they had been expected to do something about the refugees. What angered him was the realization that all the effort that had gone into forecasting what the Communists would do, and into preparing an appropriate response, had been in vain. He complained to McGeorge Bundy on the phone later in the day, "Why didn't we know?"

But first he telephoned Dean Rusk in Washington for a more comprehensive picture of the situation than the comparatively brief telex message provided. He wanted to know if there were any signs that the access routes were being blocked and whether West Berlin was in any way affected. He was relieved to hear that the answer to both was no. Rusk said there was no sign of panic in West Berlin, but like Brandt and the Soviets, he feared an East Berlin uprising that might spill over into the West and that could lead to Soviet military intercession with unpredictable consequences.

Rusk said, however, that from all reports the situation could not be considered critical—certainly not yet. There was no need for the president to rush back to Washington. "Time was not of the essence," Rusk said later. "We had previously discussed the refugee problem and were sure the Russians and East Germans would have to plug that hole. But they were not moving against West Berlin."

---

[3]It seems remarkable that the president was not alerted earlier. It remains possible that he was informed but that the seriousness of the situation was not fully appreciated, a fact that the White House would not have wanted publicized.

As Kennedy had made clear, the United States was prepared to go to war to keep the access routes open or defend the freedom of West Berlin. What might or might not occur in East Berlin, no matter how heavy-handed and deplorable, had never been considered a possible justification for war. The point of greatest significance for the president at that moment was that a Communist internal security operation, which this seemed to be, in no way heightened the threat of nuclear confrontation with which the president had been living since his encounter with Khrushchev in Vienna.

Some administration figures made no effort to disguise their absence of concern and their relief that the situation was not worse than it seemed. When told by Ausland that morning, "People are going to ask what we're going to do about this," Assistant Secretary of State Kohler had replied, "Let's not worry about it. That refugee flow was getting out of hand." According to McGeorge Bundy, Kennedy himself did not feel a sense of relief, more a "sense of irritation, accompanied by an awareness that this was not the issue on which we had decided we would have had to take a forceful stand."

The Communists' barricading of Berlin was, nevertheless, an illegal act, unilaterally violating four-power agreements. Even if no forceful response was contemplated, the United States, as primary "protecting power" in West Berlin, was obliged to issue a public condemnation. Rusk read Kennedy a prepared statement observing that the East German authorities, in a confession of failure of the Communist system, had denied their own people access to West Berlin. Satisfied that the statement did nothing to complicate or aggravate a situation that was still in the making, the president gave his approval and it was duly released to the press:

> Available information indicates that measures taken thus far are aimed at residents of East Berlin and East Germany and not at the Allied position in West Berlin or access thereto. However limitation on travel within Berlin is a violation of the four-power status of Berlin and a flagrant violation of the right of free circulation throughout the city. . . . These violations of existing agreements will be the subject of vigorous protest through appropriate channels.

Kennedy and Rusk thought that this statement soberly and responsibly dealt with the situation, at least until the dust settled. The United States registered its unqualified disapproval of the Communist action, but in planning to protest "through appropriate channels," it was signaling Moscow that in the volatile situation that prevailed, no hasty, scatterbrained overreaction was being contemplated.

The statement was also calculated to avoid encouraging an East German uprising. At the time of the 1956 Hungarian rebellion against the Soviets, the United States had, with some justification, been accused of encouraging the rebels by lauding their hunger for freedom while never intending to come to the aid of Hungarians who dared to take to the streets against Soviet tanks. Nothing was to be said this time that might be taken as promoting civil disturbances in East Berlin.

Besides, no one yet imagined that splitting the city would turn out to be the high-water mark of Soviet action. The Soviets were still expected to trigger the real confrontation with their threatened move against the access routes. It was thought that civil disturbances in East Berlin could goad them in that direction sooner than they had intended and before America's military buildup in Europe had gotten into full stride. All chances of negotiating an end to the Berlin squabble from strength would thus be undermined.

Kennedy and Rusk agreed that British Foreign Secretary Lord Home was right to have warned that panic pronouncements could prove self-fulfilling. No crisis atmosphere was to be nurtured. The president advised Rusk not to cancel his plans to go to a baseball game that afternoon. He himself was going sailing again. Everything was to appear perfectly calm and controlled.

Ironically, as the Communists moved ahead with settling the Berlin problem their own way, people in Washington were reading in their Sunday newspapers reports, which had been written earlier, that Kennedy was planning a major "peace offensive." It was reported that the president might make an appearance at the United Nations General Assembly in September to kick off a campaign there dramatizing the Soviet threat to peace in Berlin and its foot-dragging on arms control. Whatever thinking at the White House had gone into preparing for that appearance would have to be modified in the light of the campaign the Communists had already kicked off in the streets of Berlin.

Dean Rusk's public statement may have reassured the Soviets that the Americans were not going to overreact, but it stunned West Berliners. Was that all their protectors were going to do? There were armed Communist troops on the sector border. East German machine guns were trained west. The city was being cut in two. Ulbricht was making fools of the Americans. And the United States was only going to "protest through appropriate channels"!

General Watson kept a close watch on developments. But his primary concern at that moment was the military situation—in particular, the deployment of Soviet forces around Berlin. Soviet troops stationed at Teltow, just south of Berlin, were actually closer to his headquarters than the troubled sector border. With things in flux and Soviet intentions uncertain, Watson realized that his garrison, his command post, and the entire American establishment in Berlin would be overrun if the situation escalated. Compared to that, barbed wire being strung on the Soviet side of the sector border didn't seem to amount to much.

In Britain Prime Minister Macmillan was heading for a hunting holiday in the north of England and didn't intend to cancel it. Though officers of the American Berlin Mission agonized over the unruffled response from Kennedy and Rusk, Macmillan believed the situation, although not yet dangerous, could turn so, "partly because the Americans have got very excited." He was convinced the best approach was to stress the importance of negotiations. The possibility of western countermeasures did not seem credible to the British leader, nor to the London *Times,* where an editorial writer was pounding out his comment on the situation for Monday morning's edition of the paper: "All that the West can do at the moment is to protest against this further infringement of the Berlin agreements and the freedom of East Germans." With Foreign Secretary Lord Home vacationing in Scotland, the task of coordinating British reaction was left to the prime minister's secretary, Philip de Zulueta. "I suppose," Macmillan wrote in his private journal, "the newspapers will criticize us for being on holiday during the Berlin crisis, but actually this is nonsense."

Had there been any criticism of De Gaulle's absence from Paris at the time, he would not even have deigned to recognize it. The French president was at his country home at Colombey-les-Deux-Églises, maintaining a haughty seclusion. All senior officials and just about everybody else at the French foreign ministry were also away on their annual vacations—the Quai d'Orsay, like much of the rest of Paris, was pretty much closed down for August. In Bonn Chancellor Adenauer, who had returned from his summer holiday that morning, issued a strong condemnation of the border closure but, like the Americans, had little to suggest.

In Washington that Sunday afternoon, with Rusk having gone to his baseball game and Kohler having gone home, Berlin Task Force members decided there wasn't much they could still do that day. They scheduled a meeting for the morning and also went home. Returning from vacation and expecting to see people at work, Pete Day hurried over to the State Department, but finding no one manning the Task Force suite, he went home too.

Around 3:00 P.M. James O'Donnell received a telephone call at his Washington apartment from journalist Marguerite Higgins, who was an old friend and, like O'Donnell, a charter member of the Berlin Mafia. Higgins was calling about another matter, but she pointed out that her neighbor—in Chatham, Massachusetts—was General Clay whom they had both known when they were covering the Berlin blockade. She said she was going to talk to Clay about the Berlin situation and asked O'Donnell what Washington was doing about it. O'Donnell, who had spoken with colleagues at the State Department earlier that day, told her what he knew.

Not long after Higgins had talked to Clay, the general also telephoned O'Donnell for an update. O'Donnell told him the State Department line was basically to lie low and do nothing because there was nothing the United States could do in East Berlin. Clay, who retained a feeling of special responsibility for Berlin, was distressed by that attitude. He said that he might volunteer to go back to Berlin for the American government to try to salvage the situation.

O'Donnell suggested that if Clay was serious, he should contact Attorney General Robert Kennedy, the president's brother, who had greater access to the president than anyone else in Washington. Clay replied that though he had great respect for John Kennedy, he couldn't abide his brother. O'Donnell explained that Marguerite Higgins was nevertheless a good friend of the attorney general, which made him the best available channel for Clay to get a message through quickly to the White House. Clay discussed the matter with Higgins, and she called Robert Kennedy who passed word on to the president. But there it stood for the moment, although O'Donnell informed German correspondent Lothar Loewe, who had proved so useful an informant that morning, that Clay would be volunteering to go to Berlin. He also told German journalist Peter Boenisch, who telephoned him from Berlin that night. O'Donnell hoped the news would make West Berliners feel that they weren't being abandoned by the Americans. But Loewe was too convinced at the time that the White House crowd "was a bunch of amateurs" who couldn't grasp the situation. And though Boenisch passed word along to Willy Brandt's adviser and friend Egon Bahr, it did not go further. The story, which was premature anyway, was therefore stillborn.

As August 13 drew to a close, the barbed-wire barrier was virtually complete. Work to fill remaining gaps continued under floodlights. The East German Communists and the Soviets had good reason to be satisfied. Little by little, protesters on both sides of the border were detaching themselves from the clusters of demonstrators and trudging home. The operation was, however, still in its early stages. There was much more to come. Would the Americans, who had promised to remain firm in defense of their rights in Berlin, react on Monday with the same restraint they had displayed on Sunday? How would East Berlin workers respond when they gathered at their factories and construction sites in the morning, and exchanged views and shared feelings?

A lot of East Berliners had to quickly rethink their personal situations. The Grenzgängers were now out of work. Dropping in with a colleague at the Adlon Hotel in the East that night to refresh himself at the bar after a long, hard day's work, Reuters man Kellett-Long was greeted by the doorman, which was interesting because there hadn't been a doorman there since the war. It became even more interesting when Kellett-Long recognized the doorman as the man who, until the previous day, had been doorman at the Hotel Am Zoo on the Ku'damm in West Berlin. He was still wearing the same cap, but with the name of the West Berlin hotel torn from above the brim. Here was one commuter who had wasted no time relocating.

10
Postmortem

I N the days, weeks, and months ahead the Berlin crisis would assume awesome proportions. The barbed wire strung along the sector border and the even more drastic moves the Communists were about to make were only a prelude to a greater threat than Kennedy could have imagined when confronted by Khrushchev at the Vienna summit meeting in June. But even as that first day, *Stacheldrahtsonntag* ("Barbed Wire Sunday"), drew to close, it seemed astounding that the Allies had not known, or even suspected, that the Communists would plant a virtually impenetrable divide down the middle of Berlin to stop the refugees. It was a huge project, requiring extensive, elaborate preparation.

After Ulbricht had been given permission to build the Wall at the Moscow Warsaw Pact meeting during the first days of August, Honecker had installed himself and his staff at police headquarters in East Berlin. From there he was in "constant contact" with the commanding officers and staffs of the armed forces, district committees of the SED, central government departments, and the municipal councils of the major cities.

Few of the officials with whom Honecker dealt were told his exact intentions when he gave orders and made requests. Members of the Central Committee of the SED did not have to explain themselves. But it must have been apparent to many that he was engaged in a major undertaking, involving a large-scale security operation, and not a few must have had a pretty good suspicion of what was about to take place. Berlin was a city of spies, divided loyalties, and rumors. People were passing back and forth all the time. It was a situation in which confidentiality was virtually impossible to maintain. Yet the Allies were caught totally, unqualifiedly by surprise.

Balancing too long on the edge of a crisis in which another party is prime mover generates a kind of mental torpor. The options are reviewed and analyzed over and over again until they seem to have only a paper reality, remote from here and now. After a while dramatic factors—threats of nuclear conflagration, troops geared up for armed clashes in the middle of a metropolis—lose their capacity to generate new ideas. The unrelenting sameness of a protracted tense situation is stupifying.

So it was with Berlin as the climax approached. There developed a mind-fix that blunted the imaginations of western intelligence personnel. They concentrated on the access routes because unless those were kept open West Berlin was in trouble, and possibly lost. The appropriate contingency plans were devised and worked over. If the Soviets did such-and-such to interfere with those routes, the Allies would respond thus-and-so. If the East Germans presumed to do this-and-that on the routes, the Allies would react with that-and-this. A whole catalogue of responses had been divised to cope with everything from petty harassment to a full Communist blockade.

But in examining Ulbricht's options in dealing with the refugee problem, which was a totally different issue, the analysts had developed tunnel vision. They could only imagine him slapping tight controls on traffic between Communist East Germany and Communist East Berlin, in effect turning *all* of Berlin rather than just West Berlin into a political island. Since such a move would not affect Berlin's four-power status, it was nothing to get excited about.

At the British Mission Bernard Ledwidge had been told by well-informed Norwegian colleagues based in West Berlin that the East Germans had planned instead to seal off the Soviet Sector from West Berlin the previous weekend and that the operation had been canceled at the last minute. But that had seemed like just one more rumor. Indeed, at that point Honecker had just received the go-ahead and had a lot of preparatory work yet to do on his massive assignment.

Gaston Koblentz, a resourceful newsman who infuriated his colleagues by wandering through that city of suspense with a knowing grin, was not prepared to dismiss the idea so readily. He reported in the *New York Herald Tribune* that Ulbricht had asked Khrushchev to close the border between East and West Berlin—and without delay. But even if that were more than just another rumor, it didn't mean much. Ulbricht wanted the Soviets to do a lot of things for him, including handing him all of Berlin on a plate. Flora Lewis reflected prevailing thought in the journalistic, diplomatic, and intelligence fraternities in West Berlin when she reported to the *Washington Post,* "No one here expects an effort to shut off the traffic across Berlin at this point."

That the Soviets might permit the East German Communists to split the city in two had, in fact, not been completely overlooked by Allied intelligence, and particularly not by the American Berlin Watch Committee. The job of that standing group, made up of United States Army, CIA, and State Department intelligence analysts in Berlin, was to give the first alert when trouble was brewing. It had examined and discussed the possibility of a move in the middle of Berlin to choke off the refugee outflow but had dismissed it as too farfetched to deserve serious attention. It knew something was going to happen "pretty darn soon" but was not able to say with conviction exactly what it would be.

When John Mapother, an intelligence officer who had been dealing with the Berlin situation in Washington since 1958, was transferred to Berlin at the end of July, he questioned people there about whether it were possible for the Communists to throw a cordon around West Berlin rather than around the perimeter of the entire city. "The answers I got," he said,

> persuaded me that it would be too much of a problem. There were too many doors and windows to be sealed. There were buildings that opened in East Berlin on one side and in West Berlin on the other side. The conception of sealing the city down the middle was one that people in the know found too difficult to take on board and see as realistic.

Later there would be countless people who said they had warned before the fact that the Communists would quarantine West

Berlin to stop the refugees. Such people were as easy to run across afterward as they had been scarce on the ground before. There was a flamboyant American newspaper correspondent who had arrived in town the week before and who said later that he had known it would happen but hadn't reported it to his newspaper because he would have endangered the life of the East German source of his information. Martin Hillenbrand, who was directing the operations of the Berlin Task Force, said if there were westerners who knew in advance, "they must have squirreled that information away because it didn't reach Washington."

A report in the *New York Herald Tribune* two weeks after the border closing operation began said that the Communist plan had been known to the Allies since 1958 and had been labeled "Operation Chinese Wall" by American and West German intelligence agents. The newspaper account said an East German official who defected to the West had brought with him a document describing the plan that called first for a barbed-wire barrier to be built on the sector borders, then for its replacement by a cement block fence, and finally by the erection of concrete "palisades." It was said that Brandt had reported the plan to American intelligence officers. However, the West Berlin mayor denied that he had any suspicion whatever before August 13 that the East Germans might divide the city. He believed the East Germans would consider it sufficient to introduce "very severe, very strict controls on travel between the east and west sectors—on every car, every train, maybe introduce passport controls —and tighten controls between East Germany and East Berlin."

In view of the improbability of what happened, the few people —one CIA operative in Berlin at the time says he knew only two— who spoke up were thought to be fantasists, or self-seeking bunkum artists, of whom Berlin had more than its fair share, or had their suggestions dismissed as just more speculation churned out by the rumor mill. The senior CIA officer there thought Ulbricht would be committing political suicide if he tried to seal off East Berlin from West Berlin. Others believed he was determined to take control of all of Berlin in due course and wasn't about to settle for only the half that was his already.

One man who was convinced the Communists would divide the city, and said so with a passion, was Stephen Koczak at the Berlin Mission. But even other hardliners there believed Koczak was too obsessed with the Communist menace for his views on what was likely to happen to be given the attention they later turned out to have deserved. One mission member who served with him said Koczak had "a brilliant mind which produced brilliant ideas but because he was thought to feel so strongly about issues generally, other minds closed against his suggestions. When he came up with an original idea, people were as likely as not to think, 'Oh, Steve's got one of his notions.' " Koczak's credibility at the time was also damaged by his seriously strained relations with his superior, Thomas Donovan, chief of the mission's Eastern Affairs Section. Donovan believed a lot of people were getting far too excited by Soviet threats. It was a case of insurmountable personality and policy clashes between two men who were supposed to be working closely together. Both were soon to leave the Foreign Service, each soured by his Berlin experience.

Another man who refused to dismiss out of hand the idea of Berlin being split in two by the Communists was Colonel Ernest von Pawel, chief of the American Liaison Mission in East Germany. It seemed to him the most rational way for the Communists to deal with the refugee problem. Furthermore, after several years of duty in East Europe, it was his belief that "If you think a wall is the least likely option, then that is where I place my bet because we've never outguessed the Soviets yet." He pointed out that it would not be the first such barrier the Germans had built, having sealed off Warsaw's Jewish ghetto with a wall during World War II. But von Pawel had no evidence to back up his theory.

Nevertheless, there was good reason to take von Pawel's hypothesis and Koczak's conviction seriously, though it wasn't until after the event that telltale clues were easier to spot. The clampdown on cross-border movement during the Evangelical Church Congress the previous month could now be seen as a dry run by the East German security authorities. The so-called *Sputnik Bahn,* an elevated train line the Communists had tried to build at great expense in money and labor more than a year earlier in an effort to provide local East Germans with extra public transport that skirted West Berlin, could now be recognized as long-range planning for splitting the city. Western intelligence had picked up reports that unusually large amounts of barbed wire and cement posts were being stockpiled in and near East Berlin. But the East Germans had been talking about major East Berlin construction projects. It was not unreasonable to believe that some effort was being made to launch those projects as a gesture toward refurbishing East Berlin's depressing image. Even those who remained suspicious assumed that the construction materials were being stacked not to split the city but as part of the expected move to cordon off East Berlin from East Germany.

Dolchstoss ("stab-in-the-back") rumors began circulating in West Berlin during the first few days after the barbed wire had been strung. It was suggested that the United States had known the Communist plans in advance, that they had even been tipped off by the Soviets. This tip-off, it was suggested, accounted for the absence of any forceful American response. The story was originally spread by the Soviets, who with feigned discretion whispered it about that there was no chance of war because Moscow had informed the Americans of what was coming. The Americans, they said, had understood that the refugee exodus had to be halted for the sake of peace and stability in Europe. Having been nonplussed by Washington's mild reaction, some Germans believed it.

Rumors spread that Khrushchev himself had briefed John McCloy about the operation when McCloy had visited him at Sochi two weeks earlier. It was said also that Marshal Koniev, when he held a reception for the chiefs of the Allied liaison missions to mark his arrival in East Germany a few days before the border-sealing operation began, had tipped his hand by assuring them that whatever was about to happen would be a purely internal matter for East Germany.

Years later when Walt Rostow's memoirs reported that Kennedy had told him prior to border operations that the East Germans might have to build a wall to stop the refugees, diehards took that as further confirmation that the Americans had known beforehand. They believed Rostow's account explained why the president had responded so calmly and at such a leisurely pace. Some Germans remain convinced even today that a deal was made between the Americans and the Soviets, that Berlin was sold down the river by its protectors, and that reunification of Germany was thereby made even more remote. The myth of American betrayal of Berlin may one day be revived to cast a shadow over relations between the United States and Germany.

.   .   .

Erich Honecker did an extraordinary job of secretly organizing the sealing off of West Berlin. It is remarkable that no one in the West detected his crash preparations for that vast undertaking. Even more remarkable, very few East Germans knew about it until the troops and trucks were ordered to roll. Sometime later, John Mapother got to know an East German army colonel, a defector, who had been commander of one of the troop units deployed on the border that Saturday night, Sunday morning. He said he had not been told exactly what was going to happen until 10:00 P.M. Saturday night, two hours before the operation commenced.

It was a daring blitz action in the most pugnacious of German military traditions. According to General Maxwell Taylor, Kennedy's personal military adviser, known for his reluctance to accept easy answers to tough problems,

> If someone had suggested [it] as a possible course of action to me, I think I would have said it was highly improbable. . . . We later reviewed the intelligence that came in during the two weeks preceding [the operation] and found only fragments which have pointed to this event taking place. Movements of engineering material were reported. However, I still can't blame the intelligence people or those of us who had access to the intelligence for not anticipating [what happened].

Nevertheless, Allied intelligence services did not come out of the affair with their reputations untarnished. They were the natural butt for criticism and ridicule. British correspondent Terence Prittie recalled that just before the border closure, he was assured by a senior British intelligence officer in Berlin that "the present crisis will end in anti-climax after the [West German] elections [in September]. . . . This is naturally my own theory . . . but I have a maddening habit of being right on most occasions."

Most curious was the failure of the West Germans to know what was going to happen. Their intelligence services were reputed to have had first-class espionage networks throughout East Germany. Yet they had not been able to forecast what the East Germans would do. General Reinhard Gehlen, the head of the Bundesnachrichtendienst, the West German Federal Intelligence Service, insisted later that the criticism was unfair because he had "received and passed on reports of an imminent sealing of the sector boundary."

If he did so, those reports were either lost in a bureaucratic shuffle or dismissed as humbug. In any case West German officials did not pass such reports on to the Allies; nor did Gehlen's men, who had close links with their Allied counterparts, trouble to tip them off. Even among those who believed the Communists capable of the most cunning behavior, only von Pawel and Koczak are known to have predicted developments more or less accurately, and they did so through logical deduction rather than because of evidence.

The only reasonable excuse for the intelligence failure was the fact that in conception, the project could be dismissed as a logistical nightmare. But that underestimated how far the Communists were prepared to go to keep the German Democratic Republic from being bled dry.

Stragglers showed up at the Marienfelde refugee center early Monday morning, some weeping, overcome by the trauma of their escape. Some had made their way across border wasteland, flattened during the war, which wouldn't be completely secured by the Vopos until later in the day. Several escaped through cemeteries that straddled the sector boundaries, which also hadn't yet been fully wired off. Two young men made their way to East Berlin from the East German industrial city of Karl-Marx-Stadt and, finding the easier way to the West that they had charted blocked, they stripped down, dove into the Teltow Canal, and arrived dripping in West Berlin in nothing but their underpants. A couple with a young daughter crawled to West Berlin through a border-straddling drainage pipe. Some simply used wire cutters to break through in places where they thought they would not be spotted by guards or patrols. These belated escapees employed a mixture of ingenuity and recklessness in their desperation to find a route out. But this was the tail end of the exodus. From then on, the numbers would dwindle sharply.

By dawn's early light the Communists had made good their intention to reduce the number of border-crossing points to only thirteen. Through those thirteen, West Berliners, West Germans, and foreigners were allowed to cross from West to East and back again after having their passports or identity documents examined, and after convincing the border guards that they were not bent on causing trouble and were not carrying subversive literature or contraband. But the only East Berliners and East Germans being permitted to cross the other way through the Communist checkpoints were the rare few on official business for the East German authorities.

They were not required by West Berlin police to answer any questions or go through any control procedures. There were no restrictions on the trickle of people coming west.

It was uncertain in the tense atmosphere that prevailed how long foreigners residing in or visiting East Berlin would be permitted the freedom of movement no longer enjoyed by East Germans. At the Reuters East Berlin office Kellett-Long got a telephone call from a Soviet diplomat with whom he had become friendly. "How are you?" the Russian asked.

"Pissed off," Kellett-Long replied. "I don't want to get stuck here."

"How's Mary?"

"Like me—okay but apprehensive."

"Tell her not to worry," the Russian said. "If worse comes to worst, we will fly her out through Prague."

If his Russian friend had meant to reassure Kellett-Long, he was only partly successful. His message meant that Mary would be safe, but worse might come to worst (war was considered a real possibility) and he might still be locked in there.

Foreigners living in West Berlin were also apprehensive, but we did not suffer the same sense of isolation. However, I found going east, even by car, to size up the situation had become an intensely disagreeable experience—the barbed wire, the control posts manned by armed guards, their submachine-gun-toting back-ups in reserve not far away, the questioning about destination and purpose, all of this in the center of one of the great cities of Europe. It triggered the queasy feeling of entering a prison camp.

To Berliners abruptly cut off from contact with loved ones, what had happened was a matter of profound grief. To those who had been habitual border crossers—whether for work or pleasure—it was a tyrannical, disorienting intrusion in their lives. To those of us who were observers, transients, passersby, it was grim and depressing.

To West Berliners as well as East Berliners, it was as if a glacier of a political ice age, having previously come to rest, had suddenly taken a surge forward, smothering what lay in its path. Even words took on a crushed, distorted aspect. A photographer positioning himself to take a picture of the barbed wire and armed guards from the eastern side was stopped by a Vopo. "This is free Berlin," he was told. "Taking pictures here is forbidden."

In *Passport to Pimlico,* a British movie made in 1949, people were required to have their passports stamped as they went from one part of London to another. It was a delightful comedy, made hilarious by the absurdity of the notion. Being checked out by the armed guards in the middle of Berlin, being crisply ordered to drive on when I wanted to linger for a close look, being eyed dolefully by people in clusters a hundred yards into East Berlin as if I had come from some fabled Babylon and would, unlike them, be permitted to return there when I wished, was also absurd. But rather than being hilarious, it was loathsome. It was impossible not to think that despite their condemnations of fascism, the Communists of East Germany were the true heirs of Adolf Hitler.

To guard against the possibility of popular discontent spilling over into action, armed Vopos were posted in front of all major buildings, and particularly at the Soviet Embassy on Unter den Linden. Troops were still held in reserve on side streets near the border. Their rifles slung over their shoulders, the soldiers lined up for breakfast at field kitchens. Tanks, troop carriers, and armored cars remained positioned in strategic locations, ready to roll if summoned. East Berliners walking by them looked the other way, as if refusing to acknowledge the humiliation they represented.

In an effort to dispel the bitterness felt even by the great number of East Germans who never intended to abandon their homes and jobs but who resented being locked in, East Berlin radio stations broadcast interviews with East Berliners who professed to be delighted with the events of the preceding day. One woman, bubbling with satisfaction, said she was enormously relieved that her young daughter was finally safe from the kidnappers who had been spiriting children away to the West. Another woman said she was grateful that the people of the German Democratic Republic, who had for so long endured the disruption of their lives caused by currency speculators and slave merchants in West Berlin, would no longer be exposed to those wicked elements.

No one in those interviews, or in commentaries that accompanied them, mentioned barbed wire. Reference was made only to the *Massnahmen*—the nameless "measures" that were transforming the face of the city and life of its people. Not a word was said about Berlin being split in two. Though Vopos near the border had distributed the leaflets detailing the new restrictions on travel, no one on East German radio mentioned that an East Berliner who now tried to go West risked his life.

There was no announcement that telephone communication between East and West Germany, maintained after phone links between East and West Berlin had been cut years before, had been severed along with postal links just before dawn, leaving East Germans and East Berliners even more cut off from external contact. There was no in-depth analysis of what would no longer be permitted, how individuals would be affected and might react, what might still be in store, or the anxiety to be seen on the faces of people in the streets.

In its columns *Neues Deutschland* stressed the advantages that had accrued to East Germans overnight: "Families would now be protected from the enticements of slave traders, peoples' industrial and commercial enterprises would be protected from headhunters, the public order would be protected from criminals, the security of the nation would be protected from warmongers." On the radio Gerhardt Eisler confidently forecast that "one day the red flag of the working class will fly over all of Germany," a comment that, when more widely reported, sent a shudder through West Berlin.

East Berliners who congregated as near to the wire as they were permitted appeared to share none of the relief and satisfaction of the people interviewed on East German radio. They looked on in solemn silence. Many came hoping to catch a glimpse of relatives on the other side of the border, some of whom were refugees who had previously made their escape but who feared that if they reentered East Berlin to see kinfolk, even with their new West Berlin identity papers, they would not be permitted to leave again.

There were poignant sights to be seen that morning. An elderly East Berlin woman broke into a broad smile as she spotted her son west of the barrier, and then, almost instantly, dissolved in uncontrollable weeping at the realization that they could come no nearer. A man on the west side held up his wide-eyed, bewildered baby for his parents in the East to see and coo at from too great a distance for the infant to notice. A young man and a young woman, separated by the wire, their faces masked by profound sadness, called out to each other but were too timid to do so loudly enough to be heard. Others just looked at each other wordlessly.

A few of the Vopos on duty between them focused their eyes on the ground or on the far distance, seemingly distressed by this emotionally charged atmosphere. Others, scanning the weepers, wavers, and message callers on their side of the wire for signs of trouble, were vigilant rather than perturbed. They needn't have worried. People standing east of the wire were thoroughly cowed and easily dispersed when ordered to move on.

But pockets of protest existed elsewhere in the East. More than once that day, East Berliners told western correspondents that the Americans should tear down the barbed wire. "Give the goatee [Ulbricht] twenty-four hours to remove it himself," one man said. "If he doesn't, then do the job for him."

The Communists weren't worried about disgruntled or aggrieved individuals. Those who made too much of a fuss were hustled away by the Vopos, but so much effort was required to maintain the overall security operation that the police couldn't yet be bothered to launch a systematic crackdown on complainers. That would soon come, but for the moment, attention away from the border was concentrated instead on the workers of East Berlin as they gathered at their work places that morning. That was where trouble could erupt. Party activists in the factories and at the construction sites had been instructed to explain in great detail the benefits the people of the Socialist Fatherland would derive from the border "measures." Nevertheless, there was deep and widespread unease among the workers.

At lunchtime some men outside a factory not far from the city center muttered bitterly about what was happening. "This is no way to treat us," one of them complained, ignoring my presence though, as far as he knew, I could easily have been a Communist informant. "They didn't have to do it; we are not criminals," another said. They made no explicit political complaints, but neither did any of those men speak out in defense of the "measures." (Meant as a euphemism, "measures" quickly became something else; it was mouthed with caustic emphasis, as if it were an insult to intelligence.) Two teenagers from the Free German Youth organization who had been mingling with the workers went off to report to a Vopo officer nearby. The Vopo made notes, presumably for action to be taken later in the day when there would no longer be a group of malcontents gathered together to react when the police singled out the more outspoken ones among them, the potential counterrevolutionary ringleaders.

Press reports the following day told of the arrest of western agents who had tried to foment trouble by stirring discontent among the workers. It wouldn't be long before the people of East Berlin would learn that grumbling in public was a luxury they could not afford. East Germans would soon no longer need the urgings of West German Minister Ernst Lemmer to "refrain from committing reckless acts" that might provoke Communist retribution. They had more potent warnings on their own side of the wire.

Four days earlier, on Thursday, driving out of East Berlin after vainly seeking confirmation from East German government spokesmen of reports that stiff antirefugee action was imminent, I exchanged pleasantries with a Vopo on duty at the Brandenburg Gate. "Where are you going?" he asked. I told him I was heading for a café on the Ku'damm for a cup of coffee. He smiled and joked, "Got room for one more?" But on Monday, some thirty-six hours after the clampdown had begun, when I stopped to be cleared through the gate, that same Vopo, whose double take indicated he recognized me, stiffly asked for my passport. He looked at it, handed it back, scanned the floor of the backseat of my car for any unauthorized passengers, saluted, and briskly waved me on. No pleasantries this time. No smiles. Berlin had a new order, and it bit deep.

The Communists did not want to close the Brandenburg Gate. The gate, like most of the fine, old architectural treasures of Berlin, was situated in East Berlin, just a little ways in from the British Sector. It was the single most recognizable symbol of Berlin, and they were reluctant to be blamed for defacing it with barbed wire. But the crowds of angry West Berliners congregated on the far side of the gate were becoming increasingly unruly. If a few thousand of them tried to surge through those monumental arches into East Berlin, they might be uncontrollable. There was no point in taking chances. Things were proceeding too well.

On Monday afternoon a troop of Vopos marched through the gate to form up shoulder-to-shoulder just west of that magnificent monument, but still within East Berlin. Armored cars and water-cannon vehicles rolled into position behind them. And behind them the bales of barbed wire were brought forward. Like most of the rest of the border between the two parts of Berlin, the gate was now being sealed.

If the Communists thought that would disperse the demonstrators on the far side, they were mistaken. West Berliners gathered in front of the closed gate in ever larger numbers as the day wore on, despite police attempts to disperse all unauthorized demonstrations near the border. The vision of a clash between unarmed civilians and the armed Vopos was a nightmare that seemed about to be transformed into bloody reality as the demonstrators began inching forward. Protesters threw stones at the Communist guards, at East German armored cars in front of the gate, and at a Soviet bus that arrived for the regular changing of the guard at the Soviet war memorial. West Berlin police reinforcements were rushed to the spot to press the crowd back, and the West Berlin authorities quickly issued a decree banning all demonstrations within a half mile of the border.

The consequences of the clampdown were felt elsewhere in West Berlin as well. With the cross-border commuters no longer able to get through, West Berlin's labor force was immediately slashed by 7 percent. Factory managers took a close look at their personnel rosters to see how badly their production levels would be hit. Skilled and unskilled workers were lost. Service industries were particularly affected. With many chambermaids caught behind the wire, beds in some hotels went unmade and rooms uncleaned. Waiters did not show up for work in some restaurants, and the remaining waiters in others had to double up as dishwashers.

The dimensions of personal reaction among West Berliners ranged from the tragic to the trifling. A cleaning woman who worked for an American family collapsed in hysterical weeping because her daughter, who lived in East Berlin, was supposed to undergo serious surgery that day. With telephone communications cut and doubting that she would be permitted to cross the border, she feared she would have no way of learning how her daughter fared. Less agonizing was the case of a man who worked in West Berlin's old main post office building, which housed the radio transmitting studio used by foreign radio correspondents. He had gone to see his mother in East Berlin the previous week and had left his raincoat there—a chic thing for which he had paid a fancy price in Düsseldorf the previous *Fasching* ("carnival") time. Would a western correspondent, who didn't have to worry about crossing into and out of East Berlin, be kind enough to visit his mother, send his filial greetings, and retrieve that precious garment?

Five thousand West Berlin workers, outraged that their city was being chopped in two, marched on West Berlin's Town Hall to demand retaliation against the Communists. Brandt sympathized with them but urged them not to be provoked into rash action. He said he was pressing for a strong response from the Allied commandants. Brandt himself was, for purposes of morale, considering closing offices of the Communist SED in West Berlin and was looking into control of the S-Bahn, which had been run throughout the city by the East Berlin authorities since the war. But there was, in fact, little he could do that would change things.

The Monday morning meeting of the Berlin Task Force at the State Department was a well attended, lively session. All sorts of questions were raised. Was the barbed wire only the first step in a bigger Communist operation? Was the next move just around the corner? If so, what was that next move likely to be? Was the border barrier permanent? (In the early hours of the previous day Reuters had cautiously reported from West Berlin that "It was not clear immediately whether the borders would be closed for long or perhaps for only . . . until necessary controls had been put into effect.") If the barrier was to be permanent, what were the implications for the viability of West Berlin as a western outpost? How would the confidence and morale of America's allies, particularly West Germany, be affected?

There were no answers to those questions, nor to the question that most troubled members of the Berlin Mafia in attendance— What was the United States going to do? Task force members heatedly rehashed what had gone before—the president's identification of *West* Berlin, rather than all of Berlin, as America's concern; the signal sent to the Soviets that East Berlin was theirs to do with as they liked; the absence of a more forceful response the day before. One participant said that feelings of some in the task force "ran so high, you could cut the tension with a knife." But with details of the Communist operation still flowing in from Berlin, and with task force director Foy Kohler's eyes still focused firmly on the far more serious concern—the fate of the access routes—the approach of the task force was less "What do we do now?" and more "What will they do next?"

Elsewhere in Washington others felt a similar sense of being upstaged by the Soviets. That feeling led to agonizing over how to capture the initiative. Robert Amory, deputy director of the CIA and a friend of National Security Adviser McGeorge Bundy, recalled,

> Mac and I sat around at first alone early in the morning and he said, "What the hell do we do now?" . . . I was quite freewheeling, at least with him, and I didn't worry about making policy recommendations. I said, "Mac, there is one thing you can do right here and now, and that is to vividly enhance your commitment to Berlin. I think you ought to send a cable to Norstad . . . to send another combat team in this afternoon over the autobahn." Then Taylor came in, and Mac said, "What do you think about that, Max?" Max said, "That's a hell of a bad idea. We're in a dangerous situation here. This would be further maldeployment. Any troops that we have in Berlin will be casualties in the first six hours of fighting. We can't afford to give up 5,000 good armed men out of the NATO shield [in West Germany] to that." Mac was more or less on my side and we pressed that all day. But Kennedy decided in favor of Max Taylor and the Joint Chiefs agreed with Max.

General Taylor was worried because the NATO shield was thought to be desperately thin. The American reinforcements promised by Kennedy had not yet reached Europe. Only two out of the twelve West German divisions were combat ready and most of the French Army was still in Algeria. American military chiefs were not prepared to take chances that Khrushchev was bluffing when he threatened war if he didn't get his way. Assessing comparative strengths as far as they knew them, they feared they might have no alternative but to go nuclear if the situation came to armed conflict over Berlin before the American military buildup was completed.

They tended to see the small Allied garrisons in West Berlin not as a political asset, keeping the Communists at bay, but as militarily insignificant, doomed to be lost if things turned hot. General Clarke in Heidelberg, who checked the resources at his disposal as he reviewed his defensive tactics, knew that "Berlin was not a [militarily] viable community. It could have been taken at any time." The generals dealt with cold military facts. How strong were the forces at their disposal? What could they do if the guns went off? What couldn't they do? Trip wires and such stuff were for politicians. Reinforcing a militarily hopeless position was just plain crazy.

Kennedy's White House aides were equally caught up in a frenzy of calculations about the dangers, so relentlessly stressed by the Soviets, of calamitous armed conflict. In a National Security Council memorandum on Monday Walt Rostow said,

> We should take the view that the weakness and incompetence of the Ulbricht regime is leading to a situation which might trigger a general war unwanted by the major powers. We do not propose to let this irresponsible regime lead us by the nose into war. We [should] therefore [be] asking for four power negotiations.

McGeorge Bundy told Kennedy,

> I find unanimity in your immediate staff for the view that we should take a clear initiative for negotiations within the next week or ten days. . . . This opinion is strengthened by the border closing episode which can be described as one reason more for calling talks—because of the dangerous and explosive weakness it reveals in [East Germany].

Little thought was devoted in the White House to suggestions that anything be done about the barbed wire. No one proposed that it be torn down as an unacceptable violation of four-power control. For one thing, it still wasn't clear how long the Communists planned to keep it up. For another, as Bundy said, "It was apparent from hour one that this was an action on their side of territories sharply staked out." Bundy told Kennedy, "1) This is something [the Communists] have always had the power to do; 2) It is something they were bound to do sooner or later."

The British agreed. Edward Tomkins said, "We [at the Foreign Office] accepted there was little we could do to stop the Russians from acting in a unilateral manner in their sector," and there was no doubt that the East Germans were acting with Soviet approval. Not even at the American Berlin Mission, where feelings were more fiery, was there any call for action against the barbed wire. Howard Trivers, political adviser at the mission, believed that "if we had crossed the line to remove the barbed wire, I am convinced that [the Communists] would not have sought to resist. They would have moved back 200 or 400 yards and commenced to rebuild the barbed wire fence there." If that were also torn down, they would have moved further back again and rebuilt it again. "We would have been obliged to keep moving further and further into the Soviet Sector." It was generally acknowledged that if that was the way things developed, the situation would have quickly become both ridiculous and dangerous. Allan Lightner said it was later believed that the Communists would not have resisted when Allied troops rolled over the first barrier built by the Communists, nor would they have fought back when the Allies knocked down the second barrier, but that the Soviets would have resisted with overwhelming military force at a third barrier, an encounter from which he could have seen "nothing but tragedy resulting, certainly a terrible humiliation for the West."

Even if an Allied move to prevent Berlin from being split had not been resisted, such a move could have touched off the much dreaded popular uprising in East Germany for which there were wildly exaggerated expectations. Soviet tanks would have been brought out into the streets and tempted to go in hot pursuit if the uprising spilled over into West Berlin, as it so easily could have. What would the Allied commandants do then? Could they send their own few tanks (the Americans had only twenty-seven of them in Berlin) to drive the Soviets back? They couldn't very well instruct the West Berlin police to push demonstrators for freedom back into East Berlin to avoid such a clash. Nor could they order American, British, and French troops to crush anti-Communist demonstrations. Distasteful as it was, Allied interests coincided with those of the Soviet Union in trying to prevent anything that might produce such hopelessly unacceptable options.

However, there were possibilities for action. General Taylor, momentarily suspending his military caution, suggested that the Allied commandants notify the Soviet commandant in East Berlin that they were coming over to talk things over and to make it clear that they were going to enter East Berlin at a point that was not among those designated as open to westerners. They should serve notice that they would use force to cross over if obstructed. But the idea was thought too risky and got no backing in the White House.

If General Clay had been in command in Berlin on August 13, the situation might have been different. "This was the place," he later said,

> where if the commandant in Berlin had acted, even if he had been in violation of his instructions, he would have succeeded and he would have been forgiven and he would have become a very great man. All he had to do in my opinion that night, was to have run trucks up and down the street unarmed—unarmed soldiers in the trucks.

No sooner would the wire be put up than American soldiers would run over it. Clay was convinced the Soviets did not want war and would back down. It was, of course, easy to be bold after the fact, but Clay's later performance in Berlin indicated that he might very well have done what he suggested. But he was not there that night, and the barbed wire stood.

Inevitably, various other responses that might have changed things occurred to people afterward. The Allies could have expanded on General Taylor's abortive suggestion, notified the Soviets that the crossing points designated by the East Germans were unacceptable, and set up crossing points of their own. The barrier would have been left in place but it would have signified western determination to remain in at least partial control of the situation. Or the Allies could have announced they had no intention of obeying the orders of the East German minister of the interior and intended to send military vehicles through all the border crossings that had been open before, forcing the Soviets to show their hand openly.

Another idea conjured up well after the event focused on the fact that the Soviets had conspicuously abandoned responsibility for East Berlin. The Allies could send troops from the three western garrisons into a portion of East Berlin and claim it for West Berlin. The Soviets would hurriedly return to reclaim it. The Allied troops would then withdraw, but a farce would have been made of the East German barbed-wire spectacle.

Even if ideas of that kind had been broached while there was still time, it is unlikely that they would have gotten past the talking stage. Not only would they have been rejected as heightening tensions, but people also would have seen them as showing the United States prepared to bully East Germany while fearing to stand up to the Soviets. An indication of how reflex was Washington's acceptance of the Communist initiative in Berlin was a memo from Kennedy to Rusk on Monday asking, "What steps will we take this week to exploit politically propagandawise the Soviet–East German cut-off of the border. . . . The question is how far we should push this."

Berliners raged and grieved, but what the Communists were doing to them and their city meant far less to the president than the awesome fact that he had been prepared for a war in which millions of people, including Americans, might have died, and suddenly it looked like it wasn't going to happen—not yet. The ambassadors in Washington of the three western powers and senior State Department officials met and agreed that "some sort of counter-measures" had to be taken. The Americans gave assurances that Washington's reaction would go beyond paper protests. There was some talk of banning East German commercial representatives from western countries and imposing economic sanctions on East Germany. But no firm proposals were advanced, no agreement was reached, and no sense of urgency was drummed up.

In West Berlin officials at the American Mission who had long engaged in cultivating contacts among West Berliners as a matter of policy as well as personal inclination were deluged with calls from prominent local figures who wanted to know what action the United States intended to take. Still banned from making formal statements, they privately took every opportunity to reaffirm America's vow never to abandon West Berlin to the Communists. Edward R. Murrow, head of the United States Information Agency, who happened to be in the city at the time, sensed the desperate need there for an American morale booster. Murrow told the staff at RIAS, "There is no Berlin crisis. It is Khrushchev's crisis. He has, in the vernacular of our western movies, told us to 'get out of town by noon tomorrow.' We do not choose to depart." Though folksy, defiant, and reassuring, his statement had nothing to do with the barbed wire or the despair Berliners felt as the hours passed and Communist action remained uncontested.

In Paris and London, as in Washington, there was still little to indicate that the Berlin developments aroused much concern. The Quay d'Orsay issued barely a word on the subject. The British pooh-poohed suggestions that economic countermeasures might be considered. They stood by their attitude that the West should match whatever action the Soviets took but not go beyond it in any way that might provoke a stronger Soviet action and thus lead to escalation —and so far the Soviets had taken action only on their own turf. Though he had been in long telephone consultation with Edward Tomkins of the Foreign Office Western Department, Foreign Secretary Lord Home, vacationing at his Scottish estate, declined to fuel the crisis. He told reporters, "I hope to do plenty of walking and inhale some good Scottish air to get rid of the Whitehall cobwebs."

West German government spokesmen said the border closure would have serious consequences for the East German regime. But Chancellor Adenauer, though making appropriate noises of outrage, devoted most of his energies to running for reelection. His most newsworthy comment that day was a shabby allusion to the illegitimate birth of his opponent, West Berlin Mayor Brandt.

To the Soviets, day two of the operation appeared to have passed smoothly. There had been no notable disturbances by malcontents in East Berlin or any of the other East German cities. Whatever problems had arisen had been quickly, efficiently dealt with by the East German security services. The refugee problem seemed solved. Only 150 escapees got through on Monday, many by swimming the fifty yards across the Teltow Canal on the banks of which more stringent security precautions were already being introduced. Nothing had been heard from the Americans, the British, or the French. There was no reason for Moscow to object to implementation of the planned next step in the East German operation.

11
Lives, Fortunes, and Sacred Honor

O N Tuesday morning, before West Berlin had fully digested what had already happened, the East German authorities issued a new decree. West Berliners would henceforth require special authorization if they wished to drive their cars into East Berlin. The Communists said abuses of the hospitality of the German Democratic Republic made this measure necessary. Some West Berliners were alleged to have used their vehicles to smuggle espionage agents into the East or to disrupt public order.

It was true that some West Berliners had been risking arrest at the border by using their cars for smuggling. But they had not been trying to sneak people in; they had been trying to sneak refugees out, hidden in the trunks of their cars or pushed down beneath rear seats. Not many had succeeded, however, because the Vopos had become increasingly meticulous in their inspection of border-crossing vehicles. The measure was really a muscle-flexing exercise by the East Germans, firming up the sector border as the frontier of their Communist state, thumbing their noses at the western powers, and—having as yet to run into problems—continuing to test the limits of western tolerance.

A comparative trickle of refugees continued to get through. Some used documents smuggled into East Berlin by West Berliners who were still able to pass both ways on foot through the Communist checkpoints by proving their identity. If they took the risk of carrying along extra borrowed or forged West Berlin identification papers, those could be passed on to East Berliners, who—if the photos looked anything like them—were then likely to be waved through to West Berlin by the Vopos on the border with a minimum of checking. But the Vopos caught on quickly. Admission and exit procedures for West Berlin pedestrians were tightened and a touch of menace was added. They had to line up at the checkpoints to explain their reasons for wanting to visit East Berlin. Sometimes on their way out they were also asked to provide details of where they had been. What was more, they faced the prospect of being searched. Any East German found to be in possession of West Berlin identification papers faced three years in prison.

The Communists then turned their attention to a conundrum that had done so much to convince western intelligence that Berlin could not be split in two—the rows of sturdy, old, city-center tenement buildings on the border, situated in the Soviet Sector but looking and opening out on western sectors. The thousands of people who lived in those buildings, almost all of them long-time residents, had always crossed back and forth over the border simply by stepping in or out of their front or rear doors. Though they lived in East Berlin, people across the street in similar tenements in West Berlin were their neighbors. Choking off that traffic was a formidable challenge for the East German security officials charged with unconditionally disconnecting the two parts of the city.

When they were able to divert some of their men from duty at the wire, they had the Vopos lock and nail shut west-opening doors of those buildings to ensure that people would not continue to use them as escape routes by residents or nonresidents seeking an exit from East Berlin. In one case a woman living on the second floor of an apartment answered a knock at her door, opened it, and was startled to see a young man race past her without a word and jump from her window into West Berlin. That problem would have to be dealt with.

On Tuesday the western commandants got around to registering their formal protest with the Soviet Berlin commandant, Colonel Andrei Solovyev. Despite the serious violations of the four-power agreements, their protest employed only routine language and made no suggestions that the Allies might consider countermeasures. Nevertheless, the following day Solovyev replied briskly, "Your protest cannot be taken seriously. As you know the commandant of Soviet troops does not meddle in the affairs of the German Democratic Republic."

The Allied commandants knew that to be nonsense. They knew that the Soviets were still very much in charge. But Solovyev was telling them that as far as Moscow was concerned, four-power Berlin was a thing of the past. Not only were the Communists dismissing western insistence that they could not unilaterally make such a decision, they were making demands, with implied threats, of their own. Annoyed at continuing demonstrations on the western side of the barbed wire, the East German regime announced that West Berliners, for their own safety, should not come any closer than one hundred yards to the East Berlin borderline.

Such gall did nothing to lessen the fury of the West Berliners or their anguish at the absence of any meaningful reaction from Washington. Joachim Boelke, a young journalist at the West Berlin newspaper *Taggesspiegel* at the time, recalled that "some members of the United States Mission were furious, as I was furious, that it was impossible to get the message through to Washington. We waited from day to day for something to happen."

But the White House, though still braced for trouble on the access routes, was unruffled by the Berlin developments. It remained convinced that the division of Berlin made no significant difference to the power balance in the city. The Soviet Sector was still the Soviet Sector, and the western sectors were still under western control. The president and his advisers were prisoners of western publicity, which for years had been dramatically portraying Berlin as "the divided city," really two cities—one Communist and one free. So, aside from the refugees, nothing was different except, possibly, as columnist David Lawrence pointed out in the *Washington Evening Star,* "it really means that there now is less chance than before of a shooting war between the Soviet Union and the western democracies."

Some senior American officials and presidential advisers did not even know that the western powers exercised residual rights in East Berlin; that American, British, and French military vehicles drove through the Soviet Sector every day on flag-showing missions; that American officials in Berlin regularly drove in as well without seeking permission; and that they had a right to do so. The Soviets, seeking to avoid premature trouble on that point, had instructed the East Germans to let those vehicles pass, even after the barbed wire was up. Martha Mautner at the State Department said that she had

> a big fight with a couple of people up the line who didn't quite understand the theology of Berlin. There was an awful lot of cynicism about that theology. But anyone who was involved realized that you had to stick very, very close to it in dealing with the Russians or you'd end up with the shorter side of the salami.

Mission political adviser Howard Trivers believed that "The United States government did not push for countermeasures because there were too many people at the top who espoused the view that [the erection of the city-splitting barrier] might be 'good' in the context of overall US-Soviet relationships." Indeed, Kennedy told his appointments secretary and intimate Kenneth O'Donnell, "This is [Khrushchev's] way out of his predicament. It's not a very nice solution, but . . . a hell of a lot better than a war."

As the East Germans, under the vigilant eye of their Soviet "advisers," escalated the clampdown step by careful step, the attention of the Berlin Task Force remained focused instead on the likelihood that the Berlin shenanigans were a sideshow for an imminent Soviet move to squeeze the West out of the city altogether. Contingency planning for a new Berlin blockade was pored over, debated, and updated with exhaustive thoroughness. How could West Berlin's essential supplies situation be improved? Could a 1948–49-style airlift be mounted if necessary? At what stage should force be used to keep the city's lifelines open? What countermeasures should be implemented if the Soviets tried to blockade the city again—perhaps taking action along the East German–West German border, perhaps sniping at Soviet interests elsewhere in the world, perhaps going to the brink of war?

Minds were fixed on the threat to the access routes virtually to the exclusion of everything else. Foy Kohler told John Ausland, "I hope this business in Berlin doesn't take attention away from the crisis" when a lot of people believed the crisis was already upon them. Upon hearing that veteran diplomat and presidential adviser Charles Bohlen (among others) had described the Communist closure of the border as "a great failure of the Soviet system," Willy Brandt muttered, "One more failure like that and we won't be around anymore."

Whether it was a Communist failure or a triumph, the West did not know how to deal with it. State Department legal adviser and White House consultant Abram Chayes said, "We decided in the end that there was no appropriate response, that any response was either over reactive or under reactive." Chayes said the Soviet move was essentially "not an aggressive but a defensive act."

Marching troops into the Soviet Sector to shoo away the East German guards and dismantle the barrier would, on the other hand, have been seen as an aggressive act against defensive Communist positions, no matter what the four-power agreements said. Presidential military adviser Maxwell Taylor said later that even in retrospect he would not have supported the use of force to keep Berlin from being divided, even though he believed the Soviets would have backed away from a direct confrontation. The abortive "roll back Communism" crusade was no longer part of the American government's foreign-policy thinking, and that applied to Communist East Berlin as well as Communist East Europe. It was also beyond possibility in the climate of anxiety that existed that the necessary agreement could be reached among the Allies for military action by the small Berlin garrisons.

Caught by surprise, the western powers were fortunate not to have had to make a deliberate decision to let East Berlin go by default. That would have been hard to do. It would have generated much friction in their ranks; the West German government could not have agreed to it and survived. It would also have caused Kennedy considerable domestic political embarrassment. But it meant the Allies were not prepared to take retaliatory action against Soviet interests elsewhere to extract from Moscow something of value from the affair.[1] As a consequence, the West had nothing to show for its

[1]Later in the crisis, having fine-tuned contingency plans for responding to Communist action, members of the Berlin Task Force thought some of those plans should be tried out in response to Communist harassments. They sought to arouse interest in Washington for surveillance of Soviet ships in the Mediterranean. Their plan was just to stay close to the Soviets so they would know they were being watched but to refrain from doing anything to them. In contrast to Soviet moves, it was a low level response, totally without conflict potential, just to see how the Soviets would react. But when it was put up to the Pentagon, senior officers there

acquiescence—neither the junking of the Soviet demand that West Berlin become a "free city" nor guarantees over the access routes. At minimum cost to themselves, the Communists were solving the refugee problem, which had been doing East Germany colossal damage, which was threatening the stability of the East German Communist state, and for which they had themselves been responsible. It was a trump card the West, still waiting for the real crisis, was tricked out of playing.

Like General Simpson's men on the Elbe a decade and a half earlier, some officials at the Berlin Mission were chomping at the bit. Ever since the early hours of Sunday they had been struggling to keep abreast of developments, answering a flood of inquiries from Washington and the American Embassy in Bonn, liaising with the British and French missions, writing and transmitting their reports, reassuring West Berlin officials, fielding countless inquiries from resident correspondents and the army of journalists flooding in from all over the world, and trying to catch up on lost sleep. Howard Trivers had to leave the hubbub of the mission compound and go home to draft his (futile) report on possible western countermeasures. Now they were finally able to take brief breaks from their hectic pace to examine the long-term significance of what they were living through.

Like American Ambassador Walter Dowling in Bonn, Allan Lightner was pleading with Washington for a more substantial response to the situation than the United States had so far offered. A CIA official assigned to Berlin said, "Neither I nor the people I was working with had any doubt that the East Germans would pull back in the face of the slightest positive unfriendly reaction from the West." Mission officials could see no reason why General Watson should not be authorized at least to dispatch troops from his garrison to the border to demonstrate America's armed presence in the city. They also thought the United States could engage in more energetic diplomatic activity. Washington could issue a tough statement declaring that an acute situation had arisen endangering world peace and demanding an immediate four-power foreign minister's confer-

---

began talking about training schedules for the fleet and for the air force and how such activity would divert their forces from their prime military mission, which was to be at readiness at all times to deal with threats to American interests.

ence, perhaps to be held in Berlin itself. Washington would not be overreacting, but neither would its allies or the Communists see the United States as the castrated giant the Chinese and Ulbricht had tried to bludgeon Khrushchev into believing it was. George Muller drafted a memo to that effect and handed it to Lightner. But Lightner regretfully said there was no point in sending it on because, as had been made clear to him, "Washington is handling this."

Many felt this was a charitable description of what was going on in the nation's captal. In Berlin America's low profile was made to seem doubly negligent and misguided when word spread that a Vopo who had jumped the barbed wire reported that he and his comrades had been given no ammunition for their weapons. Their superiors were taking no chances that they might panic and use them if the Americans advanced to tear the wire down. There were doubts about whether this story was true, or whether (as was actually the case at first) it was true only for lower ranks, or—if it had been true at first—whether it was true any longer. The question of whether the Communist guards had ammunition was answered on Tuesday when shots were fired at but missed a couple who had jumped into the Teltow Canal and were swimming to the West Berlin bank.

The phased Communist operation had again been taken one step further, with the West looking impotently on. But the realization of the fact was finally beginning to filter through to the White House that though Kennedy was fortunate not to have a catastrophic war on his hands, he did have a very serious problem in Berlin, and his reaction was making it worse.

Assistant Secretary of State Foy Kohler later conceded that the American government "did not initially fully anticipate the traumatic reaction of the West Berliners and West Germans." "Anticipate" was, however, the wrong word. The fact was that Washington —waiting for the *real* Berlin crisis—did not recognize the extent and significance of that traumatic reaction for a full three days after it had set in. But there was no mistaking it on Wednesday afternoon when more than a quarter of a million people, one in every eight West Berliners, jammed into the big square in front of the West Berlin Town Hall for a demonstration called by Mayor Brandt in an effort to channel frustrations away from the twin dangers of despair and violence.

The people there were no longer stirred up only by the barbed wire. They were outraged by what the Communists had been able to get away with, but—as far as they could tell—the future of West Berlin was at stake as well. Were the Communists always to have their way? Was West Berlin, like East Berlin, destined to be ultimately absorbed into Ulbricht's Democratic Republic? Would the Vopos one day be patrolling their streets too?

Anxiety over the absence of tangible proof that the West was prepared to face up to the Communist challenge was fueled by another shooting incident—submachine-gun fire sprayed at a car driven by a middle-aged East Berlin woman who, with her teen-aged son in the passenger seat, crashed successfully through to West Berlin.

Bitterness about Allied inaction was intensified by the headline of the Berlin tabloid *Der Kurier*—"MARSHAL KONIEV TIPPED OFF THE WEST"—which gave wide circulation to the rumor that the Soviets had cleared the border closure with the Americans in advance. When he saw that story, Brandt's aide Egon Bahr telephoned the American Mission and said, "I need a clear-cut denial within a half-hour, otherwise, instead of gathering in front of Town Hall, there is a danger West Berliners will gather in front of the American Mission on Clayallee." Officials of the main "protecting power" did not appreciate implied threats, but they felt very much on the defensive. Bahr was called back with a firm denial in twenty-five minutes.

Not to be outdone as the voice of the people, another West Berlin newspaper, *Bild Zeitung,* complained about West Berlin being left in the lurch by its supposed guardians: "THE WEST DOES NOTHING—KENNEDY IS SILENT, MACMILLAN IS OUT HUNTING, ADENAUER SNEERS AT BRANDT." The newspaper then proceeded to do some sneering of its own about the Allied response: "They speculate. They get in touch. They prepare steps. They try to take a common stand. In the meantime our fellow countrymen are bloodied on the Communist barbed wire!" Some West Berliners suggested sarcastically that the Allies were so upset by what had happened that they (the Allies) might go on a hunger strike.

The placards carried by people in the square for the big demonstration showed how deeply disillusion had sunk in. In addition to those that condemned Ulbricht and the Communists, some were targeted against the West: "WE WERE BETRAYED!" "DEEDS NOT PROTESTS!" "QUIET, PLEASE. PEOPLE ARE STILL ASLEEP."

It was to the frustration of his fellow Berliners that Brandt was going to address himself with great care but much emotion. He realized that the people of his city needed both reassurance and direction. Their confidence had been badly shaken. They were bewildered, vexed, and worried. "People," he recalled, "were afraid something might happen to them. I did not believe that but certain things had to be said."

West Berlin housewives were already out on panicky shopping sprees, stocking their pantries with nonperishable staples. The telephones of moving firms specializing in West Berlin-to-West Germany transport were jammed with calls from people making bookings or inquiries. Popular anxiety could not be pooh-poohed or sweet-talked away; neither could the fury that had several times since Sunday led mobs of young West Berliners to rush the barbed wire in an attempt to tear it down, which their American guardians appeared too timid to do. Only by showing that he shared their anguish could Brandt hope to guide their responses. He was also not unaware that his performance could have some bearing on the results of the forthcoming West German elections.

The mayor gave a stirring speech, delivered in his deep, permanently strained-sounding voice, which added to the effect of his distress and controlled fury. "Berlin," he rasped, "expects more than words. Berlin expects political action!" He said the prestige of the Allies and the fate of the western world were at stake. He warned that Berlin should not be permitted to become "another Munich" (where Britain and France tried to avoid war by appeasing Adolf Hitler in 1938 on the eve of World War II).

Brandt directed the thoughts of the assembled crowd toward the tribulations of the people in the East. "Our countrymen in the Soviet Sector and the Soviet Zone," he said, "now carry the heaviest burden." He promised those on the other side of the border that they would not be forgotten and appealed to East German police and troops to ignore orders to shoot at their countrymen.

The mayor also revealed that he had written a letter to Kennedy drawing the president's attention to the anxiety of the people of West Berlin. In that letter, the details of which were not publicly revealed at the time, Brandt warned of the consequences of the failure of the Allies to take action:

> The illegal sovereignty of the government of East Berlin has been recognized. . . . I consider this a serious turning point in the postwar history of this city, such as has not been experienced since the blockade. This development has not altered the will to resist of the population of West Berlin, but it has succeeded in casting doubt upon the capability and determination of the Three Powers to react. . . . The Soviet Union has used the [East German] People's Army to achieve half of its proposals for a "free city." Act Two is only a question of time. After Act Two we would find a Berlin which resembles a ghetto. Having lost not only its function as the refuge of freedom and the symbol of hope for reunification, it will also be cut off from the free section of Germany. Then, instead of a refugee movement into Berlin, we might see the beginnings of a flight out of Berlin. I consider it appropriate in this situation that the Western Powers demand . . . the reestablishment of Four Power responsibility.

Brandt also told Kennedy that the Allies should reaffirm assurances of their continued presence in West Berlin until German reunification was achieved. He urged the president to bring the Berlin situation before the United Nations and to reinforce the American garrison in the city.

Neither his disclosure that he had written to the president, nor the letter itself, did anything to endear the Berlin mayor to the White House. Kennedy was riled that Brandt had publicly mentioned the letter before he had received it. He also objected to Brandt's lecturing him after he had devoted so much of his time and energy to the Berlin crisis and after he had repeatedly given absolute assurances of America's determination to defend West Berlin and Western Europe.

That very day United States Secretary of the Army Elvis Stahr had frozen in military service almost one hundred thousand men soon due for discharge from the armed forces. Stahr had also alerted more than one hundred army reserve units that they might soon be called to active duty. He had announced that three thousand more troops would be sent to Europe and had ordered that the number of combat-ready divisions in the American strategic reserve be doubled. All this, administration officials said, was hardly a sign that the United States was reneging on its obligations.

Some in Washington suggested that Brandt's letter to Kennedy was just a stunt to gain points in his election contest with Chancellor

Adenauer. Adenauer was indeed furious at both the letter and at the fact that Brandt was in the Berlin limelight. Some American newspapers said Brandt—"a mere mayor"—was trying to dictate American foreign policy, which could not be permitted to concentrate on Berlin to the exclusion of other issues. Some accused him of being a demagogue, trying to stir up the West Berlin crowd—which was unjust because Brandt lived in fear of a violent explosion of anger in the city.

Nevertheless, Brandt's letter contributed to the growing realization at the White House and the State Department that a very important aspect of the Berlin crisis had been neglected: the effect it would have on West Berliners and, even more dangerously, on West Germans who were asking with increasing concern whether the United States could be relied upon to protect them if they too came under pressure from the Soviet Union.

Newspapers throughout West Germany questioned whether, in view of the recent events, the United States could claim to be the guardian of freedom. Was there really an advantage to being linked to the western alliance if this was the best it could do? Little reassurance was derived from a report in *The New York Times* that the Kennedy administration believed that the long-awaited Berlin crisis hadn't yet occurred. From Bonn Ambassador Dowling dispatched a warning that further changes brought about in the situation by the Communists, even if they only amounted to their tightening of the screws in East Berlin, could direct public support in West Germany toward a radical reorientation of that country's foreign policy. A group of West German students sent Kennedy a black umbrella, reminiscent of the one carried by Prime Minister Neville Chamberlain, who had knuckled under to Hitler at the 1938 Munich meeting. (When that was reported, a West German pacifist group urged Kennedy to send the umbrella back to them so that they might return it to the students "in a drastic way.")

A report from the Berlin Mission, telling of a crisis of confidence developing in the city, could easily have been taken as another of the recurring outbreaks of Berlinitis among the Americans stationed there. Not so easily dismissed was a message from Berlin sent outside regular channels to the president by Edward R. Murrow, in whose judgment Kennedy placed great value. Murrow told the president that the United States was badly misplaying the situation. He said the people of West Berlin had been demoralized by the absence of a meaningful American response to the border closure. He urged that efforts be made to correct the "psychological climate."

Another call for the United States to derive greater advantage from the situation came from the man Kennedy trusted most—his brother, Attorney General Robert Kennedy. In a memorandum to the president the attorney general pointed out that "We have been handed a propaganda victory of tremendous dimensions on a silver platter and we are just not taking advantage of it." He claimed that if the Americans had acted as the Communists had, there would be riots and disturbances around the globe. Why, he wanted to know, was the United States failing to alert the world to the enormity of what the Communists were doing in Berlin?

The Soviets were relieved that the White House had accepted the division of Berlin without a fuss. But they were aware that pressures were mounting on Washington to adopt a stronger line. Moscow accordingly took steps to avert a change in the American stance. Andrei Smirnov, the Soviet ambassador to Bonn, paid a well publicized call on Adenauer to deliver a message from Khrushchev assuring the chancellor that the Soviets had no intention of exacerbating the situation. Smirnov urged that the West also refrain from heightening tensions. In a message meant to be transmitted to Washington Smirnov told the West German leader that Moscow believed there was no need for anyone to get excited because the danger of war had now receded.

But the signals emanating from Berlin were now stronger than any the Kremlin was sending. The United States could no longer comfortably conclude that its vital interests in the city had remained untouched and untarnished. The crisis of confidence was real and spreading. Kennedy and his advisers might protest that America's commitment to the freedom of West Berlin was undiminished. They might explain that the problem was purely psychological. They might insist—to the fury of the Berlin Mafia—that in closing off East Berlin the Soviets had admitted a failure, not achieved a victory. But it was glaringly obvious that such words did nothing to calm the anxieties of West Berliners and West Germans. America's leadership of the West was being tested. John Kennedy had to pass that test if that leadership was to retain its credibility.

Ironically, it was the timid British who moved first to display western resolve not to be pushed around. While officials in London suggested that countermeasures in Berlin were out of the question because they might distract the world's attention from the barbarity of the Communist action, a detachment of Royal Green Jackets showed up at the Soviet war memorial in the British Sector near the Brandenburg Gate to enclose the memorial in a barbed-wire cage, with a space left at the rear for entrance and exit.

When a Soviet officer realized what was happening, he drove through the gate, the Vopos quickly opening a gap in the wire for him, and angrily confronted the British officer on the spot. He demanded that the fence around the memorial, dedicated to the men who had heroically given their lives in the fight against fascism, be removed immediately. The British officer—resisting a temptation to say simply, "You're on our patch, mate!"—informed him that they were simply protecting the memorial against West Berliners who were enraged by what was happening to their city. Fuming, the Soviet officer insisted that his commandant should have been consulted first. But he drove back through the gate to East Berlin, and no more was heard about it. When this act was compared to the determined British efforts to avoid confrontation with the Soviets at all costs, a White House official allowed that "the British come in two sizes."

Late Thursday night West Berlin police on duty near the barbed wire at Potsdamer Platz reported unusual activity on the far side of the barrier. The Communists were stacking concrete blocks and deploying an extra detail of guards. Soon workmen, closely watched by armed Vopos, began shifting the concrete blocks into place just behind the wire. The East Germans were launching the next phase of the border-closing operation. They were building the Berlin Wall.

If the Americans, British, and French had done nothing about the barbed wire except issue a protest, there was reason to assume they would not do anything about the concrete that was to replace it. Only five days had passed since Barbed Wire Sunday, but now the wire—messy, not completely effective, and needing to be patrolled by far too many guards—was to make way for a more permanent, tidier fixture.

The dimensions of the Wall were not immediately apparent. Ranging from five to six feet high and topped with barbed wire, the new barrier at first seemed meant only for specific lengths of the border that the East German security forces considered most vulnerable to border crashers or to trouble from West Berlin demonstrators. In fact, preparations for such a formidable obstruction clear across the entire East Berlin–West Berlin frontier had been part of the plan from the beginning, though the Soviets withheld final authorization until it was confirmed that a vigorous western response to the earlier stages would not be forthcoming.[2]

Like the barbed-wire barrier, the Wall was going up safely back from the actual borderline. There was still to be no encroachment on West Berlin, no provocation that might elicit an Allied response. No territorial changes were involved. Having already locked them in, the Communist authorities were merely locking the East German people in more securely. Those still trying to flee the republic would have a much harder job of it than before. As the Wall took shape, East German troops could be relieved of border duty and sent back to their barracks. Vopos could be shifted to other duties. Members of the Worker Battle Brigades could be sent back to their factories and offices. The guards still on duty at the border would not have to concern themselves with the antics of demonstrators on the other side of the barrier. It was said that the new barrier would defend the German Democratic Republic from militarists, saboteurs, spies, and others bent on undermining socialist construction. For Kennedy, Macmillan, and De Gaulle concrete instead of wire changed nothing. A barrier was a barrier.

But even before reports that the Wall was going up reached the White House, Kennedy had been persuaded that the United States had been made to look impotent in Berlin and that this could have dangerous consequences. Intelligence and Research at the State Department warned that to the extent the "Soviet maneuver" in East Berlin was not successfully challenged, "it strengthens Moscow's hand vis-à-vis the West on the Berlin question." Though convinced that America's message to the Soviet Union—"thus far and no further"—was sufficient, the president decided something had to be done to overcome the sense of betrayal felt by West Berliners and to neutralize the paranoid suspicions of the West Germans. He would send General Clay, the hero of the airlift, on an official visit to Berlin,

---

[2]Many who were involved with the situation at the time still believe that the Soviet fall-back positions included ultimately abandoning a city-center barrier altogether and reverting to the rejected idea of tight controls between East Germany and East Berlin.

to be the living symbol of America's determination not to be squeezed out of the city. Clay had formally volunteered his services in a brief note to the White House on Tuesday.

This presented a problem for the president. Clay was a prominent Republican and had been active in supporting the candidacy of Kennedy's rival, Richard Nixon, in the presidential election campaign. For domestic political reasons he would have to be balanced off on the trip by a prominent Democrat. On Thursday night Kennedy called Vice-President Lyndon Johnson away from a dinner party and asked him to fly to Berlin the next night. Johnson was to go with Clay (rather, vice versa) as the president's representative, unequivocally reaffirming by his words and his presence America's reliability and commitment to the defense of the freedom of West Berlin.[3]

That wouldn't be all. General Clarke in Heidelberg had already been alerted that he was to dispatch a battle group of American troops up the autobahn from West Germany to West Berlin to reinforce the American garrison in the divided city. The troops were to arrive in Berlin Sunday to be ceremonially received and welcomed there by Johnson.

Saturday turned into a day of almost frenzied celebration in West Berlin. Johnson and Clay landed at Tempelhof airfield to a ceremonial welcome from local dignitaries and found the streets lined with flower-throwing, cheering crowds. All signs of demoralization and anxiety vanished as the West Berliners, and the tabloids that had done so much to arouse their fear and trepidation, accepted the visiting Americans as the reassurance they had begun to fear would not be forthcoming. An experienced crowd pleaser, Johnson stepped out of the official limousine whenever he could to mingle with the people, shake their hands, and accept their jubilant, excited greetings.

Practiced political campaigner that he was, the vice-president was in his element. When Kennedy had asked him to go to Berlin, he had at first declined, saying it was too dangerous. He had to be

[3]When Johnson stopped off to see Adenauer in Bonn en route to Berlin, the chancellor pointed out to him a sign reading "Action, Not Words" carried by an old woman with whom the chancellor said he personally would want neither.

gently informed that he was being ordered to go. According to McGeorge Bundy, "Johnson approached anybody else's decision about what he should do with the utmost wariness. But once he got to Berlin, he thought it was great." How could anyone treated like a hero think otherwise?

The crowd that overflowed the square in front of the Town Hall to hear Johnson bring a message from Kennedy was even larger than the one that had filled the square three days earlier to hear Mayor Brandt try to calm their fears. A translator was on hand to repeat Johnson's words in German, but the crowd often did not wait for the running translation before bursting into loud cheers. People were moved not as much by his words as by Johnson's reassuring presence among them, though the speech was the most stirring the vice-president had ever delivered:

> To the survival and the creative future of this city, we Americans have pledged in effect what our ancestors pledged in forming the United States—our lives, our fortunes and our sacred honor. The president wants you to know and I want you to know that the pledge he has given to the freedom of West Berlin and to the rights of western access to Berlin is firm. . . . This island does not stand alone. . . . Your lives are linked not merely to those in Hamburg, Bonn and Frankfurt. They are also linked with those in every town in western Europe, Canada and the United States, and with those on every continent who live in freedom and are prepared to fight for it.

General Clay spoke also, briefly, but Berliners didn't need his words to know he was with them in spirit as well as body, and they cheered as clamorously for him as they had for Johnson. The faces of the people who were jammed up against one another in the square were radiant with relief and pleasure. When they didn't peer content-edly up at the balcony from which their illustrious guests addressed them, they glanced at each other, nodding and grinning, as if to say, "Everything is alright now." And when the speeches were over and the national anthems had been played, a magnificent hush fell over the square for the tolling in the Town Hall tower of the the Freedom Bell, which Clay had brought to Berlin in 1950 after the airlift.

The sound of the bell in those circumstances was profoundly thrilling, and the hush that had settled over the 350,000 people assembled there was as soul stirring as their earlier exultation had been. (Two years later, when Kennedy himself visited West Berlin and received a similarly ecstatic reception from the crowd in the Town Hall square, the dour Adenauer, who had always been suspicious of emotional excess, muttered gloomily to Dean Rusk, next to whom he was standing, "Does this mean Germany can one day have another Hitler?")

The fifteen hundred men who comprised the First Battle Group of the Eighth Infantry Division of the United States Army, under the command of Colonel Glover S. Johns, Jr., had bivouacked at Braunschweig not far from the East German border on Saturday night. They had been drawn from forces stationed at the United States Army base at Mannheim well back from the border. Under the circumstances General Clarke felt it was wiser not to spare any of his frontline troops—a decision that revealed how precarious the situation was considered.

The battle group was to proceed to Berlin in six columns of 250 men and forty vehicles each. They were to set off through East Germany at intervals so that any obstruction along the way would not lead to a snarl on the road. The columns were to remain in radio contact with each other. Even more important, they were to remain in contact with General Clarke through a command post near the West German–East German border. And Clarke was to have an open line to General Norstad in Paris and to the White House.

Before climbing into their vehicles for their trek across East Germany, the men in the battle group were assembled to hear about their mission from Colonel Johns, who would be leading the front column on the journey. The colonel told them that they were going to Berlin to protect freedom. The eyes of the world would be on them. They were told they might be stopped. They were not to acknowledge the right of any Soviet or East German to question them, inspect their vehicles, or demand identification. In accordance with long-standing agreement the colonel would be handling all of that with a Soviet officer when they first crossed into East Germany. They were told that they probably would not run into trouble but that they were, nevertheless, to be prepared.

Although detailed orders had been issued for the operation, the Pentagon had neglected to mention in those orders whether the troops should be armed with ammunition for their weapons for their trip across East Germany. General Clarke took it upon himself to have them issued with ammunition. "Suppose," he said later, "the Russians had tried to stop our men and a reporter had found that the soldiers had not been issued ammo? Wouldn't I have looked ridiculous?"

The decision to send the battle group up the autobahn to West Berlin had not been lightly taken. Several of Kennedy's key advisers didn't like the idea at all. They said that sending Vice-President Johnson to Berlin was symbolic enough and that daring the Soviets or East Germans to stop the battle group as it roared up the autobahn was needlessly tempting fate. Generals Taylor and Lemnitzer thought it was unwise to "put additional troops in an undefensible area." But the president was by now convinced that his Berlin gesture had to be comprehensive and convincing. He wanted no more backbiting from the West Germans or hardliners in his own entourage about the failure of the United States to respond forcefully to the Soviet challenge. Small though it was compared to the Soviet divisions deployed in the area, the battle group would demonstrate the determination of the United States to maintain its presence in West Berlin, regardless of what the Communists might be inflicting on East Berlin and East Germany.

Kennedy was, however, apprehensive of the Soviet reaction. *Time* magazine quoted a White House aide as saying on the eve of the operation that "talking to Kennedy was like talking to a statue. There was the feeling that this mission could very well escalate into shooting before morning." The president was worried enough to put American air and ground forces in Europe on the alert and to instruct his military aide, Brigadier General Clifton, to remain personally in touch with developments from the situation room at the White House right through Saturday night Washington time—when the battle group would be traversing East Germany—and to wake him if the operation ran into difficulties.

As it turned out, there was a problem almost immediately. Through an agreement made years before that the Allies had long since regretted, the Soviets were authorized to make a head count of western troops heading for Berlin through East Germany. But when, according to standard procedure, the Soviet officer on the East German side of the border counted the troops while they were still in their vehicles, the number did not tally with the manifest. After a

recount, which also did not tally, Colonel Johns, who wanted no
delay, had his men fall out so that the Soviets could more easily count
them.

Having "amicably resolved" this difficulty, his column, followed by the others, moved on to Berlin. Colonel Johns' remedy
would cause problems later. Never ones to pass up a chance to turn
a one-time gift into standard operating procedure, the Soviets from
then on insisted that American troops in trucks heading for Berlin
up the autobahn dismount to be counted.

The rest of the journey for the battle group was uneventful. All
other traffic had been cleared from the autobahn, and Vopos were
stationed on all the bridges under which the troops passed. Each of
the battle-group columns was escorted front and rear by jeeps of the
East German army and was thus compelled to travel no faster than
twenty-five miles an hour, which—along with rest breaks en route
—meant that Colonel Johns' front column did not get to Berlin until
half-past-noon, by which time Lyndon Johnson had been out again
happily mingling in the streets with Berlin crowds and handing out
not only handshakes but also ballpoint pens as mementoes of his
visit. The vice-president was extracted from this enjoyable duty by
West Berlin police and his Secret Service entourage and whisked
away to the point where the autobahn through East Germany
crossed into West Berlin, just in time to take the salute as Colonel
Johns and his men rolled into town.

Word of the imminent arrival of the battle group had been
widely publicized. Thousands of West Berliners had congregated
near and around the reviewing stand that had been hastily erected
for Johnson, Clay, Brandt, Watson, and other dignitaries, who—
with the help of an army band and the cheering populace—turned
the arrival of the troops into a triumphal occasion.

The troops went straight to McNair Barracks to be fed (though,
because of the pace of events, some had to go hungry till that night)
and to be formally addressed by Johnson, who told the men, "All the
resources of the mightiest nation in the world stand behind you." At
five in the afternoon, by which time the last column of the battle
group was completing its journey down the East German autobahn,
West Berlin was treated to the first American military parade
through the center of town since 1945. The battle group rolled right
down the Ku'damm. Again the streets were jammed with people.
Again they cheered, and some cried. They threw flowers, which some

of the soldiers tucked into their helmet straps. Colonel Johns said it was the most remarkable reception he had experienced since the liberation of Paris from the Germans.

Less dramatically, a British military train rolled into town carrying eighteen armored cars and sixteen scout cars to help beef up the British garrison. Macmillan had resisted American pressure to send a token force of troop reinforcements, but as with the American battle group, it was the gesture rather than the details that mattered. By nightfall on Sunday, a full week after the barbed wire was first stretched across the sector border, West Berliners felt they no longer had reason to fear a Communist take-over.

"Flashpoint Berlin" continued to exist on a plateau of excitement and drama. For correspondents who flocked in from all over the world, it was a stirring news story. The pictures and details of the Wall as it grew, and of the divided city coming to terms with its new existence, were grist for any editor's mill: people lining up at both sides of the barrier to wave at each other, shouting greetings and weeping; the heavy hand of the police state tightening its grip on East Berlin; the West Berliners, who seemed to inhabit another universe, daintily dipping forks into hunks of chocolate truffle *gâteau* at Kempinski's on the Ku'damm while refugees not fifteen minutes away gambled with their lives to slip or crash out of Germany's first workers and farmers state. Just about everywhere a person turned in the city, there were the makings of an image rich in human or political significance.

Of special political significance was the fact that what had previously been a Berlin problem had been transformed by the Soviets into a West Berlin problem. The Communists made no secret of their confident expectation that the western powers and even the West Germans, caught up in their corrupt materialistic pursuits, would soon lose interest in the outpost city on which they were spending a fortune in grants and subsidies. West Berlin, they predicted, would wither on the vine. Business and industry there were already badly hurt by the absence of the Grenzgängers, locked in behind the Wall.

West Berlin was having to adjust to a new set of circumstances. Influential Americans were no longer coy about saying publicly and without apology that the western powers could not have been expected to do anything about the Wall. They even suggested that the border closure to stop the refugees may not have been such a bad thing after all. Syndicated columnist Joseph Alsop, a hardliner bowing to accomplished fact, pointed out in dozens of newspapers across the United States that

> the western nations have no more obligation to the right of jail breaking for the East Germans than for the Poles, or the Hungarians, or the wretched Chinese. . . . If western nerves remain steady, and if Khrushchev is convinced the West means business [in standing by its commitments] there is hope for a good outcome.

The emphasis on steady nerves was important because barely had Vice-President Johnson reported to the president on his mission than the Soviets were once again making menacing gestures.[4] In a note to the United States Moscow warned that it might take action against what it called the misuse of the air corridors through which West Berlin had been supplied during the blockade. This drew a vigorous warning from the White House that no such interference would be tolerated.

That had no bearing on the change of circumstances in East Berlin. To indicate they were impressed neither by the Johnson–Clay visit nor by the arrival of the battle group, the East Germans proceeded with the next phase of their border-closure operation. Five of the twelve remaining crossing points in the city were sealed. Of the seven still open, the East German interior minister decreed that four were to be for West Berliners and two for West Germans. Only one would be for Allied personnel and other foreigners. In addition, the East Germans announced that West Berliners no longer would be permitted into East Berlin merely by showing their identification papers. They would require special permits. Still testing the limits, the East Germans warned, more firmly than before, that people in

---

[4]There had been a less publicized aspect to the vice-president's Berlin visit. He had insisted that Mayor Brandt, who had other things on his mind, arrange for stores, which were closed, to be opened for him on Saturday night and Sunday so that he could acquire palpable mementoes of his trip to the frontline city. The store managers were summoned from their homes so that a selection of shoes for Johnson to choose from (two pairs of each; his feet were different sizes) could be delivered to the Berlin residence of Ambassador Dowling where Johnson was staying and so that he could pick a royal-porcelain-china service and a collection of ashtrays to be handed out to friends.

Berlin Wall's start in 1961 remembered in ceremony

German chancellor recalls fear as child living in communism

DEUTSCHE PRESSE-AGENTUR

REUTERS

A man places a rose on a piece of paper with the name of a person killed while trying to escape from East Berlin by crossing the Berlin Wall. A ceremony on Saturday at Berlin's Brandenburg Gate paid tribute to the city's Cold War victims.

BERLIN — Berlin on Saturday commemorated the construction of the Berlin Wall — isolating the west of the city for 28 years — which began 50 years ago on Aug. 13, 1961.

Chancellor Angela Merkel said the occasion underlined the importance of supporting freedom and democracy around the world.

"The injustice of constructing the wall reminds us, to this day, to stand for freedom, democracy and civil rights at home and abroad," the chancellor said.

Merkel, the daughter of a Protestant pastor, was born in West Germany but moved to the East with her family at a young age.

"I personally — as I was 7 years old in 1961 — remember the terror that the construction of the wall triggered in my family. We were also separated violently from aunts and grandparents," Merkel said.

"It is all the more unforgettable how happy the fall of this terrible structure made us Germans in 1989," she added.

President Christian Wulff said Germany had to encourage more freedom within its borders by helping immigrants integrate in Germany and by allowing people to reach their full potential.

He recalled the activism that brought the wall down, saying: "The Wall did not fall; it was toppled."

Wulff also mentioned the people who died along the border separating East and West Germany, as well as those imprisoned or persecuted for political reasons.

At the same time, he said, millions more were affected as they were denied the opportunity of determining their own lives.

The Berlin Wall, which began 50 years ago as barbed wire and guards preventing people from crossing into West Berlin, was erected by East German authorities to stem the flow of citizens escaping the Communist regime.

another, and experts said consumers who want to know why should look in the mirror.

Many factors contribute to the nation's sputtering recovery. But consumers, whose spending on everything from groceries and gas to clothing and coffee makers accounts for more than two-thirds of economic activity, are not buying like they used to.

Without an increase in purchases, economists hold out little hope things will turn around soon.

"Consumer spending still represents close to 70 percent of our gross domestic product, so without a fairly robust consumer sector, the outlook for overall economic growth is not good," said Norman Robertson, economic adviser to Smithfield Trust Co., a Downtown investment firm, and one-time chief economist for Mellon Bank.

Yet it's not your fault, analysts said. How could anyone lucky enough to hold onto a job be expected to spend, given that wages remained flat or declined for more than a decade? People who are not employed have encountered difficulty in finding jobs, and high unemployment makes it tough to change jobs or negotiate better pay.

Economic woes / A6

» LOAN LOWDOWN: Bank lending will open up "when there's a degree of clarity about the economy."

» ENERGIZED: Gas-powered firms might blossom during tough times, analysts say.

CONFIDENCE · A6

Perry joins GOP presidential fray

Texas governor raps Obama's record, takes credit for creating slew of jobs

McCLATCHY NEWSPAPERS

CHARLESTON, S.C. — After more than a decade as his state's longest-serving governor, Texan Rick Perry moved onto the national political stage on Saturday by declaring his entry into the 2012 presidential race, transforming the scramble for the Republican nomination by adding another name to the list of those vying for the right to challenge Barack Obama for the nation's top elected office.

PERRY · A10

West Berlin were not to come within one hundred yards of the sector border.

This last decree was finally recognized by the western powers as, literally, going too far. Everything else had happened in East Berlin. Now the East Germans were presuming to assert control over part of West Berlin. The western commandants reacted immediately and uncompromisingly. In addition to lodging the standard protest with the Soviet commandant, they moved troops to the sector border to show, as British troop commander Brigadier Goff Hamilton said, that they had "no intention of being told where the west sectors begin and end."

Troops of all three western powers were deployed right up against the Wall. American tanks rolled to within several feet of the East Berlin demarcation line. Armored cars of all three garrisons patrolled up and down along the west side of the Wall, and machine-gun nests were set up well within one hundred yards of the line. The Allied moves didn't change things in East Berlin, but they showed the Soviets that, for the moment at least, whatever they still had planned would have to be done within the confines of East Berlin.

The following day three American army buses, carrying soldiers from the newly arrived battle group for a sight-seeing tour of East Berlin, were halted at the Friedrichstrasse checkpoint when Vopos demanded to inspect the identity papers of the men on board. The convoy captain flatly turned them down. The American Provost Marshal, Colonel Robert Sabolyk, was quickly summoned and told the Vopos, "These buses are going through in thirty minutes. If they are held up, we will know what to do about it." When the buses started forward again, after the Vopos had had a chance to get instructions from their superiors, no move was made to stop them. Later, an East German water cannon sprayed two American soldiers standing just west of the Wall but stopped immediately when an American officer drew a tear-gas grenade. It was apparent in both cases that the East German guards had been instructed to take some liberties but not to push the Allies too far, which did not prevent them that day—eleven days after the operation began—from shooting dead an East Berliner trying to swim to the west across the Teltow Canal. It was the first recorded killing of a would-be refugee.

As reports came in of more people cut down while fleeing, a Vopo who went west said that despite orders, he and many of his fellow policemen only pretended to aim at escaping refugees. They did not want to murder people and deliberately fired their weapons wide of the mark. But though bullets missed some of those who fled, the number of casualties—shot dead or wounded or drowned trying to swim to a West Berlin shore—grew, particularly after Vopos and Grepos were brought in from Saxony to replace East Berliners on border duty. Saxons had a reputation for being less inclined than Berliners to agonize over disagreeable orders. They were thought to be less reluctant to shoot people fleeing the republic.

Meantime, the Wall continued to creep along the border like an insidious growth, taking an even more nightmarish aspect where the buildings in the Soviet Sector were on the border line between East and West Berlin. Doors and windows of tenements there were bricked up, though not before some refugees escaped through them —and not before at least one of them tried but failed. Fifty-nine-year-old Ida Siekmann threw a mattress out of her window into the West and, after agonizing indecision on the window sill, jumped after it, hitting the concrete sidewalk instead. She died from her injuries before she could be brought to the hospital. Another woman was later caught in a squalid tug-of-war between Vopos trying to drag her back through the window of her border apartment while West Berlin firemen in the street below tried to pull her down to freedom. The firemen finally won that cold war in miniature.

The West Berlin fire department stood ready to dispatch men with safety blankets whenever word came that someone appeared ready to leap into the West from a window of a border tenement not yet fully bricked up. The Vopos took action to discourage them. There were several incidents in which firemen were alerted by people in the street that someone seemed ready to jump, but when they rushed to the scene and spread the blanket, they were bombarded from above with paint or stones. Later, all the East Berlin border buildings were forcibly evacuated, their residents housed elsewhere, the entire border area leveled. The ever-advancing Wall rose where people once had lived.

As the summer wore on and refugees continued to dribble through, makeshift lookout towers, much like those on the East German–West German frontier, were erected along the inner-city border to give guards a clear view of unauthorized persons making for the Wall. Sections that foot patrols could not adequately cover were turned into free-fire zones in which anyone spotted could be shot without question or warning. Shots were heard along the Wall at night, often followed by screams of pain. Tall grass, where it grew near the border, was trimmed to deny fugitives a place to hide until they could attempt to escape after nightfall. Frogmen strung barbed wire in border waterways, and patrol boats cruised the waterways to fish out swimmers who evaded the wire. Despite these precautions, people continued to get through.

An East German professional photographer gained permission from an officer at the Wall to take press pictures of the guards defending the Democratic Republic against the slave traders and militarists. As he clicked away, he backed toward a border crossing, then turned and raced across. One man fashioned a homemade American army uniform from bits and pieces and walked through a checkpoint without being challenged. Another did the same with the uniform of a Soviet officer. A man crashed through the Wall in a five-ton dump truck, his wife at his side.

A woman brought flowers to the guards at a border crossing, handed them over with praise and thanks, and ran toward the West. A Vopo sergeant on duty raced after her, waving his pistol and shouting, "Stop! Come back! I'll shoot!" effectively preventing his colleagues from taking aim. They both soon checked in at Marienfelde. After that incident, and after reports of guards accepting bribes to let people through appeared in the western press, East German newspapers announced that several Vopos had been approached by people offering money to let them flee the republic but had quickly arrested those who had tried to corrupt them. It was impossible for people to know whether that was true or only an effort to discourage would-be bribers.

The more ingenious or daring the escape, the more it was evident that the escape hatch was effectively closing and that the East German security forces could begin cracking down in earnest on dissident and obstructive elements that, prior to August 13, had been undermining the construction of the socialist state. Those in the East who openly criticized the erection of the Wall did so at great risk. East German newspapers explained it was no crime to use "workers' fists" to teach badly needed lessons to such people. Squads of Communist vigilantes moved about serving out rough justice to "enemies of the people." It was decreed that persons "endangering public safety and order" could be moved from their places of residence and assigned different jobs.

Work conditions in the factories and on the farms, difficult before the Wall, became increasingly onerous. In an effort to make up for lost production, workers were required to meet inflated output quotas. There were work rehabilitation camps for malingerers, for those who failed to volunteer for special work details, and for those who were reported to be subversives. Kangaroo courts were called into session to try people accused of defaming the state and its leaders, or for assisting spies or slave traders in the West—a convenient blanket charge that served when nothing more specific could be found. The prisons were soon jammed with people who objected to the Wall and to the subsequent police crackdown and who said so, either defiantly or without realizing who was listening. Meetings were called all over East Germany—in factories and in village squares, in community centers and sports halls—to congratulate the regime for its "anti-fascist, anti-militarist measures." Local people knew it was advisable to attend such gatherings. With everything under control, socialist planners could finally begin working out programs for creating the kind of economy and society they pined for.

That many East Berliners pined for something else was evident despite the police-state atmosphere, and not only in the continuing escape attempts and the general mood of dejection so conspicuous in the streets of East Berlin. Frustrated refugees with their suitcases and expressions of despair were no longer seen in the hall of the Friedrichstrasse train station. They had long since trudged home to come to terms as best they could with the way of life they had sought to put behind them. But that station remained an extraordinary place.

East Berliners were not permitted through the control booths to go West on the trains that stopped at Friedrichstrasse, but it was the only station in the East open to visitors arriving from West Berlin. There were armed guards in abundance and a careful screening procedure to make certain that people from the West were neither on the list of excluded persons nor carrying forbidden literature and to block people from the East from slipping through to the platform where west-bound trains stopped.

All that was remarkable enough at a main city-center train station. Even stranger was the character of the new shift of East

Berliners loitering in or near the station hall. They could not entertain hopes of making a sudden break through the guard positions.
Escape there was totally out of the question. Some were there because they expected visitors from the West whom they could no
longer meet halfway and who, like myself, could pass through Vopo
controls by showing personal documents. Some East Berliners hung
around the station because the setting and sight were as extraordinary to them as it was to me. But many were there because that
station and the west-bound trains they were forbidden to approach
were the closest thing they would ever again get to whatever material
and spiritual rewards they longed for on the other side of the Wall.

12

The Rogue Symbol

As reports of the crackdown in the East filtered through to the West, the euphoria generated by the weekend proceedings in West Berlin proved remarkably short-lived for many there. After the cheering had stopped, after Johnson and Clay had gone home, after the battle group had settled in at McNair Barracks, the facts of the case rose even more chillingly to the surface than before. West Berlin leaders, who had been too busy and too choked with rage and anxiety until then to study the terrain soberly, started to grasp what suddenly appeared to them to be the full significance of what had happened at the border.

Though pleased with the arrival of the American troop reinforcements and the friendly tone of a Kennedy message hand delivered by Johnson, Willy Brandt was pained by the president's reply to his own controversial letter. "My own objection," Kennedy had written, "to most of the measures which have been proposed—even to most of the suggestions in your own letter—is that they are mere trifles compared to what has been done." Remarkably, Kennedy's words stating the obvious were even more disturbing: "... this brutal border closing evidently represents a basic Soviet decision which only war could reverse. Neither you nor we, nor any of our Allies, have ever supposed that we should go to war on this point."

No one could deny that, but it now became clear to Brandt that his hopes for Germany had been built on an illusion. He had never expected nor wanted anyone to wage war to reunify Germany, but it was now clear for the first time that for the Americans and the other Allies, questions of reunification were "either rhetorical or long-range." That was proved by their acquiescence to the division of Berlin. It was an unnerving, unsettling revelation. When Edward Tomkins flew over from London in September, Brandt did not seem to him to have a firm idea of what he wanted done. But his disillusionment would, in time, have momentous consequences for Europe and for East–West relations.

Brandt's adviser Egon Bahr realized immediately after the Johnson–Clay visit that

> the Wall was like a terrible traffic accident. The victim is taken to the hospital, operated on, wakes up after surgery, and is taken to his room where friends are waiting. They tell him he is lucky he didn't lose his life. Then his friends go away and he discovers that one of his legs has been amputated.

East Berlin was gone; taken away.

West Berliners drew little encouragement from a comment extracted from Macmillan by reporters who had pursued him onto the eighteenth green at Gleneagles Hotel in Scotland, where he had gone to get in some golfing before returning to the cares of London town. "Nobody is going to fight over Berlin," the prime minister said confidently, as if dismissing the city as not worth fighting over. Then he added, "I think the thing has been gotten up by the press." The British leader clearly wasn't overly upset by developments.

But in West Berlin personal and public priorities were transformed overnight. To Manfred Rexin, then a young Berlin Social-Democratic-party activist, Adenauer and the domestic policies of his Christian Democratic government in Bonn had earlier been the nemesis. Suddenly, instead, the overriding menace had become Ulbricht and the possibility that he might have his way with West Berlin and inflict on it the police-state controls to which East Berlin was being subjected.

A wave of concern about the city's future swept through the western sectors. Sealed off from East Berlin and East Germany, West Berlin would no longer be able to fill the role that had kept it viable deep behind Communist lines. It could no longer be the "beacon of liberty in the red sea," "the haven for refugees from tyranny," "the shop window of freedom." Would the protecting powers still consider it worthwhile garrisoning forces in so exposed an outpost in the circumstances that now prevailed? Had West Berlin become redundant? Situated well inside East Germany, it was still the front-line city. But its continuing allegiance to western values had become a defiant gesture rather than an effective advertisement for the failure of Communism.

For the people of West Berlin that gesture remained crucial. Their freedoms, their ways of life were at stake. For others far away from the Wall, whose primary focus was on the danger of nuclear holocaust by miscalculation, the value of the gesture could become questionable. Was it wise, for both diplomatic and military reasons, to meet the Soviet international challenge in a patch of land behind Soviet lines? Had West Berlin been transformed from an asset into a liability? Many in the rest of the world couldn't grasp what all the fuss was about. Indian Prime Minister Pandit Nehru, a champion of self-determination for oppressed peoples, commented on first hearing of the division of city that the East Germans were legally justified in closing the sector border. He had to be informed of the legal as well as the human aspects of what had happened before he changed his mind.

There was a question also about whether people in West Germany would be prepared to sustain West Berlin in its new circumstances. Like big cities everywhere, it had been renewed and kept vibrant by a constant transfusion of new blood, new people from the provinces and lesser cities, from West Germany as well as East Germany. Now, as Walt Rostow asked, "Could West Berlin, walled off, remain a city worthy of a young man's investing his life?"

Dean Rusk's announcement of plans for negotiations with the Soviet Union over Berlin, probably in September, once more nourished suspicions that the United States was desperately anxious not to provoke Moscow. It again aroused the endlessly recurring suspicion that Washington would be willing to give more ground in Berlin than it had already. Kennedy told Rusk he wanted "a stronger lead on Berlin negotiations." It was rumored (without foundation) that the United States might be prepared to close down the American-run RIAS radio station and perhaps reduce the recently enlarged American garrison in return for paper guarantees on West Berlin's independence and the access routes from the Soviets, who—as they had already shown—couldn't be trusted to honor agreements and who would continue to nibble away at the western presence until it was all gobbled up.

Reading the despairing cables coming in from Bonn and Berlin describing popular sentiment and fears, Kennedy was convinced that West Germans and West Berliners needed a daily fix of reassurance, which was beneath the dignity of the American government to provide. But a message from Adenauer made him realize this was no time for petulance. The West German chancellor warned that, in the absence of a more convincing reaction to the Communist exploits in Berlin, neutralist notions were spreading in his country. He said those attitudes could fundamentally endanger the future of the western alliance. The West may have hedged before, but now, said the chancellor, countermeasures were essential to revive morale.

The problem for Kennedy remained the same—what countermeasures? Those that were proposed were either too trivial—like cutting off cultural links with East Germany and perhaps ruling out western attendance at a forthcoming East German trade fair—or too great—like economic sanctions, which were being held in reserve as a planned response if the Soviets fulfilled their threat to move against the West Berlin lifelines. It would be foolish to provoke Soviet action with a move planned as a counter to Soviet action.

Washington had been coming to the conclusion that West German pronouncements were meant primarily for public consumption. A paper prepared by the Historical Studies Division of the State Department later showed that Bonn's public demands for action were far stronger than those formally recommended by West German officials at Allied meetings. Adenauer publicly urged economic countermeasures and even hinted at a possible economic blockade by the West against the entire Soviet bloc. But when it came to talks at quadripartite gatherings where countermeasures were actually to be drawn up, the West Germans made no requests for such extreme action. The Americans had suggested, for example, that West Germany might abrogate its trade agreement with East Germany, but Allan Lightner learned that this proposal "went over like a lead balloon when it was discovered that Adenauer was very much opposed to it." It was believed in Washington that the chancellor's public demands for stiff countermeasures were part of his effort to offset Brandt's Berlin advantage as election day drew closer.[1]

Nevertheless, Kennedy accepted as genuine the warning about the possible danger of neutralism spreading in West Germany. He had, in fact, done so even before receiving Adenauer's letter. Reports from the American Embassy in Bonn had issued similar warnings. There was, however, no reason to believe that the West Germans were anything but profoundly anti-Communist and deeply committed to western values. Kennedy was therefore not going to be panicked by Adenauer into precipitate action. But he had, in fact, already sought an answer to questions about West German confidence and had found one, though not one he liked overly much. He would send General Clay back to Berlin to take up residence as his personal representative in the city.

There were two reasons why Kennedy was reluctant to pick Clay for the job. For one thing, the general was known to be a strong-willed, impulsive man, not prepared to accept orders gracefully if he did not agree with them. McGeorge Bundy warned Kennedy, "Clay will be a burden to you if he takes a line more belligerent than yours." Also, Clay's Republican party connections automatically associated him with several prominent Republicans who had been sharply critical of Kennedy's Berlin stance. After Kennedy had returned from Vienna, Richard Nixon had charged that the administration was plagued with a "Hamlet-like psychosis which seems to paralyze it every time decisive action is required," and he had later called Kennedy's dispatch of the battle group to Berlin an "empty gesture," which Khrushchev might see "as weakness rather than strength." Republican National Chairman William Miller charged that the administration was displaying a "general attitude of appeasement."

But Kennedy was tired of being distracted by the relentless, nagging nervousness of West Germans, West Berliners, and American hardliners from probing whether Khrushchev was prepared to talk sensibly about disarmament, as well as about Berlin. Not expect-

---

[1]Shortly after the launching of the border-sealing operation, Adenauer had foolishly suggested at an election rally that the Communists were building the Wall to help Brandt get voted in as chancellor. No one believed that was even remotely true. Instead, it permitted Brandt to score an election point by saying, "The old gentleman [Adenauer was eighty-five years old] really cannot grasp what is going on anymore."

ing simple answers from Moscow, he was convinced there had to be a dialogue with the Soviets, if only to find out where they stood. He didn't intend to be kept on a leash by Teutonic fears and frets. The West Berliners trusted Clay as they trusted no other outsider. If his arrival in their midst as the president's personal representative didn't finally reassure them and the West Germans of Kennedy's reliability, nothing short of declaring war on the Soviets would.

Claims in the West that the Berlin Wall illustrated the failure of Communism may have done nothing to allay anxiety or boost drooping spirits in West Berlin, but they were not without a solid grounding in reality. The fact that Communist rule was unable to compete with the West for the minds of people where there was a free choice was a deep embarrassment to Communist leaders. Nowhere was this more keenly felt than in the Kremlin where, despite his ferocious speechifying, Khrushchev was still unable to convince the Soviet hierarchy that he was making progress toward the fundamental goal of booting the western powers out of Berlin. It was just not happening, and there was nothing to indicate that it was going to happen.

Feelings in the Soviet Union remained strong that the Allied powers had no business being in the divided city, scene of one of the most historic Soviet triumphs in the Great Patriotic War. Soviet hawks exploited Khrushchev's Berlin frustrations to back their incessant calls for increased military strength to match that of their American adversaries. That meant diverting expenditure from other programs and projects and pumping it into escalated military spending, concentrating especially on the costly development of advanced nuclear weaponry. Hoping to shield the sagging Soviet civilian economy from the ravages of military priorities, Khrushchev was reluctant to comply. He said it was not his intention "to saddle the [Soviet] people with unnecessary hardship." But his had been a losing battle ever since Kennedy had publicly and unequivocally committed the United States to the defense of the western presence in Berlin.

As the Wall wound inexorably around the western sectors, the Soviet leader was faced with a dilemma. Having expected the Americans to succumb to his rocket rattling and obligingly tiptoe out of Berlin, taking the British and French with them, he found that he had been forced deeper and deeper into an expensive confrontation he had never expected or wanted the Soviet domestic economy to finance and in which there was no guarantee of success. He was now too deeply committed to resist hard-line pressures on budgetary priorities. He had no choice but to cave in and divert even more domestic resources to the Soviet confrontation with the American superpower.

Despite his personal assurance to Kennedy that the Soviet Union would not be the first to break the moratorium on nuclear testing, and though the United States and Britain had sent clear signals that they were interested in negotiating an extension to the test ban, Khrushchev announced on August 30 that the Soviet Union had resumed nuclear testing in the atmosphere. A Soviet government statement said, "To discourage an aggressor from criminally playing with fire we must let him know and see that there is in the world a force . . . ready to repulse any challenge to the independence and security of peace-loving states and that the weapon of retribution will smite the aggressor in his own lair." Defending the move, Khrushchev told visiting left-wing British members of parliament Sir Leslie Plummer and Konni Zilliacus that it was meant to shock the West into serious negotiations over Berlin. He explained that the tests were being resumed "to cool the hotheads in the capitals" of western powers. Kennedy's reflex response was an earthy Anglo-Saxon expletive. Presidential aide Arthur Schlesinger put it differently:

> I fear that Khrushchev has decided to make the USSR the embodiment of terror and power in the world in the expectation that all "lovers" of peace, terrified of war and recognizing the futility of trying to alter Soviet policy, will concentrate their energies on making the West give way over Berlin.

From the moment he took office, Kennedy, like Khrushchev, had been under pressure to resume nuclear testing. He himself had insisted during the election campaign the previous year that the Republican administration that preceded his had permitted a "missile gap" to develop between the United States and the Soviet Union, with the Soviet Union taking the lead in nuclear capabilities. His critics said he knew it wasn't true. Whether he did or not, after taking office and gaining access to confidential information on comparative military strengths, no more was heard from him about a Soviet nuclear lead.

However, a battery of American military experts, foreign affairs analysts, and professional cold warriors had maintained a barrage of warnings that Soviet progress in nuclear weapons technology had made the tests essential. The joint chiefs of staff urged the president to resume testing, as did the Joint Atomic Energy Committee of Congress. A public opinion poll indicated that Americans backed a test resumption by a two-to-one majority.

Fearful of triggering a tit-for-tat escalation in testing, Kennedy had resisted such pressures. He sanctioned preparations for new underground tests, partly to avoid being completely upstaged by his domestic critics. But he held back from actually authorizing even those "clean" tests. Aside from the danger of launching a new nuclear race, he felt that resuming the tests would complicate his exhaustive efforts to pin down acceptable conditions for negotiations with the Soviets. Now the complications were there anyway. What was at stake was far more serious than Berlin.

Kennedy immediately huddled with his chief aides to work out an appropriate response to the Soviet action. The suggestions included the immediate detonation of a test device, to show that the United States wasn't unprepared for whatever the Soviets had in mind, and even knocking out the Soviet test site with one well placed nuclear bomb. But Kennedy wasn't going to be stampeded into an impetuous reaction. He labeled the Soviet move "a threat to the entire world" and issued a statement saying that the United States would do whatever its national interest required. He said the Soviets were testing "not only nuclear devices but the will and determination of the free world to resist such tactics and to defend freedom." A week later, after publicly and fruitlessly offering the Soviets an opportunity to renew the test ban, he quietly gave the green light for the resumption of underground testing by the United States.

In London, Paris, and other major capitals, antinuclear movements—which had long been heavily tinged with anti-Americanism —found themselves placed by the Soviet decision in the unfamiliar position of demonstrating against the Soviet Union, though not with the ferocity they reserved for anti-American demonstrations. Those they were able to resume once the United States began testing as well.

The new Soviet tests—"atomic blackmail" Kennedy called them—triggered a new wave of nuclearphobia across the United States. The director of the Office of Civil Defense Mobilization had already publicly appealed for additional funds to promote American awareness of nuclear dangers. That did nothing to ease fears. Nor were people comforted by blueprints prepared by civil defense officials for backyard and cellar nuclear shelters, which could be made of concrete, steel, or even earth, which would cost only $150 and prove as effective as those that a new crop of entrepreneurs, who had set up "survival stores," were offering for sale at prices ranging from from $1,500 to $50,000. Advice was widely given on how to stock the shelters in order to survive in them until the danger of radioactive contamination had lessened—two-weeks' supply of food and water, first-aid kit, flashlights, battery radio, periscope, chemical toilets, sanitary napkins, deodorants, games for kids.

Magazines and newspapers printed maps showing the lethal fallout areas of nuclear explosions. A map in *Time* magazine showed that within an area of up to one mile from ground zero, everything would be vaporized; shelters would provide no protection. Within a five-mile radius of ground zero, heat radiation would incinerate virtually everything. Radioactive particles would be scattered over 150 miles from ground zero. People said that if there were a nuclear attack, they'd rather die when it happened than survive to live with the consequences.

Nor were the Soviets spared nuclear anxiety. Sorensen says Khrushchev's son-in-law, Aleksei Adzhubei, told him a joke circulating in the Soviet Union about advice to Russians on how to deal with fallout: "Question—What should I do if a nuclear bomb falls? Answer—Cover yourself with a sheet and crawl slowly to the nearest cemetery. Question—Why slowly? Answer—To avoid panic."

Kennedy tried to make avoiding panic a guiding principle. Khrushchev had threatened and lied to him on the nuclear issue, and Kennedy was sorely tempted to respond dramatically. However, he delayed authorizing atmospheric testing by the United States until the following spring, after his efforts to gain agreement from Moscow for restoring a test ban had failed. At the same time he pressed ahead with constructing a flexible-response military capability so that the United States would never again find itself in a position where its only credible response to a military challenge would be to go nuclear.

National security experts in Washington drew up a program to provide guidance for graduated moves in a crunch. First there would be representations through diplomatic channels, followed, if necessary, by conventional military measures, and finally the escalating use of nuclear weapons. In discussions with the British, French, and

West Germans, American officials underplayed the nuclear options that, in the words of one American official, "were not very attractive."

Nevertheless, to reassure Americans and to signal Moscow that the United States would not be intimidated by the rattling of nuclear weapons, Assistant Secretary of Defense Roswell Gilpatrick did some weapon rattling of his own in a speech "cleared at the highest level":

> . . . this nation has a nuclear retaliatory force of such lethal power that an enemy move which brought it into play would be an act of self-destruction on his part. The United States has today hundreds of manned intercontinental bombers and many more medium bombers capable of reaching the Soviet Union, including 600 heavy bombers and many more medium bombers equally capable of intercontinental operations because of our highly-developed in-flight refueling techniques and world-wide base structure. The US also has six Polaris submarines at sea carrying a total of 96 missiles, and dozens of intercontinental ballistic missiles. . . . We have a second strike capability which is at least as extensive as what the Soviets can deliver by striking first. Therefore, we are confident that the Soviets will not provoke a major nuclear conflict.

Those words did little to dispel the atmosphere of dread that the Berlin crisis had spawned and that the nuclear testing had thickened. John Ausland, who was more knowledgeable than most about the chances of armed conflict, said he had been very much afraid that a shooting war would break out until he was told by a Pentagon officer whose judgment he respected that if things reached a danger point, "All we have to do is put the Strategic Air Command on alert and the Russians will freeze."

Government agencies and military commands are things of habit. They have standard operating procedures, deviations from which raise eyebrows, raise hackles, and raise hell. Even before General Clay set off for Berlin to take up his job as President Kennedy's personal representative there, it was obvious that he was a wild card being introduced into a game in progress and that the rest of the deck wasn't taking kindly to the idea.

At the State Department Dean Rusk was worried that Clay would go beyond merely being a symbol of American commitment.

Martin Hillenbrand feared that the general, who had been out of government service for several years, didn't understand that times had changed since his determination to stand by the city had shattered the Soviet attempt to blockade Berlin. Hillenbrand believed Clay "was not quite aware that we now had to consider a different framework for action than that which prevailed when we had had a nuclear monopoly." Ambassador Dowling in Bonn resented the dispatch of Clay to the city. He took the move as criticism of his own performance as official head of the American Mission in Berlin, which was not an unreasonable interpretation to put on it.

If Clay had thought the "West Point Protective Society" would gather around him, he was soon disabused of that expectation. The Pentagon did not take kindly to the idea of the White House plucking a general out of military retirement to supersede active service generals in the field. Both General Norstad and General Clarke were offended by the Clay appointment and the trouble they were sure it would cause in the chain of command. Norstad passed word along to the White House that he believed Clay's presence would complicate an already complicated administrative setup. Years later, Clarke, who declined even to acknowledge that he had once been a student of Clay's at West Point, said with some bitterness, "I never did find out what [Clay's] status was."

Nor was Clay's appointment happily received by those of Kennedy's White House aides who believed that though the situation remained precarious, a rapprochement with the Soviets over Berlin was possible provided neither side did anything to aggravate the situation. Clay's presence in the city, with the blessings and authority of the American president, could hardly be interpreted as a bid to calm things down.

Though a shy man personally, and though leaving in casual encounters an impression of great modesty, Clay had a swashbuckling manner and a fierce temper in action. He believed with a passion that he knew more about Berlin and Soviet tactics in Germany than anyone else. He intended to teach the novices in the White House, the State Department, and the Pentagon how to deal with the situation. Having faced down the Soviets during the blockade, he was convinced that the only way to handle them was to stand firm, that they regarded any concession as an invitation to demand more. He also firmly believed that the Soviet Union would always back down when the United States did something that could be overcome only by the use of force.

Clay regarded himself not simply as the president's special representative, instructed to "report, recommend and advise." He went to Berlin believing he would take charge of American policy and action in the city. He had firm opinions on what had been happening and firm ideas on what should be done about it. Those ideas, which had not been discussed in any great detail before he left for Germany, tended not to coincide with those of the president. The White House was sending Clay to Berlin to reassure the Berliners; he believed he was going there to take on the Soviets.

According to one State Department official, when Clay went to Berlin to deal with the problem there, "he *became* the problem." That was, of course, hyperbole. But it was true that the general's actions and messages in the following months repeatedly caused the White House much concern and some grief. McGeorge Bundy, viewing the situation from the White House, saw Clay as "difficult. At least once a week, he would send a cable saying if A, B and C didn't happen or if the current instruction or intent to do D and E should persist, he couldn't answer for the consequences."

One day during the crisis, someone who had been in the State Department at the time of the blockade asked Bundy, "Have you begun to get the weekend cables from him yet?" He explained that when Clay was in charge of the Berlin situation during the airlift, it always seemed that on Friday, at the end of a long, hard week, he would gather the week's frustrations and cable them back to Washington, "if not with the intent, certainly with the consequence that it spoiled our weekend."

There were, no doubt, many moments during Clay's 1961–62 tenure in Berlin when Kennedy regretted having sent him there. According to Bundy, however, Kennedy's feelings remained for the most part at "a level of mutual irritation much lower than a loss of confidence by the president." That was just as well for Kennedy because the president's freedom of action in dealing with Clay was limited by international and domestic political considerations. Even if he had wanted to, he could not have fired the general without disagreeable repercussions.

When the general arrived in Berlin on September 19 (two days after the West German elections in which Adenauer retained the chancellorship but was compelled by the gains made by Brandt's Social Democrats to form a coalition government with the smallish Free Democratic party), cheering crowds again gave him a hero's welcome. For many, Clay's return neutralized fears about the future. Had Kennedy recalled him, Berlin's shaky morale would have been totally shattered and the repercussions in West Germany would have been momentous.

Aside from that, if Kennedy had permitted an open breach to develop between Clay the Republican on one side and his own Democrats on the other, Berlin policy might have been turned into a political free-for-all in Washington. The result was that Clay, never one to be intimidated by authority anyway, was in a position to treat with little deference signals from the State Department and the White House in Washington, from the American Embassy in Bonn, from General Clarke in Heidelberg, and from General Norstad in Paris that he proceed cautiously as he set about trying to regain the initiative for the United States in the Berlin showdown. Clay was to do things of which they all disapproved. One Berlin Task Force member recalled, "He was a loose cannon. He was a prima donna putting on an act and we were a bureaucracy trying to run a long-term, complicated operation."

Geoffrey McDermott, the British minister in Berlin, was not alone in believing that Clay was not merely second-guessing when he told Lyndon Johnson that had he been in Berlin on August 13, American tanks would have rolled that day (though Clay later said it was trucks rather than tanks that he would have sent across). Some believed he would have had the barbed wire brushed aside because they knew he was a man of action; others because they thought him reckless and impetuous. He certainly wasted no time proving one or both of those views to be accurate. Upon arriving in Berlin he asked General Watson to have a concrete wall built on a military training range so that his troops could practice knocking it down. Bitter at the criticism for inaction unfairly directed at him personally by some West Berliners—"Why blame me; I didn't build that blasted Wall!" —Watson was pleased to comply. Clay then ordered the resumption of American military patrols on the autobahn in East Germany, suspended years before when the Soviets objected to them. The general also immediately took on the nagging problem of the village of Steinstücken.

Steinstücken was officially part of West Berlin but separated from it by a narrow neck of East German territory. To get to West Berlin proper, the people of Steinstücken—a community of some three hundred families—had to cross Vopo lines. The Vopos had harassed them even before August 13, but the harassment had intensified since the building of the Wall. It was apparent that the East Germans were preparing to lay claim to the village and that western officials, fearing a dangerous escalation, couldn't figure out how to deal with the situation. It was a small, vulnerable place, hardly worth risking a war.

Clay immediately set about trying to sort out that problem. He told General Watson to send two companies of troops up to the border to punch a hole through to Steinstücken. When General Clarke, who happened to be visiting Berlin from his Heidelberg headquarters, heard about it, he was both astounded and outraged. Profoundly aware of the West's hopeless military position in Berlin, Clarke asked Watson whose idea it was. When Watson told him it was Clay's, Clarke asked him pointedly, "Al, don't you know who you work for? Don't you know who writes your efficiency report?" Watson knew. The troops, already assembled for the operation, were ordered back to their barracks. "Afterwards," Clarke said, "I called Norstad on the phone and told him what I had done. Norstad said, 'Thank God you were in Berlin.' "

Clay was not so easily discouraged. Denied the troops to open a corridor to Steinstücken, he ordered up a helicopter and flew to the village to assure the people there that the United States considered them under the protection of its military garrison, which wasn't exactly the kind of reintroduction to Berlin the White House had planned for him. The East Germans called it "a warlike move." Others felt the same way. The British served notice to Washington that they weren't at all satisfied that the president's personal representative in Berlin fully appreciated the danger of an armed clash over comparative trifles.

Clay ignored the fuss. The following day he dispatched another helicopter to the village, this time carrying military policemen, three of whom stayed behind to establish an American presence there. Again, the East Germans were furious, and when seven refugees from East Berlin who had taken refuge in Steinstücken were flown out, they threatened to open fire on helicopters flying that route. It was an empty threat. No shots were fired, and the Steinstücken problem, which had previously caused some anguish and much befuddlement, was seen to have been briskly resolved, though not everyone in Washington was overjoyed with the means employed.

The White House and the State Department had been trying to fix on a way to signal Moscow that the United States, while standing firm, wanted to tone down the level of tension in Berlin. Kennedy was drafting a speech for delivery to the United Nations General Assembly a few days later, which reaffirmed America's commitment to the freedom of West Berlin but recognized "the historic and legitimate interests of others in assuring European security." Yet here was Clay stirring things up over an insignificant bit of territory nobody had even heard of before. Kennedy had even greater reason a few weeks later to wonder if he really should have sent Clay to Berlin when it seemed that the general was on the verge of provoking an armed clash between the United States and the Soviet Union in the middle of Berlin over what looked like another triviality.

The control post set up by the Americans in a prefabricated shack on the western side of the border at Friedrichstrasse was designated Checkpoint Charlie.[2] It was the only crossing point for surface traffic that Allied personnel and civilians and other foreigners entering East Berlin were permitted by the Communists to use. (The crossing point at the Friedrichstrasse subway train station, which could be used by non-Germans as well as Germans, was a mile down the street in East Berlin.) Checkpoint Charlie was manned by American—and later also by British and French—military police. As a precaution, military and other official Allied personnel registered at the checkpoint when entering and leaving the East.

On the night of October 22, after checking in at the checkpoint, Allan Lightner, the senior American civilian official in Berlin, drove with his wife into East Berlin. They were going to a performance there of a visiting experimental Czechoslovak theater company that had attracted much critical acclaim. Several officials of the other Allied missions in West Berlin had already gone across to see the performance that night, but the Lightners did not get far.

On the Communist side of the crossing point a Vopo officer stopped their Volkswagen and asked to see their passports. In ac-

[2]Checkpoints Alpha and Bravo were at either ends of the autobahn through East Germany.

cordance with established practice and instructions for official American personnel, Lightner and his wife refused to show them. Their car bore official American license plates that were adequate identification when crossing into East Berlin as far as the Americans were concerned. If any problem arose on the border, American personnel were to demand the presence of a Soviet officer. Under no circumstances were they to deal with East German officials. That would have been tantamount to diplomatic recognition of East Germany as well as recognition of East Berlin as part of East Germany.

Despite Lightner's demands, the Vopos would neither let his car pass their checkpoint without passport inspection nor fetch a Soviet officer. After sitting there a half hour, Lightner tried to spurt forward in his Volkswagen but was slowed by the zigzag obstacles at the checkpoint, and the car was quickly surrounded by Vopos. He was told he would not be permitted to enter East Berlin without showing his passport no matter how long he sat there.

From the very start the American military policemen who manned Checkpoint Charlie, one hundred yards across the border from the Communist checkpoint, had observed the incident. The MPs reported to Lieutenant Colonel Sabolyk what was happening. The provost marshal immediately informed General Clay. Clay instructed Sabolyk, who was about to rush there anyway, to go to the scene to try to sort things out. A platoon of infantrymen, four M-48 medium tanks, and two armored personnel carriers were ordered to Checkpoint Charlie as well. The East Germans were not meant to misunderstand the message Clay was sending.

It was too late for the theater in East Berlin, but much more was now at stake. Sabolyk first tried to persuade the East Germans at the checkpoint to let the Lightners through without further hassle. When they refused, insisting that all civilians had to show their identity papers when entering the German Democratic Republic, the provost marshal asked Mrs. Lightner to get out of the Volkswagen and return to the American Sector. She agreed only when she was told that General Clay had ordered her back in view of what was about to happen.

Once she had been escorted back through Checkpoint Charlie by an American officer and was clear of the scene, two squads of four American troops led by a lieutenant, all with M-14 rifles at the ready, moved forward, took up positions on both sides of the Lightner car, and—with Lightner at the wheel and alone in the vehicle—escorted it past the Communist checkpoint into East Berlin. The East German guards, though scowling, made no effort to obstruct this procession. Lightner drove about two blocks, cruising very slowly so as not to outdistance his escort, and then returned to West Berlin.

Joined there in the Volkswagen by mission press officer Albert Hemsing, he turned his car around and drove back into East Berlin, unescorted by the troops. When the Vopos again insisted that he and Hemsing show their passports, Lightner signaled with his hand, and the troops came forward again to escort him once more past the grim-faced East German guards. Lightner later said, "If the East Germans had tried to stop us . . . say by shooting one of us, we would have had to kill all of them. . . . All hell would have broken loose."

As the incident approached its climax, Howard Trivers, the political officer at the American Mission, arrived at the crossing and spotted Major Lazerev, the acting Soviet political adviser, standing at the border, between the American and East German checkpoints. He walked over and asked him what was going on. Lazerev seemed perplexed. He said that he was sorry about the incident. He said that the Vopos (who hadn't realized they were dealing with a senior American official) had acted improperly and that "remedial measures" would be taken. Though the East Germans had earlier tried, unsuccessfully, to get other American officials to show their passports for inspection at the border, they had taken that next step in the phased border operation without clearing it with the Soviets. They were quickly and sharply ordered back into line. When Lightner again tested the border that night, he was able to drive right through without being obstructed and without having to summon his armed escort.

But rarely missing an opportunity to turn a chance incident into an advantage, the Soviets took a closer look at what had happened and decided that the unauthorized East German maneuver was, perhaps, not such a bad idea. The East Germans were, after all, claiming sovereignty over East Berlin and were, therefore, well within their rights in demanding to see Lightner's passport. It was consistent with everything that had been happening and everything they had been saying, ever since the first bale of barbed wire had been unrolled on the border. Independent initiatives by Ulbricht were not to be encouraged, but the passport ploy was worth another try. It would be one more step toward consigning Berlin's four-power status to oblivion. The following day, with Soviet approval, the East Germans formally announced that only Allied military personnel in uniform would be permitted to enter East Berlin without displaying their identity papers. Western civilians, even if they had official status, would be required to show their passports.

Had the State Department been given advance notice that the East Germans would personally involve the American minister in an undignified border squabble, it probably would have issued instructions that there should be no quibbling over the passport issue. Washington had already repeatedly shown itself reconciled to Communist jurisdiction over East Berlin and its boundaries. Howard Trivers was of the conviction that "Had it not been for General Clay's presence in Berlin at that time, there is little doubt that the American military and civilian authorities in Berlin would have been obliged to crawl back ignominiously. . . ." When Kennedy was first told of the incident—with Lightner's intended destination in East Berlin misreported—the president is said to have snapped, "We didn't send him over there to go to the opera in East Berlin."

But Clay, taking full advantage of his position as the president's personal representative, was operating on a totally different wavelength. He placed great importance on the fact that by long-standing agreement to which the Soviets were a party, Lightner had as much right to move about freely in East Berlin as in the western sectors of the city. The general was a devout adherent of the theology of the Berlin situation in which unrestricted access to the East for Allied personnel, the refusal to show passports, and other seemingly trivial observances were symbols of the entire structure of established relationships, a structure that would collapse—jeopardizing the American position—if the symbols were disregarded.

Clay's understanding—rather, his misunderstanding—was that he had been sent to Berlin to make certain no more ground was lost to the Communists. In the Lightner incident he had to react immediately or not at all. The general had sized up the situation and had acted on his own initiative. Now, as he made his plans for his next move, he realized he needed strong, solid backing. The State Department was already nervous about the use of the troops in the Lightner incident. There were toes he had to step on or, at least, step around. He performed that maneuver by invoking the authority conferred upon him by virtue of being the president's personal representative.

He put through a call directly to Kennedy, who in an unguarded moment had told the general to contact him if he ran into any problems, and explained what he had in mind.

He was going to challenge, with a show of military force if necessary, the East German decree that only Americans in military uniform could enter East Berlin without showing their papers. He told the president that if the Communists weren't stopped, they would continue to nibble away at western rights. The general said that it was humiliating for the United States to feel obliged to obey the instructions on border crossing issued by the regime of a third-rate power it did not recognize. He said something had to be done to counter ever-growing Communist audacity or there would be no end to it.

Kennedy, who needed no lectures on defending American interests, was not convinced that the issue of passports on the East Berlin border was the right issue or the right place to make a stand. Besides, the Soviets appeared to have been sending signals that they wanted to cool things down. But aside from distrusting such signals, Kennedy liked and respected Clay. He was grateful that despite being a political opponent, the general had taken on for the administration, at considerable personal inconvenience, what very likely would turn out to be a thankless assignment. He also simply needed Clay in Berlin. Sustaining morale in West Berlin and West Germany was still a tiresome necessity. He had heard reports of the backbiting Clay had endured from people the general believed should have been backing him, and Kennedy did not want to risk provoking Clay into throwing up the job in disgust. So Clay got the go-ahead he requested from the president, and the Berlin crisis entered a new phase.

On the morning of Wednesday, October 25—with American officials, military police, and correspondents milling about and a crowd of some five hundred onlookers held well back on the western side—two young American military police officers, looking overly stylish for the occasion in their civilian clothes but very military with their crewcuts, drove through Checkpoint Charlie in a civilian Opel sedan bearing official American license plates. When Vopos halted them on the East Berlin side for refusing to show their passports, they turned back to Checkpoint Charlie and picked up a waiting escort of three United States Army jeeps carrying battle-ready soldiers conspicuously clutching their rifles. With one jeep in front and two behind, the sedan drove without stopping through the Communist checkpoint. The East German guards made no move to obstruct them.

This was, however, not going to be a one-shot affair. A half hour later, ten American M-48 tanks and three armored personnel carriers rumbled up to the border and took up positions near Checkpoint Charlie. With tension rising, journalists—and a pretzel seller who had managed to slip through to peddle his wares to tank crewmen —were shoved by military police into the adjacent Hallo bar ("Hungarian Specialties") and Café Köln, from which some climbed to the roofs to observe the proceedings. There followed a succession of tests of the East German claim to jurisdiction at the crossing point. Each time an official American civilian vehicle was stopped by the Vopos, the combat-ready jeeps were sent in to escort it. Each time, the Vopos stepped grudgingly aside when the jeeps rolled up.

With the Americans driving in and out, flouting the East German's regime's passport decree, Ulbricht's claim to sovereignty looked very flimsy by nightfall. It was the most significant setback the Communists had experienced since the border-sealing operation had begun. The Soviets, who had sent their embassy's military attaché and political adviser through Checkpoint Charlie to reconnoiter American armored strength and positions at the border, weren't at all happy about it. This was to have remained an East German operation, but on Thursday night, after further successful American probes of the border crossing, thirty-three Soviet tanks rolled into East Berlin and parked in a lot not far from the Brandenburg Gate. It was the first appearance of Soviet armor in the city since the East German uprising of 1953.

On Friday the Soviet commander, who had been awaiting orders from Moscow, sent ten tanks down the Friedrichstrasse and positioned them facing the border, a little more than one hundred yards from where the ten American tanks were deployed. For the first time American and Soviet tanks faced each other, if not in anger then certainly not as friends. Both the American forces in Berlin and the Soviet forces in East Germany had been put on full alert.

General Clay, at an emergency operations center set up at American headquarters on Clayallee, was in direct communication with the American commander at the checkpoint, Lieutenant Colonel Thomas Tyree. Tyree had had his tank crews load cannon shells into their gun racks, ready for firing. The machine guns atop the tanks were at half load. But Tyree recalled, "My major concern at the time was not to prepare my men for a fire fight but to make sure something unexpected did not occur, such as a nervous soldier accidentally discharging his weapon." He was, however, prepared to send his tanks into East Berlin if necessary to protect the probes dispatched by Clay across the border to affirm the American right of unrestricted access to East Berlin.

People around the world worried and waited as word was fed back from Checkpoint Charlie on what was and was not happening. One of the news agencies paid a huge sum for exclusive use of the telephone in the apothecary right on the border line. All the other correspondents played catch-as-catch-can with the phones in the cafés. As always, rumors abounded. *Es geht los um drei Uhr* ("It's going to happen at three o'clock"). (What's going to happen?) General Clay is on his way to the border to direct the operation personally. (What operation?) Lieutenant Colonel Sabolyk has slugged a Vopo. (Firmly denied by the provost marshal.) With the tanks virtually snout to snout and word of their encounter flashing around the world, a lot of people in a lot of places were growing anxious. However, at the checkpoint, after the first tense hour or so, it began to seem like a game, especially with the pretzel seller back and making a small killing unloading his stock to the soldiers and others standing around doing nothing in the middle of a city street.

The British, whose mission personnel had already been showing their passports to the Vopos when crossing into East Berlin, wanted to know why the Americans were engaged in such military posturing "over an essentially minor issue." Kennedy also began to wonder what the point of it all was. He telephoned Clay who assured the president that the Soviets did not want war over Berlin any more than he did and that there would be no shooting. Despite his qualms, Kennedy told Clay he had his full support. But at the State Department, Foy Kohler told his staff, "I think we've had enough of this."

The Soviets felt the same way. On Saturday morning, under orders directly from Moscow, the Soviet tanks withdrew from their border positions, sixteen hours after they had arrived. A half hour later, the Americans followed suit. As far as Clay was concerned, the operation had served its purpose—to show that Moscow, not the East German regime, was still in charge of East Berlin. "The fiction," he said,

> that it was the East Germans who were responsible for trying to prevent Allied access to East Berlin is now destroyed. The fact that the Soviet tanks appeared on the scene proves that the harassments which were taking place . . . were not those of the self-styled East German government but ordered by its Soviet masters.

Whatever moral victory was scored was, however, soon diluted by (unpublicized) instructions from Washington that American civilian officials should refrain from entering East Berlin for the time being. After Clay's triumph on the issue they couldn't very well begin showing their passports to the Vopos, and the State Department wanted no new Berlin confrontations to damage chances of getting talks going with the Soviets.

The growing divergence between Clay and Washington was as yet not widely known. And few people knew that General Clarke in Heidelberg was asking, "What in the hell did Clay think he was doing? You don't spit in the face of a bulldog." Clarke viewed the operation, and Clay's hijacking of his troops and tanks, with great resentment. Asked later by historian Honoré Catudal, "Would we have retreated if the Russians had used force to try to turn back our armed escorts into East Berlin?" Clarke, tough soldier that he was, replied, "I would hope so."

West Berlin's military vulnerability also colored the views of General Norstad in Paris. In command of Allied forces in Europe, Norstad was furious that he had been excluded from prior knowledge of and planning for the confrontation with the Soviets. NATO had drawn up plans detailing when and how military forces would be deployed in the Berlin dispute. Those plans had been approved by the various NATO powers after lengthy consultations. There was nothing in them that covered Clay's maneuver at the checkpoint, which exposed the United States to the possibility of having to back down in the face of far superior fire power, as his critics pointed out. The question was, After you bring our few tanks to the Wall, what do you do next if the Soviets either do not show up or do show up and just stay there? Norstad not only had not been consulted on the operation, he had not even been officially informed. He sent an angry cable to Berlin, which concluded, "I will not be ignored!"

However, West Berliners had been delighted that the Americans had demonstrated that they were prepared to defend them, by force if necessary. And the Soviets had learned that the changes they wished to impose on the situation would no longer draw only routine protests from the United States.

13

Endgame

THERE were now three alien presences in once-proud Berlin—the Allied presence, the Soviet presence as represented by the Communist regime, and the Wall. Though there were—and would be for months—places along the border where the barbed wire had not yet given way to concrete, the Wall had quickly replaced the Brandenburg Gate as the symbol of the city.

Sounds of gunfire east of it each night testified that more people were attempting to escape than the comparative few who were succeeding. During the day people in the West stood on chairs they had brought to the Wall to try to spot loved ones on the other side. Not permitted close enough to do the same, people in the East stood where they could, squinting, hands cupped over eyes, scanning the top of the Wall, now capped with barbed wire, for a familiar face. On both sides elderly men and women, forlornly trying to make contact, wafted white hankerchiefs back and forth, as if transmitting coded semaphore messages laced with sorrow. People held up placards with greetings or family news in the hope that they could be read on the other side.

Worries about the viability of West Berlin after the Wall were no longer academic. Fearful of the future, three hundred people, on average, were leaving the city every day to settle in West Germany,

where the attractions remained considerable—statistics showed
there were six unfilled jobs for every unemployed person there. The
new exodus was helped along by circulation-grabbing headlines in
the popular press asking "Is West Berlin Now Being Sold Out?"
West Berlin newspapers were full of advertisements of real estate for
sale. Businesses as well as individuals and families were abandoning
the front line. Many people who were not yet leaving were nevertheless "putting a foot" in West Germany, buying property if they could
afford to and following leads for jobs. Some married couples and
families, who had not long before debated whether to leave their
homes in East Germany, now debated whether to leave West Berlin
as well.

Inducements were devised to keep people from going. Income
taxes were cut for West Berliners. Cash bonuses were paid to low-
income workers. Substantial tax and other financial advantages were
offered to businesses. Large loans were offered to young married
couples. No effort was made to downplay the fact that a young West
German man could gain himself an exemption from being drafted
into the army by moving to West Berlin.

One night a young woman knocked on our door to offer us
money. It was, she explained, *zitter Geld* ("fear money"). Every
resident of Berlin was being given a reward simply for living there!
—one hundred marks for an individual; in a family, one hundred
marks for the husband, fifty marks for the wife and each child. But
the drift out of the West Berlin continued.

The city was being hurt in other ways as well. The Hilton, once
fully booked every day, was half empty. Businessmen from afar saw
less reason to visit Berlin, and fewer journalists were sent to the city
to cover a story that was beginning to grow stale. Correspondents
reporting from Berlin found that their stories about Wall shootings,
Communist demands, Allied protests, and local morale problems
were having a tough time competing for space in their newspapers,
on television, and on radio news programs. The world's concerns had
moved elsewhere.

In Bonn as well as Berlin, political scientists, sociologists, financial specialists, and other experts were put to work to devise ways
of convincing West Berliners not to desert the city. Such studies were
undertaken by the Americans as well. There was no sense in keeping
a garrison in the outpost city if the people they were there to protect
went astray.

.   .   .

Despite persisting rumors that the West would abandon Berlin in due course, no such possibility was considered by Allied leaders. Their determination to defend the freedom of West Berlin and the access routes through East Germany remained firm. In Washington, in addition to the unceasing deliberations of the Berlin Task Force and the studies undertaken by the Pentagon and the National Security Council, political-military exercises were held at Camp David to give additional substance to the thinking on what the Soviets might do and how the West might respond in an escalating conflict.

Those participating in these "war games" were divided into the control team, the blue team (representing the United States), and the red team (representing the Soviet Union, East Germany, and other Warsaw Pact nations). At the start of the game, the control team would set the stage with a crisis situation scenario—for example, not only a blockage on the access routes but also related developments in East Germany, West Berlin, Moscow, and Washington. The blue team would then describe how it would react, the red team would respond to the ensuing situation, and the control team would project the situation forward from their responses to present a new crisis. A game would last three days, after which the control team would offer a critique.

It was not a way of formulating policy. It was primarily a close reconnaissance of the terrain. Players better understood Soviet thinking when forced to come up with decisions they thought the Soviets would make. Players representing the United States found it helped expand their thinking; hypothetical positions they were taking often proved more vulnerable than they had imagined they would be.

It proved a useful exercise also because participating players, often men who had been dealing independently with the Berlin problem, grew better acquainted. The sessions were, however, not without heated clashes. At one point the normally mild-mannered Henry Kissinger exploded in anger at what he considered a foolish move by a member of the opposing team. At another point, Carl Kaysen, who was on McGeorge Bundy's staff at the White House, issued a gratuitous condemnation of the State Department, its personnel, and its procedures. Taken aback, John Ausland said, "Carl, the Soviet Union is the enemy, not the State Department." Kaysen glared at him and responded, "I'm not so sure."

. . .

Even before the tank confrontation at Checkpoint Charlie, the Soviets, stopped dead at the Wall, had begun reviewing their Berlin tactics. In September, Mikhail Kharlamov, head of the Soviet Foreign Ministry's press division, had told presidential press secretary Pierre Salinger that Khrushchev was prepared "to consider American proposals for a rapprochement on Berlin." A week before the Lightner border incident, to the barely concealed fury of Ulbricht, Khrushchev had told the Twenty-second Congress of the Soviet Communist party in Moscow that the western powers had finally shown "some understanding of the German problem and are disposed to seek a settlement of . . . the question of West Berlin on a mutually acceptable basis." Therefore, the Soviet leader said, the deadline he had previously set for signing a peace treaty with East Germany "was not really important." He told visiting Belgian Foreign Minister Paul-Henri Spaak, "Berlin is not such a problem for me. What are two million people among a billion Communists?"

Mikhail ("Smiling Mike") Menshikov, the unsmiling, hard-line Soviet ambassador in Washington, was replaced by the personally more agreeable Anatoli Dobrynin, whom western intelligence services considered less hawkish in his approach to East–West differences. Ulbricht continued trying to force Khrushchev's hand. There were no less than twenty-four incidents in the closing months of 1961 involving detention, harassment, or damage of American military vehicles in East Berlin. West Berlin police on the border were equipped with rifles and automatic weapons after Vopos, who had been equipped with such weapons since 1948, had persistently fired into the western sectors after fleeing refugees. But faced with Allied resolve on West Berlin and the American military buildup in Europe, the Soviets, though still deeply affronted by the continuing western presence in Berlin and while not abandoning their objectives, were stepping back to reexamine the possibilities. The Americans were doing the same.

When Gromyko went to the United Nations General Assembly in New York toward the end of September, he met there with Dean Rusk for "exploratory talks." If no progress could be made toward ending the Berlin dispute satisfactorily, Kennedy hoped at least to trap the Soviets into a protracted dialogue while the western defensive buildup in Europe was completed. Rusk said, "Westerners usually like to rush to agreement while Russians like to wait it out and hope to gain an advantage that way. But we decided we'd just talk, talk, talk. We'd talk just as long and just as repetitively as Gromyko would."

At the same time indications began to appear that the United States was preparing to offer concessions, though not over West Berlin, if comparable concessions could be extracted from Moscow. Apparently acting under instructions from the White House, no less a hardliner than General Clay, said with a steely grin, while briefing some American correspondents, that West Germans would have to come to terms with the new situation and "recognize the reality of the existence of two German states." This was such a remarkable turnabout for the general that UPI's Joe Fleming, who knew him well, asked him twice if that was what he really meant to say. When Clay's comment was reported, the storm of outrage in West German official circles was so intense that Clay was quickly instructed to declare that he had been misquoted and that the United States still firmly backed reunification for Germany. But Senator Hubert Humphrey, a leading Democratic party figure and close political ally of the president, spoke in Washington of "give and take on both sides." After visiting East and Central Europe, Senator Claiborne Pell suggested that no matter what Adenauer said, most Germans did not care all that much about whether their country was reunified, implying that most Americans didn't either and that facts were facts and had to be recognized as such.

When Attorney General Robert Kennedy visited Berlin the following February, he reassured Berliners that they were not alone. "An armed attack on West Berlin," he told them, "is the same thing as an armed attack on Chicago, New York, London or Paris. You are our brothers and we will stand by you." But he also made it clear that though the Wall was an atrocity, no miracle was going to bring it down. A new situation had been created, he said, and the West had to reconcile itself to it. Remaining unsaid but clearly implied was what Willy Brandt knew already—no matter what the official position, American acceptance of the division of Berlin signaled American acceptance of the division of Germany.[1]

---

[1] The attorney general was accompanied on that trip by his younger brother, Edward Kennedy, later to be senator from Massachusettes. The youngest of the Kennedy brothers took the opportunity to visit East Berlin, entering by way of the Friedrichstrasse train station, where his passport was checked and his photograph

Despite the feelers put out by the administration, the fact was that Kennedy, while prepared to discuss the future of Germany with the Soviets, was still not willing to recognize East Germany. He told President Urho Kekkonen of Finland, whom the Soviets were trying to use as an intermediary, that the United States was not going to acknowledge the Soviet-imposed division of the country and "thus weaken our ties to West Germany and their ties to Western Europe." As for Soviet offers of guarantees on the access routes in return for Allied concessions, Kennedy told Kekkonen that the Soviets were "asking us to make concessions in exchange for which they will give us what we already have. . . . We would be buying the same horse twice." Negotiations would have to be serious, not a matter of one party taking and the other being required to give.

The French declined to agree to what would be essentially a superpower dialogue with France pretty much only looking on. They remained unimpressed with the whole idea. Adenauer, resenting suggestions from Washington that he reconcile himself to the reality of two Germanies, was increasingly suspicious of Kennedy. Backed only by the British, who were even more eager for negotiations than Kennedy was, the president became increasingly exasperated with Paris and Bonn. He told French Ambassador Alphand he was weary of France offering objections to talks with the Soviets while contributing little to the western military buildup in Europe, which was the only alternative. He warned that the Allies would have to "come along or stay behind." That was an empty challenge. The last thing he wanted was to abet the Soviet objective of splitting the western alliance.

It was, moreover, soon apparent that though the Soviets might be willing to talk, their objectives remained unchanged. They were not interested in negotiations that might involve concessions of any kind on their part. Only a western cave-in would suffice. Pressure toward that end had merely been suspended until a more suitable moment. That moment was not long in coming.

Barely had the sounds of 1962 new-year celebrations faded out

---

was taken for the Communist press. The East German news agency ADN later boasted that Edward had "respected in every way the sovereignty of the German Democratic Republic." When the reports reached Washington, Foy Kohler telephoned Allan Lightner and told him the president wasn't at all happy and wanted him to do what he could to stop publicity on Edward's visit. John feared it might hurt Edward's political career.

when Gromyko suggested to Ambassador Thompson in Moscow that the Soviet Union would not object to the continued "temporary" presence of western forces in West Berlin, provided Soviet troops could be stationed there as well. It was an unabashed bid to turn West Berlin into the four-power city that all of Berlin had previously been. It was immediately, unequivocally rejected. The Soviets were, however, now again ready to shift their efforts away from fruitless diplomatic exchanges to exchanges of a more palpable kind. Once more their actions were influenced by the position of General Clay.

Clay had flown off to visit Washington early in January. A State Department spokesman called it a "routine consultation" and denied reports that the general had returned to Washington to protest at being hemmed in not by the Communists, but by his own side. The patrols he had reintroduced along the autobahn in East Germany had been removed so as not to exacerbate the situation. General Watson, through whom Clay had been able to bring out the troops and tanks when needed, was ordered in no unmistakable terms to clear all future American military moves in Berlin with General Clarke, who still refused to acknowledge that Clay had any special authority. Clay was being turned into the mere symbol of America's commitment to Berlin that President Kennedy initially intended him to be.

When he got to Washington, Clay protested to Dean Rusk that General Watson—meaning he and Watson—had to be given enough latitude to deal with emergency situations on the border. Such things, he said, could not be directed from afar. He warned that the muzzle that had been fitted on him was an invitation to the Soviets to begin nibbling away again at the western presence in the city. He was angry that his cabled complaints from Berlin were ignored.[2] He had protested earlier to the White House but had discovered that his difficulties with the State Department and the Pentagon were not high on President Kennedy's list of priorities.

In Washington Clay saw the president for an hour, but when he returned to Berlin and was questioned by his aides about what the

---

[2]The tone of Clay's telegrams had grown increasingly abusive and increasingly offended people in Washington. Some of the resulting exasperation with Clay rubbed off on Allan Lightner. Though the telegrams began "From Clay," many of them were signed "Lightner" because Lightner was the minister at the mission. Lightner had been making strenuous efforts to get Clay to tone down those messages and not to send the more abusive ones at all.

president had said, he told them that, in view of the senior position in the business world from which he had taken leave to go to Berlin (he was chairman of the Continental Can Company), Kennedy had spoken to him about the problems the administration was then having with the steel industry, which was pushing for inflationary price increases. As McGeorge Bundy has said, "Presidents talk about what's on their mind."

A fundamental problem was that Clay, with firm ideas on what should be done, was playing a unilateral game while everybody else was trying to sustain a carefully, sometimes painfully worked-out, multilateral Allied holding operation. The contradiction was too sharp to be overlooked. The same was to some extent true of the American Embassy in Bonn, which was to be sharply reprimanded for sending messages proposing unilateral American moves that, in the words of one Berlin Task Force member in Washington, "just didn't fit in."

Clay's visit to Washington earned him nothing more than an infuriating pat on the back and instructions to go back to Berlin and carry on his good work. He was incensed but realized that if he quit in a huff and refused to return, he would do more damage to the American position and West Berlin morale than he believed the administration was doing. To their befuddlement, he shunned people at the British Mission when he returned to Berlin. Washington had used them as a scapegoat. Clay had been told that their complaints about his behavior, at a time when Allied unity was essential for East–West negotiations, were part of the reason for the changes being made.

With no further American challenges to the passport-showing requirements on the sector border, with the American autobahn patrols that Clay had reintroduced removed, with the American tanks that he had kept positioned three hundred yards from the sector border now drawn back from the Wall, and with various minor acts of harassment on the autobahn from West Germany eliciting mostly routine protest notes, it became apparent to the Soviets that Clay was being roped in. The significance was, however, unclear to them, and they decided to find out what it meant by resuming suspended efforts to elbow the West out of Berlin.

This time the Soviets posed a major direct challenge to the Allies. They chose to move against the access routes, which Kennedy had vowed to keep open by armed force if necessary. The air corridors between West Germany and West Berlin, which had been used to break the Berlin blockade, were to be the stage for the renewed Soviet campaign.

On February 12, 1962, the Soviets announced that they were reserving the corridors at certain times each day for their own military aircraft. They then announced that they were reserving certain altitudes for their own use. They then insisted on certain changes in flight procedures. They backed up their words with actions more dangerous than any taken so far in the crisis.

Soviet jets took to buzzing western commercial aircraft in the corridors. They also dropped strips of metal foil along their routes to disrupt the safety radar of the planes. For a time searchlights east of the sector border were directed at western aircraft coming in to land at Tempelhof in an effort to blind the pilots. A CIA operative ironically suggested that since Washington was still insisting that Berlin was a four-power city, the American command should send troops into the East to arrest the people operating the searchlights and bring them back to West Berlin for trial.

The safety of the civilian airliners flying daily through the corridors to Berlin became a serious concern, which was the Soviet purpose. At one point the director of British European Airways wanted to suspend flights because of the danger. Lord Home, who was awakened at 2:00 A.M. one morning to deal with the situation, had to speak to him very firmly before he changed his mind. But there were grim faces in the western foreign ministries as the Soviet harassment of the defenseless aircraft continued. It was feared that all that was needed was one accident for the situation to become irretrievable. John Ausland said, "When they started fooling around with the air corridors, it was hard to see how we would get out of it without some sort of shooting." The situation also caused friction between the United States and Britain.

Although General Clay's characteristically bellicose suggestion that American jet fighters be sent through the corridors to demonstrate Allied determination to keep them open had been rejected by General Norstad, the British feared the United States, with its countless contingency plans, would be provoked into defiant gestures that might increase rather than lessen the dangers, and they said so. At one stage Foy Kohler took Lord Hood, the minister at the British Embassy in Washington, aside and gave him a stiff lecture on how timid the British were. The Foreign Office in London felt obliged to draft a long telegram to the embassy explaining in detail how that charge should be answered by giving chapter and verse on how unwavering and firm the British had been throughout the crisis.

Though it posed a greater danger, this new Soviet exercise was a more difficult undertaking for Moscow than the building of the Wall. In the case of the Wall, aggressive action—tearing it down—would have had to come from the Allies. In the air corridors, aggressive action—stopping Allied aircraft from getting through—had to come from the Soviets. Despite the dangerous harassment of flights, Moscow wasn't prepared to risk the consequences. Though some voices in Washington continued to urge stronger action, the Allies demonstrated their determination not to be budged by doing no more than putting fighter aircraft at bases in West Germany on ground alert, flying military transport planes through parts of the western air corridors that the Soviets claimed to be reserving for their own use, and maintaining uninterrupted, normal civilian air traffic to Berlin.

The Soviet action in flirting with disaster so angered the normally imperturbable Rusk that he wanted to cancel an East–West disarmament conference in Geneva, but in view of the importance attached to the subject, the White House urged him to go through with it. The meeting achieved little, but Rusk was treated to a remarkable display—the most vigorous dressing down to which he had ever seen Gromyko exposed, delivered by the British foreign secretary. Using language of which Rusk had never thought so courteous a man capable, Lord Home told the Soviet foreign minister exactly what he thought of a government that could order steps that might make civilian airliners crash. The West's unqualified determination not to back down on this issue persuaded Moscow that a totally different approach to the Berlin problem had to be devised; harassment of the air corridors soon tapered off and then stopped altogether.

Once more, Soviet moves against the western presence in Berlin were suspended. There were still recurring harassments of Allied traffic on the ground access routes and in East Berlin. But they were comparatively minor, and once more tensions eased. The files on contingency plans for countermeasures were stuffed back into the file cabinet, and General Clay seized the opportunity to withdraw from the front-line city without inflicting damage to West Berlin morale or the American image. He had no wish to remain a powerless symbol.

When it was announced that the general was going home, the American Mission was deluged with frantic calls from West Berliners who believed that his departure was a frightening omen. The general tried to assure West Berliners that they were safe from a Communist take-over. Like the United States Cavalry in western movies, he promised to return if he were needed. But though three-quarters of a million people jammed the Town Hall square to say goodbye, he was unable, nor did he try, to reconcile them to the existence of two Berlins.

By then Clay had long been shorn of power to go his own way, and West Berliners had gotten over the worst of their fear and trembling about the future of their portion of the divided city; so it no longer mattered much to the White House, the State Department, and the Pentagon whether he stayed or went. Kennedy was relieved and grateful that he went home without public complaint or accusation. After the fact Dean Rusk and most of the others whose nerves the general had rattled by his actions came to the conclusion that he had served his country and the Allied cause far better than they had imagined at the time. Feisty and insubordinate, he had demonstrated that it wasn't necessary to let aggressors have everything their own way. He had held the fort while everyone else figured out what the problem really was and how to deal with it.

A full year after their city had been divided, Berliners were still trying to reconcile themselves to their new circumstances. On August 13, 1962, the first anniversary of the sealing of the sector border, thousands of West Berliners, mostly youths, converged on the Wall for angry commemorations of the day their fellow Berliners had been trapped behind barbed wire. Tempers flared. Stones and beer bottles were hurled into East Berlin. Vopos responded with tear-gas grenades. More than twenty West Berlin policemen were injured before the crowds were brought under control. But the incident was only a curtain raiser for the explosion of popular wrath two days later when two young East Berlin construction workers tried to escape to the West over the Wall not far from Checkpoint Charlie. One got over as bullets whizzed around him. But the other, eighteen-year-old Peter Fechter, was shot as he tried to pull himself over the barbed wire atop the Wall. He fell back into the East and lay there bleeding and moaning. The seeming indifference of the armed East Berlin guards who left him there slowly dying infuriated West Berliners. Their anger was by no means diminished by a report that an American lieutenant on duty nearby, when asked to do something, said tactlessly, but in accordance with his orders, "It's not my problem." A West Berlin tabloid carried a paid advertisement saying, "West Berliners accuse American Commander General Watson of being an accomplice to murder." For the first time in West Berlin, there were shouts of "Ami Go Home!" and American army jeeps were booed while on patrol.

But anti-American feeling was, for the most part, limited to a few embittered individuals. It was far outweighed by recognition that without the presence of the Allies, particularly the Americans, West Berlin was lost. It was also outweighed by fury against the East German Communists who ordered that fellow Germans be shot down. Anti-Communist riots erupted west of the Wall for the next three nights. Soviet vehicles riding through West Berlin were stoned. One Soviet car, on its regular flag-showing tour of West Berlin, was chased by a crowd of Berliners and had to drive into an American military compound to ask for an escort, which was provided. When a bus carrying troops for the changing of the guard at the Soviet war memorial in the British Sector had its windows broken by stones, the Soviets took to bringing their men across in armored personnel carriers. The Allies immediately protested. In response, the Soviets, weary of Allied protests in the city, simply abolished the office of the Soviet commandant in East Berlin.

The Allies nevertheless told the Soviets that they would not tolerate the appearance of Soviet combat vehicles in West Berlin. They also told the Soviets that instead of using Checkpoint Charlie to reach their war memorial, as they had been doing, they should send their memorial guards through a crossing point closer to the monument. Apparently because they did not wish to make an issue of their war memorial, the Soviets acquiesced to these instructions without further fuss, though Kennedy had been deeply worried that it might lead to a new, dangerous confrontation.

In fact, the Soviets again appeared to be calling a momentary "time out" over Berlin. Though they declared, "It is necessary at long last to liquidate the occupation regime in West Berlin," the

Soviet news agency Tass announced that Moscow would make no further Berlin moves until after the American midterm elections in November. Washington welcomed the respite but began bracing itself for the long-awaited final showdown on the access routes, the *real crisis,* after election day, just two months away. Not much significance was attached to the fact that the Tass announcement about waiting till then before coming to grips again with the Berlin problem coincided with a visit to Moscow of a Cuban delegation that had gone to the Soviet Union to sign an arms agreement.

On October 16, 1962, Nikita Khrushchev summoned Foy Kohler, who had by then become the American ambassador in Moscow, to the Kremlin. Dismissing widespread American reports that the Soviet Union was engaged in a major arms buildup in Cuba as exaggerated, the Soviet leader expressed his admiration for the United States and its president and added his voice to the chorus of Soviet assurances—Ambassador Dobrynin had chimed in with one as well—that Moscow had no intention of doing anything that might embarrass Kennedy on the eve of the congressional elections.

Two days later, Soviet Foreign Minister Andrei Gromyko called at the White House in Washington and sternly told Kennedy there would finally have to be a "normalization" of the Berlin situation. Gromyko once more served notice that his country would sign a separate peace treaty with East Germany if the western powers were not prepared to cooperate, and would not be deterred by American threats. But the Soviet foreign minister also made a point of reiterating to the president that the Soviet Union was putting Berlin on hold until election day.

Kennedy briskly informed Gromyko that the United States still had no intention of reneging on its commitment to West Berlin. But the president didn't spend much time on the subject. Moscow knew the American position well enough. Nor did Kennedy have much to say about Gromyko's assurance that Moscow wanted to spare him possible electoral embarrassment over Berlin during the following few weeks. Of far greater concern to the president were accelerated Soviet arms shipments to Cuba, about which the CIA had first reported to the White House several weeks earlier. Gromyko assured the president that the United States had no reason to be bothered by them. He said only defensive weapons were being sent and that surely the American superpower didn't have to worry about being threatened by tiny Cuba.

Gromyko did not know, and was not at that time told, that Kennedy knew he was lying. High flying U-2 reconnaissance aircraft had brought back photographic evidence that the Soviets were installing offensive nuclear missiles in Cuba that had the capacity to devastate large parts of the United States. The recklessness of Khrushchev's move was frightening. The attempt to deceive the United States—to the extent of brazenly lying to the president on crucial security matters—was outrageous. The threat to the American mainland was intolerable.

On October 22 Kennedy appeared on nationwide television to inform the American people and the world of the Cuban developments and to announce his response. No more offensive weapons would be permitted through an American naval blockade of Cuba. "This quarantine," the president said, "will be extended, if needed, to other types of cargo and carriers. We are not at this time, however, denying [Cuba] the necessities of life as the Soviets attempted to do in their Berlin blockade of 1948." Kennedy further declared that if any nuclear missile were "launched from Cuba against any nation in the Western Hemisphere," it would be regarded as "an attack by the Soviet Union on the United States, requiring a full retaliatory response upon the Soviet Union."

By then the American Strategic Air Command's nuclear-armed B-52 bombers had been put on full airborne alert. Jet fighters had been moved to bases in Florida as had more than one hundred thousand troops. America's intercontinental ballistic missiles had been primed for firing. Almost two hundred United States Navy vessels had been deployed in the Caribbean with instructions to stop, board, and inspect ships that might be carrying nuclear missiles to Cuba, and to turn back any found to be doing so.

At the United Nations in New York, the Soviet delegate, who denied his country was mounting a threat to American security, said the United States was putting millions of lives at risk. British philosopher Bertrand Russell cabled Khrushchev that his "continued forbearance is our great hope" and cabled Kennedy that there was "no conceivable justification" for the action he was taking. In London crowds of demonstrators gathered in front of the American Embassy in Grosvenor Square to shout their protests and try to break through police lines. That scene was duplicated in Paris and in capital cities of many other countries. Homes of American diplomats were bombed in Montevideo and crowds staged anti-American riots in Rio de Janeiro. Countless people feared that the world was trembling on the brink of disaster.

Not only foreigners were frightened. Dean Rusk greeted Under Secretary of State George Ball the morning after Kennedy's announcement with congratulations that "You and I are still alive." Admiring a beautiful sunset in Washington, Secretary of Defense Robert McNamara wondered how many more he would be permitted to enjoy. In Moscow military leaders declared threateningly that the Soviet Union would not permit itself to be pushed around, and Khrushchev warned that Soviet submarines would sink any vessel trying to interfere with trade with Cuba.

Whatever their fears or expectations, Macmillan and De Gaulle, alerted in advance, had given their unqualified support to Kennedy's move, as did the member nations of the Organization of American States. Adenauer did as well after agonizing over whether the Soviets would seize the opportunity to move against Berlin. But no such fears were felt by those who believed that the Soviets would back down when faced with firm resistance. In Berlin Joachim Boelke said, "When I heard that Kennedy had stopped those ships, I knew the Russians would pull back. It was too dangerous for them. I said to my colleagues [at the *Taggesspiegel* newspaper]—who felt the same way—'That ends the Berlin crisis. We have survived it.' "

At the State Department, the Berlin Task Force could not afford to adopt so casual an approach. It shared Adenauer's anxieties. The situation was ideal for a renewed Soviet move against Berlin. The United States was distracted elsewhere. The smell of catastrophe was in the air. Once more, the various Berlin contingency plans were trotted out. Once more, the task force went into round-the-clock session. Once more, LIVE OAK command outside Paris prepared for the worst. And once more, the Western garrisons in the divided city were put on the alert.

In the White House too, Berlin was, according to Ted Sorensen, "first on everyone's list" as the likely target for Soviet retaliation. A special subcommittee comprised of some of Kennedy's most valued advisers was formed to duplicate the workings of the Berlin Task Force and monitor Berlin developments during the missile crisis.

As it turned out, no significant problems developed over Berlin.

One comparatively minor incident occurred at a Soviet autobahn checkpoint over the processing procedure for an American convoy. It was soon resolved, but the American Mission in Berlin, attuned primarily to local circumstances, urged that the situation be exploited to force a showdown on processing procedures while the Kremlin was preoccupied with Cuba. The State Department, however, pointed out to the mission that the United States was at that moment also up to its eyeballs in the Cuba crisis and there was no point in adding an unnecessary dimension to it.

On October 28, six days after Kennedy announced the quarantine, Khrushchev beat a clumsy retreat. He announced that the missiles, which the Soviets had so strenuously denied were in Cuba, would be dismantled, crated, and shipped back to the Soviet Union. No other nuclear weapons would be sent to replace them. In desperation over Berlin, Khrushchev had tried and failed at a demeaning deception. The implications of his humiliation, and that of the Soviet Union, would extend far beyond the Caribbean.

When the Soviets had earlier scattered word like buckshot that they would put off further action on Berlin until after the American congressional elections, Khrushchev expected to have his missiles in place in Cuba by election time. He believed they would then become an American election issue and that he would be able to use them for a proposed trade-off on Berlin. Defense Secretary Robert McNamara later told Congress, "Their stationing of nuclear armed ballistic missiles in Cuba was directly related to [the Soviet Berlin] agenda. The psychological if not the military threat that these missiles would have posed to our own homeland was apparently the trump card which Mr. Khrushchev intended to play in the next round of negotiations on the status of Berlin."

There was talk during the crisis that Khrushchev was angling for a trade-off of the missiles in Cuba for American Jupiter missiles in Turkey. But though the missiles in Turkey were obsolescent, the suggestion was rejected by the White House. Such a move might have been taken by America's allies as indicating Washington's readiness to sacrifice their defense interests to protect those of the United States. In any case it was Berlin that Khrushchev was after. Khrushchev's Cuban missiles were to be the key to the removal of the western garrisons from Berlin. West Berlin would fall first under

Soviet influence and then under Soviet control. The heroic victory of the Red Army in conquering the city in 1945 would finally be complete.

By responding so vigorously and unequivocally to the Cuba challenge, Kennedy had, however, demonstrated the shortcomings of Soviet military capabilities and determination. What was more, the Soviets now had to live with the likelihood that Kennedy, having shone brilliantly in his management of the Cuba crisis, would respond with equal vigor and control to any further efforts to squeeze the West out of Berlin. He had finally redeemed himself for the Bay of Pigs. As was clear even in the Kremlin, Khrushchev had behaved with dazzling recklessness in committing Soviet resources far from home against a power his military forces could not match.

As a last gasp of the Kremlin's shattered Berlin ambitions, Gromyko hinted to Rusk that the Soviets might be prepared to trade Soviet dominance in Cuba for West Berlin. But it was a feeble try, and Rusk told him the United States wasn't interested. Not long afterward, visiting East Berlin, Khrushchev told his unhappy hosts that the existence of the Wall reduced the need for a separate peace treaty. There were further incidents of harassment on the western access routes and further fulminations from the East German Communists, who continued to denounce West Berlin's links with West Germany as a militaristic provocation and to condemn the Allied lifelines as an encroachment on the sovereignty of the German Democratic Republic. But the end of the Cuba missile crisis had effectively spelled the end of the Berlin crisis.

Since 1958 Khrushchev had tried everything to snuff out the western presence in the city—ultimatums, smiles, promises that West Berlin's independence would be guaranteed, harassment of Allied access routes, and nuclear threats. But the western garrisons were still mockingly in place smack dab in the middle of Communist East Germany. Whatever hopes and plans the Kremlin had for West Berlin were now shelved. Soviet diplomacy, shaken by the enormity of Khrushchev's abortive gamble, went into a period of rest and rehabilitation.

However, the Berlin Wall—gray, bleak, and forbidding—remained in place. It became a tourist attraction. No trip to Berlin was complete without a look at it. West Berlin—walled in but accessible from the West—remained an island of defiance in a Communist sea. Western leaders ritually visited it and climbed viewing platforms to peer over the Wall in wonder and dismay at the armed guards on the far side, at the watchtowers, and at the death strips.

John Kennedy paid his personal respects to West Berlin a few months after the Cuba missile crisis. He looked at the Wall and over it and then stood on the balcony of West Berlin's Town Hall, over-looking the square that would later be named after him, to offer hun-dreds of thousands of West Berliners who gathered there to cheer him an eloquent tribute and a promise that they would not be forgotten:

> There are many people in the world who really don't understand, or say they don't, what is the great issue between the free world and the Communist world. Let them come to Berlin. There are some who say that Communism is the wave of the future. Let them come to Berlin. And there are some who say in Europe and elsewhere we can work with the Communists. Let them come to Berlin. And there are even a few who say that it is true that Communism is an evil system, but it permits us to make economic progress. *Lasst sie nach Berlin kommen.* Let them come to Berlin. . . . All free men, wherever they may live, are citizens of Berlin and, therefore, as a free man, I take pride in the words *"Ich bin ein Berliner."*

Over the next two years the two prime movers in the Berlin crisis were removed from the scene. John Kennedy was cut down by an assassin in Dallas a few months after his Berlin visit. The follow-ing year Khrushchev—a victim of his failure in Berlin as much as anything else—was ousted from the leadership of the Soviet Union and made to tiptoe into obscurity. The peace treaty to formally conclude World War II, which he had turned into a diplomatic ploy and a threat, was never signed. The armies of Adolf Hitler may have surrendered unconditionally a long time ago, but World War II is still not officially over.

Changes in Berlin followed. A secondary wall was built to keep people in the East from approaching the border Wall and reduce still further the small number of escapees. A deep trench was dug be-tween them for the same purpose. More watchtowers were built along the Wall, and more lightposts were put up to keep it il-luminated the night through. Dog runs were installed, and death strips were extended. Maintenance of the Wall, and the refinements around it, became a main priority of the East German regime.

Though East Berliners were still not permitted west, arrangements were made in due course for West Berliners to obtain visas to visit relatives in the East again. Welcome though that was, it could not eradicate the image of the barrier between the two parts of the city or the fact that East Germans were still being killed trying to come west. Nor could it relieve Willy Brandt of the disturbing conviction that he had been wrong to believe that the Allies, and particularly the Americans, would actually strive for the reunification of his country. If they could not prevent the division of a city, they could not be expected to do anything about the division of a country.

For Brandt—who had wanted "energetic steps" taken by the West the day the Wall was built, who reviled and despised the police-state behavior of the East German regime, who had wanted nothing to do with Communism or its practitioners—the Wall was a turning point that would prove to be of momentous significance for Europe and the world when, a few years later, he became West German foreign minister and then chancellor. The seed of his *Ostpolitik* (Eastern policy), his reaching out for reconciliation with East Germany, was planted when the barrier was lowered across the middle of Berlin on Barbed Wire Sunday. Brandt concluded that reunification of his country, if such a thing were possible, would have to wait. Some form of contact first had to be established between the two parts of the German nation. He said, "We had to look for new ways to alleviate the split—and leave the rest to the future."

Egon Bahr, who went with Brandt from Berlin to Bonn and became a prominent figure in West German politics, said, "We had to adjust to reality. Since we could not break through the Wall, we had to start negotiations, not with the Americans, not with the Soviets, but with those damned East German Communists, to get visas to cross the border."

The turnabout in West German policy initiated by Brandt was seen by his critics as an unforgivable sellout to Communist tyranny. But it led to an easing of international friction in Europe. In 1972, fourteen years after Khrushchev's first Berlin ultimatum to the Allies, the four powers that had conquered Germany in the war and the two German states that had sprung from that defeat reached agreement on the future status of West Berlin. All concerned agreed that West Berlin, though not an integral part of West Germany, would retain undisputed, close economic, cultural, and political links with the West German state. The western access routes through East

Germany would be unimpeded. The continued presence of the three western garrisons in West Berlin would no longer be disputed.

The international status of the German Democratic Republic was upgraded; the United States granted it diplomatic recognition two years later. Its Communist leaders were less than happy having to agree that control of West Berlin remained beyond their grasp. But Khrushchev's successor, Leonid Brezhnev, still struggling to make sense of the Soviet civilian economy, and Richard Nixon, Lyndon Johnson's successor as president of the United States, trying to extricate the United States from Vietnam, were relieved that a less strained, less precarious East–West climate of relations in Europe had replaced the discord that had clouded the atmosphere for so long.

Though the agreement was widely welcomed, not everybody was satisfied with the details. When American officials who had been involved with the crisis from the beginning heard that there would be a reference in the final communiqué only to the "western sectors of Berlin," rather than to all the sectors or just to "Berlin," they were amazed that Nixon and Secretary of State Henry Kissinger had agreed to the distinction. One of them cabled the American delegation that they had "worked too hard on this to give it away in a communiqué." His protest and those of others were ignored, and he was left believing it would "come back to haunt us one day." The West had never been willing to sign an agreement with the Soviets concerning only West Berlin, with East Berlin removed from the equation. It was a violation of the theology of Berlin. The fact remained that West Berlin was still one hundred miles inside Communist East Europe, and the access routes were (and are) still potentially as vulnerable as they had been before.

For the West the Berlin Wall symbolized the failure of communism to endure without recourse to force and repression. For Communist ideologists it was a necessity as they guided people along the rugged road to what they believed would be a better society and a more fulfilling life. For Communist bureaucrats and officials it meant being able to call upon the police to guarantee that the requirements of the party and the state were met, without the danger of driving the work force into exile.

But to many East Berliners and East Germans, the Wall was

just concrete and kalashnikovs, and it was confinement for reasons they could not accept, under rule to which they objected, in a place they no longer wished to be. Confronted with the armed might of a system in which even a few unguarded words could earn them jail sentences, most resigned themselves to circumstances and grew grudgingly reconciled to being behind the Wall.

For some, however, though they had jobs, enough to eat, and places to live, the situation was unendurable. Whether in search of freedom, the comparative luxuries that life in the West could provide, or a more rewarding future than they believed communism had to offer, people found ways to get past the Wall, at the risk of being imprisoned if their intentions were revealed, at the risk of being shot if they were caught in the act.

In the beginning, before the Vopos tightened their border-control procedures, it was easier to escape. One man drugged his three small children with sleeping pills and, with his wife, carried them to a less well patroled stretch of the barbed wire in a rural section of the city. There he snipped the wire with wire cutters, held the ends apart while his wife carried the children through, and followed. Fourteen people took command of an East German excursion boat on the River Spree and forced it to dock in West Berlin so that they could step ashore there and seek sanctuary. An engineer had friends in the West use a huge construction crane to lift him over the Wall in an improvised basket.

When the East Germans were first building the barrier, lookouts were posted at night in West Berlin apartments overlooking the area while accomplices in the street below hauled two long ladders to the Wall. Propping one ladder against the western side, they climbed up, snipped the barbed wire at the top, and dropped the other ladder against the eastern face of the Wall. In accordance with prearranged instructions, refugees sprinted forward from the eastern side to climb up and over into freedom.

Twenty-five people fled aboard a commuter train, driven by a refugee, which sped from East Germany into the British Sector. Another escapee fitted out the rear of his van with armor plate, lined part of the sides with poured concrete, and crashed through a border checkpoint through a hail of gunfire. Others neglected such precautions and tried to ram their unfortified vehicles through checkpoints. Some succeeded; others had their bodies riddled with submachine-gun bullets before plowing into obstructions erected to stop them.

Some visitors from West Germany who were not barred from entering and leaving East Berlin fitted tight, closed compartments into their cars. Refugees secreted inside them were spirited through checkpoints at great risk to both driver and escapee. West Berlin university students formed what they waggishly called the Travel Bureau Incorporated to organize escapes through various channels and along various routes for, among others, many of their 450 fellow students who had been trapped in East Berlin when the border was sealed.

The most dramatic escapes were under the Wall through make-shift tunnels. Some tunnels dug soon after the Wall was built were comparatively short subterranean passageways, virtually only dipping under the border barrier. One was started in the basement of an East Berlin home and clawed out by a group of men who took turns taking sick leave from work to get on with the job. A lookout mounted at a second-floor window signaled the approach of border guards by switching off tunnel lights whenever guards approached the house. When it was finished, twenty-eight people, ranging in age from eight to seventy-one, crawled through it to the West.

Another tunnel, through which 150 people escaped, went from a building on the western side to a cemetery in East Berlin, where its entrance was concealed by a gravestone. The Vopos discovered it when a woman fleeing with her infant drew the gravestone back into place after she had entered the tunnel but left the baby carriage standing empty nearby.

The most ambitious tunnel was 145 yards long and dug over a seven-month period by a group of West Berliners, mostly college students, some of them aspiring engineers, who gave up a term's work to complete the job. They started it in the cellar of a West Berlin building near the Wall and by sheer luck came to the surface again in a deserted cellar in East Berlin, the first tunneler out emerging with an automatic weapon at the ready. Like most who worked on other tunnels, they had already sent couriers who possessed West German passports into East Berlin through the Communist checkpoints to make contact with the East Berliners who were to be brought to the West through the tunnel—relatives, close friends of the tunnelers, and others they could trust. It was a worrying matter for all concerned because the East German security services had penetrated some of the tunnel-building groups in West Berlin.

When the digging was done and the tunnel was ready, arrangements were made for the escapees to converge calmly on the East Berlin tunnel mouth by ones and twos, carrying nothing that might arouse suspicion. During the actual escape, a mother crawled past her son, one of the tunnelers, whom she had not seen in months. He did not reveal his presence to her for fear she would make noise that might be heard above. Fifty-seven East Germans escaped through that tunnel before a Vopo discovered it. He was shot dead by a tunnel guard who was able to scamper back to West Berlin before other Vopos arrived to fire blindly into the tunnel and flood it with tear gas.

Dozens of tunnels were started, mostly from the West. Most were too ambitious and had to be abandoned. It soon became evident that the urge to dig a tunnel and bring people out did not suffice. Expert assistance and careful planning were needed, as well as suitable equipment and materials—timber to prop up tunnel roofs, excavation tools, trucks to haul away displaced earth, electricity for illumination. To finance all of this, money was needed; in one case NBC provided the finances in exchange for the right to film the operation for television.

Some of the tunnels were intricate, long-planned, lengthy conduits that involved dozens of volunteers enrolled in what James O'Donnell has called the "Berlin Institute of Tunnelology." In many cases the tunnels had to be dug deep to get under the pipes and cables that crisscrossed the city. The tunnelers had to cope with the danger of flooding (many of the tunnels were flooded and abandoned before they could be used), detection, and betrayal. At least five of the tunnelers were shot dead by East German police. Several others were caught and imprisoned.

Most of the tunnelers were dedicated individuals. Some were trying to rescue relatives or friends; others were motivated by a belief in human liberty and/or a hatred of communism. Their efforts became a fashionable, noble cause that attracted the full-time commitment of many young people in West Berlin. But so anxious were some East Germans to go west that shady entrepreneurial elements were soon lured by the prospect of commercial gain into tunneling operations. In some cases large sums of money were demanded of would-be refugees or their relatives in the West. To this day, "escape arranger" advertisements can be seen pasted to the railings of observation platforms overlooking the Wall in West Berlin: "Emigration Arranged from the German Democratic Republic, Unconventional, Discreet, and Reliable."

Some people who offered escape services soon after the Wall was built were from West Berlin's criminal community. They sometimes took the money and abandoned the refugees. In some cases it is believed they betrayed their clients to the Vopos. Many people maintain that criminal elements are still in the "escape arranging" business. But people also say that for the huge fee they charge for their services—between fifty thousand and one hundred thousand west marks—they do what they offer to do and actually manage to get people past the Wall.

As East German security precautions grew more sophisticated and as the no-man's-land on the eastern side of the Wall grew larger, tunnels had to be so long to get from safety in the West to secrecy in the East that they no longer became practicable propositions. People had to find other methods and other directions for their escape. And they did, but in much reduced numbers. Some escaped to Scandinavia across the Baltic Sea from the northern shore of East Germany; others demanded exit visas when staging embarrassing sit-downs in West German embassies in other Communist East European countries to which East Germans are permitted to go on vacation. There have been several cases in which East Germans have stolen the passports of visiting West Germans, sometimes after flagging down their cars on East German roads, and have used them to get through the Wall, leaving their victims to try to convince the Vopos that they did not connive in the escape. At times visiting West Germans did connive in such escapes. There was also a notorious case in which a young man in West Germany proposed marriage to a West German girl, took his fiancée to East Germany, supposedly to meet his family, then stole her passport and used it to bring his look-alike girl friend out of the East, leaving the West German girl to find her way out as best she could.

Many who have escaped have been individuals permitted access to the Wall—members of the East German security forces. More than five hundred Vopos, Grepos, and soldiers have fled to West Berlin since the Wall was erected, some by scrambling over the barrier, some by dashing through a checkpoint, some by other routes. (More than four times that number have fled directly to West Germany.) An East German coast guard cruised his patrol boat across a border lake to West Berlin while the other members of the crew were taking a coffee break ashore. As a precaution, foot and motorized guards patrol the Wall in pairs. Partners are continually rotated so that would-be escapees can not count on friendship to save them from bullets in the back if they try to make a getaway while on Wall duty.

Every so often, the East German authorities issue a number of exit visas in an attempt to defuse discontent—and to earn money, since the West German government has periodically paid what amounts to ransom payments in exchange for people permitted to leave. According to several West Berliners who regularly visit family and friends in East Berlin and East Germany, these constitute no more than a fraction of the number who would head West if they were able obtain visas. That impression appears to be confirmed by the fact that though living and working conditions for East Germans and East Berliners are now greatly improved, the Wall remains very much in place to keep them from straying. A dud street light in East Berlin can take four months to replace, but the slightest crack in the Wall is repaired instantly.

Even the most grotesque situation becomes normal if you live with it long enough. For Berliners the Wall is now, therefore, normal. No one likes it, and even the Communists make no effort to glorify it. But the Wall no longer arouses the passions it did when it first rose in the middle of the city to divide families and friends and keep people from their jobs. Berliners have reluctantly accepted it. Most do not even think of it any longer.

14
Last Look

THERE is a museum now at Checkpoint Charlie, an old, shabby building, the last house on the street before the border no-man's-land begins. Inside, in a hodgepodge of cluttered wall displays of photos and words, the story of the barbed wire, of the Wall, of the escapes that succeeded, and of some that failed is thrown at the visitor without subtlety, without sophistication. At first it seems misconceived, distasteful, unwieldy, a mistake. But it is not. It captures with great fidelity the anguish and the terror, the desperation and despair the building of the Wall begot.

The checkpoint itself, in the middle of the street, is still manned by American, British, and French military policemen, some not even as old as the Wall. On the East Berlin side of the border, the Vopo checkpoint is now equipped with parking spaces for the tourist buses that come through from West Berlin, which must undergo thorough inspection on entering and leaving. The Vopos in the prefabricated huts of the checkpoint have lists of banned persons that they scan carefully before permitting a visitor to buy a visa for five west marks and requiring him to change another twenty-five into nonexchangeable east marks. All must pay for the privilege of passing through the Wall from one part of Berlin to the other. How long it takes to

284

be cleared through depends on the size of the crowd seeking entry, the mood of the Vopos on duty, and the international situation. It is possible to be processed in five minutes or, even when there is no great crowd waiting, to have to wait an hour or more. A visitor is left with the feeling that East Berlin rather than West Berlin is walled in. Crossing into the East is still an unpleasant experience, if only because of the realization that East Berliners can be shot for trying to come the other way.

But not far east of the crossing point is Platz der Akademie, once considered the most beautiful square in Berlin. Until just recently it was a collection of stately war ruins. Now it is being renovated. The German Cathedral, the old Huguenot Cathedral, and the theater there are being meticulously restored. These efforts are part of a long-term project to beautify some long-neglected sections of East Berlin. Even in its unfinished state, the area is an agreeable sight and goes some way toward relieving the irritation of being gone over by the Vopos at the border.

At a café I share a small table with an East German engineer, a cultured, articulate man. He says I have come to East Berlin too soon. There is a lot of building and rebuilding going on, not only of the fine old monumental structures in the downtown area, but new apartment houses, hotels, restaurants, sports centers. "Much is being done here," he says. "Come back in ten years. It will all be *different* then—or," he says, as he gets up to leave, "maybe not."

At the Museum of German History, where the ground floor is devoted to what has transpired in East Germany since World War II, history is strikingly selective. There is not a word about barbed wire or the Wall or about the mass exodus of the refugees that preceded it. The four or five items devoted to that critical moment in postwar German history deal only with the defense of the Socialist Fatherland and the foiling of the attempts by warmongers and slave traders to undermine the German Democratic Republic.

In another section of the museum I am caught up in a flurry of playful blue-bloused kids from the Communist Free German Youth organization. When they learn I am an American, they cluster around laughingly and ask if I have been to Chicago or Arizona before they are hushed by a porter for making too much noise. An American diplomat who was once stationed in East Berlin and who traveled some in East Germany said that while East German officials are as suspicious and uncommunicative as Communist bureaucrats can be anywhere, "Sometimes I had the impression that the East German people like us better than the West Germans do."

The people I speak with, ask for directions, ask the time of day, buy things from in stores, are polite, agreeable, easygoing. But there is a pervasive drabness about them. It's hard to understand. Then it becomes clear—it's the uniform absence of liveliness or stylishness in the clothes they wear, as if all were backdrop extras in a movie, meant never to attract undue attention.

At the Centrum department store in Alexanderplatz, much is explained. East Berlin's major peoples' emporium is well stocked with clothes and everything else a department store should have. But strangely, for a country that now occupies a very respectable position on the world table of national economic performance, the place seems like a large Woolworth's. Though some of the stores around Alexanderplatz and on Unter den Linden display high-priced, interesting ceramics, high-quality leather goods, and other specialty items —and have credit-card stickers on their windows to indicate that western customers are their target market—there is nothing at East Berlin's main department store to compare with the quality of the goods available not only in West Berlin but also at the unmarked government-run store on Clara Zetkin Strasse in the East. There only hard foreign currencies may be used to buy imported goods—from Camembert to après-ski gear—denied ordinary East Berliners whose relatives in the West have neglected to send them gifts of money. Building for a glorious future, they are shortchanged on current material rewards for their labors—and have been since the war ended more than four decades back.

East Berliner: "We don't lead such a bad life here. Food is cheap. Rents are low. Medical care is free. There is no unemployment. I earn a good salary, but there aren't too many things to buy. All the good things we make are reserved for export. My brother lives in West Berlin. He does all right. He comes to see me now and again, but I cannot go to see him. We drift apart. Our children hardly know each other."

.   .   .

West Berliner: "I go into East Berlin three or four times a year —to see my mother. It is not far, but it is an expensive trip. I am not a rich man. In addition to having to exchange twenty-five west marks for twenty-five worthless east marks each time, and not being able to change them back when I leave, I try to bring my mother little things that are ordinary for us but are luxuries over there—real coffee, different kinds of spices, a good salami, things like that. If my other relatives over there know I am coming, they also expect me to bring them something. East Berliners think all West Berliners have a lot of money. My sister lives in East Berlin. But I never see her anymore. She is married to a Vopo, and he is not allowed to have any contact at all with people from the West."

The crosstown subway train between the Gesundbrunnen and Kottbusser Tor stations, both in West Berlin, passes six stations without slowing down or stopping. Those stations are in East Berlin and have been sealed since August 13, 1961, when the East Germans rolled out the barbed wire on the sector borders. Some of them are brightly illuminated, others dimly lit. If you look closely as they whiz by, you can see armed Vopos posted in each of them to make certain the train doesn't slow down to pick up someone who has managed to get into the station and who might be trying to flee the republic. Each day tens of thousands of West Berliners travel back and forth *under* East Berlin to work or play. For most it is the only contact they have with the other part of their partitioned city. They make that contact without so much as looking up from their newspapers or interrupting their conversations, as if it were just a bit more subway tunnel to be chugged through before they can get off the train when it reaches West Berlin once more and come to grips again with Berlin's special brand of reality.

Manfred Rexin: "Shortly before the Wall was built, I visited Jerusalem and looked at the wall that stood at the time between the Jewish and Arab sections of the city. I thought such a thing could only happen in a place where the people on the two sides had different cultures, different ethnic backgrounds, different languages, and hated each other. Here in Berlin we were one people, one culture, one background. I never believed it could ever happen here."

East German Communist: "Do you think I am blind? I hate the Wall! It is ugly. But we had no choice. We were losing so many of our best people—engineers, scientists, specialists of all kinds, and so many of our young people who were still wet behind the ears and had no idea of the kind of world we were trying to build. Without the measures we took, we never could have gotten as far as we have."

West Berlin school teacher: "The Wall is the price we pay for Hitler and the Nazis. I am afraid it will take a war to bring it down. The Wall is monstrous, but it's better than a war."

American foreign service officer: "I didn't think so at the time, but now I believe we should have torn down the Wall right away. The sight of the Allies coming in would have so confused and disorganized the Communists that they would not have been able to regroup to build the Wall further back like we said they would at the time. It would have been such a major event that the world's attention would have focused on the issue. There wouldn't have been a war. The Russians didn't want war and we certainly didn't. There might have been East–West talks that could have led to solutions to problems we have had to live with ever since."

Sir Frank Roberts: "Shortly before the Wall was built, at a party in Moscow, Frol Kozlov, the Soviet deputy prime minister, told me, 'The situation is not dangerous. After the war a line was drawn across Europe. We would have liked it to be further west. You would have liked it to be further east. We will make trouble for you, and you will make trouble for us. We will find it easier to make trouble for you, in Berlin as everywhere else. But there will be no risk of war.' "

. . .

James O'Donnell: "The Wall lurks like an iceberg in German–American relations. One day in the future, maybe around the turn of the century, a master demagogue will arise in Germany and will implant the lie—already believed by many there—that the cynical Americans sold the Germans down the river to the Russians on August 13, 1961."

Acknowledgments

While writing this book, I was fortunate to meet and speak with many people with special insight into the Berlin crisis, some casually, some at greater length. I am grateful to them all and particularly to the following for granting me interviews: John Ausland, Egon Bahr, Joachim Boelke, Willy Brandt, McGeorge Bundy, Lieutenant Colonel Michael Burkham, Major Peter Cutler, Arthur Day, William Fulbright, Martin Hillenbrand, Adam Kellett-Long, David Klein, John Kornblum, Sir Bernard Ledwidge, Lothar Loewe (by telephone), John Mapother, Karl Mautner, Martha Mautner, Francis Meehan, George Muller, Nelson Ledsky, James O'Donnell, Manfred Rexin, Sir Frank Roberts, Dean Rusk, Polizei Oberkommissar Dieter Seidel, Richard Smyser (by telephone), Sir Edward Tomkins, and Colonel Ernest von Pawel (by telephone.)

I am much obliged also to Allan Lightner for troubling to make and send me a tape recording of answers to questions I sent him, to Mary Kellett-Long for permitting me to quote from her Berlin diary, to Honoré Catudal for permission to quote from material he gathered while researching his study of American government decision-making processes in the lead-up to the crisis, and to the following for their assistance: Carlotta Anderson, Cynthia Efird, Suzanne Forbes and the staff of the John Fitzgerald Kennedy Library in Boston, Edward

Harper, Joerg Henschl and the staff of the Press Office of the Berlin *Senat,* Rainer Hildebrandt, Tom Homan, the Photographic Division of the Press Office of the Federal Republic of Germany, Polizei-hauptkommissar Rainer Schmidt, Clyde Taylor, who prodded me into reliving the crisis, Joachim Trenkner, and Dr. Bernd von Waldow. I am grateful most of all to my wife, Barbara Gelb, for everything.

Notes

The Wall

3. "the testicles of the West": Quoted to the author by Dean Rusk.
3. "If Khrushchev wants": Arthur Schlesinger, Jr., *A Thousand Days.*
5. guaranteed by East–West agreement: *Politics and Government in the Federal Republic of Germany, Basic Documents.* Leamington Spa: Berg Publishers, 1984.

The Stage Is Set

10. "From the day": Walter Bedell Smith, *Eisenhower's Six Great Decisions.* New York: Longmans, Green, 1956.
10. "Our main objective": Stephen E. Ambrose, *The Supreme Commander.* Garden City: Doubleday and Company, 1969.
10. "the main prize": Jean Smith, *The Defense of Berlin.*
11. "Not until the campaign ended": Omar Bradley, *A Soldier's Story.* New York: Henry Holt & Company, 1951.
12. "only a geographic location": John Toland, *The Last 100 Days.* New York: Random House, 1966.
14. "entirely coincides with the plan": Cornelius Ryan, *The Last Battle.* New York: Simon & Schuster, Inc., 1966.
15. "Well, who will take Berlin": *Ibid.*
15. "The Russian armies will": Winston Churchill, *Triumph and Tragedy.* Boston: Houghton Mifflin, 1953.
16. George Kennan recalled: George Kennan, *Memoirs 1925–1950.* Boston: Little, Brown & Company, 1967.
17. "for battles fought and won": James Gavin, *On to Berlin.*

17. "I can handle Uncle Joe": *Ibid.*

18. "in no condition": Robert Murphy, *Diplomat Among Warriors.* Garden City: Doubleday and Company, 1964.

18. "I told the Supreme Commander": Harry C. Butcher, *My Three Years with Eisenhower.* New York: Simon & Schuster, Inc., 1946.

19. "The only thing": *The New York Times,* 12 June 1966.

19. "If the Americans": Ryan, *op. cit.*

19. "hell-bent for Berlin": Toland, *op. cit.*

20. "Stop right where you are.": *Ibid.*

20. "All I could think of": Ryan, *op. cit.*

20. "a pretty stiff price": Bradley, *op. cit.*

20. "If I were to seize": Gavin, *op. cit.*

20. "Every soldier I know of": *Ibid.*

Discord in the Ruins

22. "Craters, caves, mountains of rubble": Willy Brandt, *My Road to Berlin.* Garden City: Doubleday and Company, 1960.

23. "It is vital now": Winston Churchill, *Triumph and Tragedy.*

23. "splendid contribution": 28 May 1945, *Public Papers of the Presidents of the United States—Harry S Truman.* Washington: United States Government Printing Office, 1961.

24. "they illegally occupy": Jean Smith, *op. cit.*

24. "Our State Department": *Ibid.*

24. "We went to Berlin": Frank Howley, *Berlin Command.*

26. Howley was left with the impression: *Ibid.*

26. "Why are you Americans": *Ibid.*

26. "Even at [the] first meeting": Gregory Klimov, *The Terror Machine.*

28. "We were quite willing to start off": Lucius Clay, *Decision in Germany.*

28. "dreams of a happy collaboration": George Kennan, *The New Yorker,* 25 February 1985.

30. "To the man in the street": Wolfgang Leonhard, *Child of the Revolution.*

31. "It is a matter of common knowledge": *The New York Times,* 12 October 1947.

33. He had publicly accepted blame: *The New York Times,* 24 July 1948.

34. "The belief in Europe": Author's interview with John Ausland.

35. "There is no discussion": Richard Collier, *Bridge Across the Sky.* New York: McGraw-Hill, 1978.

35. When the full dimensions: Harry S Truman, *Years of Trial and Hope.* New York: Signet Books, 1965.

41. People who had devoted their lives: Carola Stern, *Ulbricht.*

42. "There can be no question": Leonhard, *op. cit.*

44. Refugee statistics compiled by the Ministry for All-German Affairs of the Federal Republic of Germany.

Ultimatums and Departures

46. "The international Communist movement": John Foster Dulles's press conference, 26 November 1958.

47. "It should be clear": Jean Smith, *op. cit.*

48. "If you want war": Jack M. Schick, *The Berlin Crisis 1958–1962.*

48. Eisenhower agreed: President Eisenhower's press conference, 28 September 1959.

49. Yugoslav Ambassador: Veljko Mikunovic, *Moscow Diary.* London: Chatto & Windus, 1980.

49. "the sore blister": Nikita Khrushchev, *Khrushchev Remembers.*

50. "the rights we have": President Eisenhower's press conference, 27 April 1960.

51. "The Soviets choose": Henry Kissinger, *The Observer,* London, 21 December 1985.

60. "I walked past the open door": Mary Kellett-Long, unpublished Berlin diary.

61. "enlisted for service": V. Vysotsky, *Berlin.* Moscow: Progress Publishers, 1974.

71. a meeting of Warsaw Pact leaders: Honoré Catudal, *Kennedy and the Berlin Wall Crisis.*

Collision in Vienna

73. "Let every nation know": 20 January 1961, *Public Papers of the Presidents of the United States—John F. Kennedy.* Washington: United States Government Printing Office, 1962.

74. "How could I have been so stupid": Theodore Sorensen, *Kennedy.*

74. "watching a gifted young amateur": Transcript, oral history interview with Dean Acheson, John F. Kennedy Library, Boston, Massachusetts.

75. "remove this splinter": Sorensen, *op. cit.*

75. Llewellyn Thompson . . . now believed: Honoré Catudal, *Kennedy and the Berlin Wall Crisis.*

75. "Of all the problems": National Security Files, JFK Library.

76. "We will bury you!": Nikita Khrushchev, *Khrushchev Remembers.*

77. "All officers, especially marshals": Oleg Penkovsky, *The Penkovsky Papers.* Garden City: Doubleday and Company, 1965.

79. "after a nuclear war": Quoted to the author by Dean Rusk.

80. "the time had come": Khrushchev, *op. cit.*

80. "though you really can't reach": Author's interview with Dean Rusk.

81. "It must not be tolerated": Jean Smith, *op. cit.*

82. "He looked not only anxious": Khrushchev, *op. cit.*

82. "The president and the chairman": *Department of State Bulletin,* 26 June 1961.

83. "About par for the course": Arthur Schlesinger, Jr., *A Thousand Days.*

83. "shaken and angry": *The New York Times,* 15 November 1964.

83. Harold Macmillan . . . said: Harold Macmillan, *Pointing the Way.* London: Macmillan, 1972.

83. "Kennedy looked kind of tired": Transcript, oral history interview with Peter Lisagor, JFK Library.

83. "I just want you to know": Montague Kern, Patricia Levering, and Ralph Levering, *The Kennedy Crisis.* Chapel Hill: University of North Carolina Press, 1983.

84. "If we're going to have to start": Kenneth O'Donnell and David Powers with Joe McCarthy, *Johnny, We Hardly Knew Ye.*
84. "New Frontier": Sorensen, *op. cit.*
85. "a good beginning": Robert Slusser, *The Berlin Crisis of 1961.*
86. "At least one half": Schlesinger, op. cit.
87. "Now we've got an invalid": Hugh Sidey, *John F. Kennedy, President.*
87. "a new heaviness of features": London *Times,* 20 July 1961.
87. "I hear you bastards": Sidey, *op. cit.*
88. "had all the answers": Author's interview with Karl Mautner.
89. "They had such tremendous self-confidence": Author's interview with Martha Mautner.
91. "It would not have been to our advantage": Author's interview with McGeorge Bundy.
92. "Once the United States": National Security Files, JFK Library.
92. acceptable as "agents": Jean Smith, *op. cit.*
93. "The fundamental reason": National Security Files, JFK Library.
93. *"Um Gottes willen":* Author's interview with David Klein, note taker at the meeting.
94. "if you left a declaration": Author's interview with McGeorge Bundy.
95. "Britain's frontier was not at Dover": London *Times,* 1 August 1961.
95. "the absurd contingency planning": Macmillan, *op. cit.*
95. "he could not conceive of himself": Charles De Gaulle, *Memoir of Hope.* New York: Simon & Schuster, 1971.
95. The defense correspondent of the *Manchester Guardian,* quoted in *The New Leader,* 26 June 1961.
95. This view seemed to be confirmed: London *Times,* 11 August 1961.

The Crisis Looms

100. "We are realists": Jack M. Schick, *The Berlin Crisis 1958–1962.*
100. "who had the misfortune": *Manchester Guardian,* 17 June 1961.
100. "We should re-screen": National Security Files, John F. Kennedy Library, Boston, Massachusetts.
101. "immediately [for] the level": *Ibid.*
101. "formed the impression": Robert Slusser, *The Berlin Crisis of 1961.*
102. "The might of the Soviet Union": *Ibid.*
102. "The historic truth is": *Ibid.*
102. "All I ever hear": Kenneth O'Donnell and David Powers with Joe McCarthy, *Johnny, We Hardly Knew Ye.*
103. "An essential element in Soviet strategy": Slusser, *op. cit.*
103. "We threaten you": *Manchester Guardian,* 26 July 1961.
103. "the American people": *New York Herald Tribune,* 16 July 1961.
103. "Washington bureaucrats will": John Ausland and Colonel Hugh Richardson, "Crisis Management," *Foreign Affairs,* January 1966.
104. "a bowl of jelly": Arthur Schlesinger, Jr., *A Thousand Days.*
104. "He's imprisoned by Berlin": *Ibid.*
104. "saturated himself in the problem": Theodore Sorensen, *Kennedy.*

105. "this I thought": Transcript, oral history interview with Dean Acheson, JFK Library.
106. three "essentials": Jean Smith, *op. cit.*
107. "It seemed to us": Transcript, oral history interview with Charles Bohlen, JFK Library.
107. "bleak choices": Schlesinger, *op. cit.*
107. "Kennedy Plan" for Central Europe: National Security Files, JFK Library.
107. "We didn't have the negotiating alternative": Transcript, oral history interview with Abram Chayes, JFK Library.
108. "Let me tell you": Author's interview with Sir Frank Roberts.
109. "If Khrushchev restrains himself": Schlesinger, *op. cit.*
109. "the greatest concentration of modern forces": London *Times,* 18 July 1961.
110. An opinion poll: *U.S. News and World Report,* 19 July 1961.
110. "If we mobilize": National Security Files, JFK Library.
112. "Chip, what's wrong?": Charles Bohlen, *Witness to History.* New York: W. W. Norton and Company, 1973.
112. "a scissors and paste job": Transcript, oral history interview with Abram Chayes, JFK Library.
112. According to Martin Hillenbrand: Author's interview with Martin Hillenbrand.
113. "With all changes and clearances": Sorensen, *op. cit.*
118. "Ted, if you want": Author's interview with James O'Donnell.
118. "There was an 'Oh, my God!' feeling": Author's interview with Karl Mautner.
118. "It's West Berlin": Author's interview with McGeorge Bundy.
119. "to explore the widest possible area": Pierre Salinger, *With Kennedy.* Garden City: Doubleday and Company, 1966.
120. "entertained very hospitably": *Washington Evening Star,* 27 July 1961.
122. "The drain of workers": Nikita Khrushchev, *Khrushchev Remembers.*

Bracing for the Showdown

127. "everyone from the Task Force": Author's interview with John Ausland.
127. "It was made clear": Author's interview with Karl Mautner.
128. "to settle jointly": Robert Slusser, *The Berlin Crisis of 1961.*
129. "Not only the orange groves": *Ibid.*
129. "I will not issue orders": *Ibid.*
129. They were often on the road: Author's interview with Colonel Ernest von Pawel.
131. "the Soviets were sitting": Author's interview with John Ausland.
133. "the administration of law": *Manchester Guardian,* 10 August 1961.
133. "the principle of freedom": *The New York Times,* 4 August 1961.
135. "I argued that": Walt Rostow, *The Diffusion of Power.* New York: Macmillan, 1972.

135. "We are in West Berlin": Dean Rusk's press conference, Paris, 4 August 1961.

136. In a study of the possibilities: "Military Power and the Cold War," report prepared for the Department of Defense by the Rand Corporation, February 1961.

137. A Russian-speaking British officer: Author's interview with Lieutenant Colonel Michael Burkham.

137. One evening early in August: *Ibid.*

140. "There has never been": *The New York Times,* 6 August 1961.

140. "I don't understand": Arthur Schlesinger, Jr., *A Thousand Days.*

140. Fulbright said later: Author's interview with Senator William Fulbright.

140. "Khrushchev is losing East Germany": Rostow, *op. cit.*

141. "the situation at the time": Taped comment by Allan Lightner.

141. "West German monopolies": Erich Honecker, *From My Life.*

141. "It became more and more obvious": *Ibid.*

142. Wolfgang Leonhard has described how docilely: Wolfgang Leonhard, *Child of the Revolution.*

143. "hundreds of millions": Slusser, *op. cit.*

145. "the inflexible determination": *The New York Times,* 6 August 1961.

146. "Purpose of Moscow 3–5 August meeting": National Security Files, John F. Kennedy Library, Boston, Massachusetts.

146. "Let us sit down honestly": *Washington Evening Star,* 7 August 1961.

146. "I do not propose": quoted in Schlesinger, *op. cit.*

146. "are not for slicing sausages": London *Times,* 9 August 1961.

147. "A city is like the branch": *Ibid.,* 10 August 1961.

Something Funny at the Border

148. "If I were you": Author's interview with Adam Kellett-Long.

149. "Adam is getting tired": Mary Kellett-Long, unpublished Berlin diary.

150. food supplies on hand: Author's interview with George Muller.

150. "implement all measures": Erich Honecker, *From My Life.*

150. "under proper control": *Ibid.*

150. At 4:00 P.M. that Saturday: *Ibid.*

151. Thurow thought it was: *Die Geschichte einer Grenzkompanie des Ringes um West-Berlin,* Ministry for All-German Affairs of the Federal Republic of Germany, 1965.

151. "Something funny is going on": Author's interview with George Muller.

153. At the American military liaison mission: Author's interview with Colonel Ernest von Pawel.

154. "I strongly advise you": Author's interview with Adam Kellett-Long.

157. After checking with the British military police: Author's interview with Sir Bernard Ledwidge.

158. Minister Allan Lightner of the American Mission: Taped comment by Allan Lightner.

158. "There seems to be something": Author's interview with Richard Smyser.

159. "Soviet 19th Motorized Rifle Division": National Security Files, John F. Kennedy Library, Boston, Massachusetts.
161. "The phone kept ringing": Author's interview with George Muller.
161. Officials there realized: *Ibid.*

"Why Didn't We Know?"

166. "Surprise, when it happens": from Thomas C. Schelling's foreword to Roberta Wohlstetter, *Pearl Harbor—Warning and Decision.* Stanford: Stanford University Press, 1962.
168. "No one knew what was happening": Author's interview with Sir Edward Tomkins.
168. West Berliners "with peaceful intentions": *Politics and Government in the Federal Republic of Germany, Basic Documents.* Leamington Spa: Berg Publishers, 1984.
171. "It was hard": Author's interview with Willy Brandt.
172. "If all the commandants do": Author's interview with George Muller.
172. "Scanning the troubled faces": Willy Brandt, *People and Politics.*
177. "The cold concrete posts": Curtis Cate, *The Ides of August.*
177. "Twenty hours elapsed": Brandt, *op. cit.*
178. In Washington Berlin Task Force duty officer: Author's interview with John Ausland.
180. Embarrassingly, the most detailed early-morning report: Author's interview with Lothar Loewe.
181. "It was exceedingly difficult": Howard Trivers, *Three Crises.* Carbondale: Southern Illinois University Press, 1972.
181. "Washington, the president, the Administration": Author's interview with George Muller.
181. "didn't understand that what was happening": Author's interview with Richard Smyser.
181. "We always noted": Author's interview with Martin Hillenbrand.
183. "Why didn't we know?": Author's interview with McGeorge Bundy.
183. "Time was not of the essence": Author's interview with Dean Rusk.
184. "People are going to ask": Author's interview with John Ausland.
184. Kennedy himself did not feel: Author's interview with McGeorge Bundy.
186. "partly because the Americans have got very excited": Harold Macmillan, *Pointing the Way.*
187. Returning from vacation: Author's interview with Arthur Day.
187. Around 3:00 P.M.: Author's interview with James O'Donnell.

Postmortem

190. At the British Mission: Author's interview with Sir Bernard Ledwidge.
191. "No one here expects": *Washington Post,* 10 August 1961.
191. "pretty darn soon": Author's interview with Lieutenant Colonel Ernest von Pawel.
191. "The answers I got": Author's interview with John Mapother.
192. "they must have squirreled": Author's interview with Martin Hillenbrand.

192. "very severe, very strict controls": Author's interview with Egon Bahr.

193. "a brilliant mind": Author's interview with Richard Smyser.

193. "If you think a wall": Honoré Catudal, *Kennedy and the Berlin Wall Crisis.*

195. "If someone had suggested": Transcript, oral history interview with Maxwell Taylor, John F. Kennedy Library, Boston, Massachusetts.

195. "the present crisis will end": Terence Prittie, *Willy Brandt—Portrait of a Statesman.* London: Weidenfeld & Nicolson, 1974.

195. "received and passed on reports": Reinhard Gehlen, *The Service—The Memoirs of General Reinhard Gehlen.* New York: World Publishing, 1972.

199. "Families would now be protected": *Neues Deutschland,* 14 August 1961.

201. "refrain from committing reckless acts": Reuters, 14 August 1961.

203. "ran so high": Author's interview with John Ausland.

204. "Mac and I sat around": Transcript, oral history interview with Robert Amory, JFK Library.

204. "Berlin was not": Honoré Catudal's interview with General Bruce C. Clarke.

205. "We should take the view": National Security Files, JFK Library.

205. "I find unanimity": National Security Files, JFK Library.

205. "It was apparent from hour one": Author's interview with McGeorge Bundy.

205. "We [at the Foreign Office]": Author's interview with Sir Edward Tomkins.

205. "if we had crossed the line": Howard Trivers, *Three Crises.*

205. Allan Lightner said: Taped comment by Allan Lightner.

206. momentarily suspending his military caution: Transcript, oral history interview with Maxwell Taylor, JFK Library.

206. "This was the place": Transcript, Oral history interview with Lucius Clay, JFK Library.

207. "What steps will we take": National Security Files, JFK Library.

208. "There is no Berlin crisis": Archives, American Mission in Berlin.

Lives, Fortunes, and Sacred Honor

212. "some members of the United States Mission": Author's interview with Joachim Boelke.

212. "it really means that": *Washington Evening Star,* 15 August 1961.

213. "a big fight with a couple of people": Author's interview with Martha Mautner.

213. "The United States government did not push": Howard Trivers, *Three Crises.*

213. "This is [Khrushchev's] way out": Kenneth O'Donnell and David Powers with Joe McCarthy, *Johnny, We Hardly Knew Ye.*

213. "I hope this business": Author's interview with John Ausland.

214. "We decided in the end": Transcript, oral history interview with Abram Chayes, John F. Kennedy Library, Boston, Massachusetts.

214. Presidential military adviser: Transcript, oral history interview with Maxwell Taylor, JFK Library.

214. Later in the crisis: Author's interview with Arthur Day.

215. "Neither I nor the people": Honoré Catudal, *Kennedy and the Berlin Wall Crisis.*

216. "Washington is handling this": Author's interview with George Muller.

216. "did not initially fully anticipate": Foy Kohler, *Understanding the Russians.* New York: Harper & Row, 1970.

217. "I need a clear-cut denial": Author's interview with Egon Bahr.

218. "People were afraid something might happen": Author's interview with Willy Brandt.

218. "Berlin expects more than words": *The New York Times,* 17 August 1961.

220. "a mere mayor": Jean Smith, *op. cit.*

221. "We have been handed": Memorandum from Robert F. Kennedy to John F. Kennedy, 17 August 1961, National Security Files, JFK Library.

222. "the British come in two sizes": Author's interview with McGeorge Bundy.

223. "Soviet maneuver" in East Berlin: National Security Files, JFK Library.

224. Clay had formally volunteered: *Ibid.*

224. When Johnson stopped off: Arthur Schlesinger, Jr., *A Thousand Days.*

225. "Johnson approached anybody else's decision": Author's interview with McGeorge Bundy.

225. Two years later: Author's interview with Dean Rusk.

227. "Suppose the Russians had tried to stop": Catudal's interview with Bruce Clarke.

227. "put additional troops": National Security Files, JFK Library.

227. "talking to Kennedy was like": *Time,* 5 January 1962.

230. There had been a less: Willy Brandt, *People and Politics.*

231. "no intention of being told": Curtis Cate, *The Ides of August.*

The Rogue Symbol

236. "My own objection": National Security Files, John F. Kennedy Library, Boston, Massachusetts.

237. "either rhetorical or long-range": Author's interview with Willy Brandt.

237. Brandt did not seem to him: Author's interview with Sir Edward Tomkins.

237. "the Wall was like": *The New Yorker,* 14 January 1974.

237. "Nobody is going to fight": London *Times,* 28 August 1961.

238. "Could West Berlin": Walt Rostow, *The Diffusion of Power.*

238. "a stronger lead on Berlin": National Security Files, JFK Library.

239. A paper prepared: Historical Studies Division of the State Department, December 1963.

239. "went over like a lead balloon": Taped comment by Allan Lightner.

240. "The old gentleman": Terence Prittie, *Willy Brandt—Portrait of a Statesman.*

240. "Clay will be a burden": National Security Files, JFK Library.

240. "Hamlet-like psychosis": London *Times,* 24 July 1961.

240. an "empty gesture": Glen D. Camp, Jr. (ed.), *Berlin in the East–West Struggle 1958–1961.* New York: Facts on File, Inc., 1971.

240. "general attitude of appeasement": Harold W. Chase and Allen H. Lerman (eds.), *Kennedy and the Press.* New York: Thomas Y. Crowell Company, 1965.

241. "to saddle the [Soviet] people": Robert Slusser, *The Berlin Crisis of 1961.*

242. "To discourage an aggressor": *Ibid.*

242. "to cool the hotheads": *Ibid.*

242. "I fear that Khrushchev": Arthur Schlesinger, Jr., *A Thousand Days.*

242. "missile gap": Theodore Sorensen, *Kennedy.*

243. "a threat to the entire world": *Department of State Bulletin,* 18 September 1961.

243. "not only nuclear devices": *Ibid.*

245. "cleared at the highest level": *New York Herald Tribune,* 24 October 1961.

245. "this nation has a nuclear": United States Arms Control and Disarmament Agency, *Documents on Disarmament, 1961.*

245. "All we have to do": Author's interview with John Ausland.

246. "was not quite aware": Author's interview with Martin Hillenbrand.

246. Norstad passed word along: Author's interview with John Ausland.

246. "I never did find out": Catudal's interview with Bruce Clarke.

247. saw Clay as "difficult": Author's interview with McGeorge Bundy.

247. "Have you begun": *Ibid.*

247. "if not with the intent": *Ibid.*

248. "He was a loose cannon": Author's interview with Arthur Day.

248. Clay was not merely second-guessing: Geoffrey McDermott, *Berlin— Success of a Mission.* New York: Harper & Row, 1963.

249. "Al, don't you know": Catudal's interview with Bruce Clarke.

249. "Afterwards I called Norstad": *Ibid.*

249. "a warlike move": Jean Smith, *op. cit.*

250. "the historic and legitimate interests": *Department of State Bulletin,* 16 October 1961.

252. "If the East Germans had tried": Catudal's interview with Allan Lightner.

253. "Had it not been": Howard Trivers, *Three Crises.*

253. "We didn't send him": Curtis Cate, *The Ides of March.*

254. So Clay got the go-ahead: Transcript, oral history interview with Lucius Clay, JFK Library.

256. "My major concern at the time": Catudal's interview with Colonel Thomas Tyree.

256. "over an essentially minor issue": Cate, *op. cit.*

256. "I think we've had enough": Author's interview with John Ausland.

257. "The fiction that it was": Camp, *op. cit.*

257. "What in the hell": Catudal's interview with Bruce Clarke.

257. "Would we have retreated": *Ibid.*

257. West Berlin's military vulnerability: Author's interview with John Ausland.

Endgame

261. "Carl, the Soviet Union is the enemy": Author's interview with John Ausland.
262. "to consider American proposals": Robert Slusser, *The Berlin Crisis of 1961.*
262. "some understanding of the German problem": *Ibid.*
262. "Berlin is not such a problem": Paul-Henri Spaak, *The Continuing Battle.* London: Weidenfeld & Nicolson, 1971.
262. "Westerners usually like to rush": Author's interview with Dean Rusk.
263. "recognize the reality": *The New York Times,* 24 September 1961.
263. "give and take on both sides": *Ibid.*
263. "An armed attack on West Berlin": *The New York Times,* 23 February 1962.
264. "respected in every way": *The New York Times,* 24 February 1962.
264. "thus weaken our ties": Arthur Schlesinger, Jr., *A Thousand Days.*
265. The tone of Clay's telegrams: Taped comment by Allan Lightner.
266. Kennedy had spoken to him: Author's interview with James O'Donnell.
266. "just didn't fit in": Author's interview with John Ausland.
267. At one point the director of British European Airways: Author's interview with Sir Edward Tomkins.
267. "When they started fooling around": Author's interview with John Ausland.
268. Lord Home told the Soviet foreign minister: Author's interview with Dean Rusk.
270. "It is necessary at long last": Jack M. Schick, *The Berlin Crisis 1958–1962.*
272. "This quarantine will be extended": Robert F. Kennedy, *13 Days—The Cuban Missile Crisis.* New York: W. W. Norton & Company, 1969.
272. British philosopher Bertrand Russell: *Manchester Guardian,* 25 October 1962.
273. "You and I are still alive": Elie Abel, *The Missiles of October.* Philadelphia and New York: Lippincott, 1966.
273. "When I heard that Kennedy": Author's interview with Joachim Boelke.
273. "first on everyone's list": Theodore Sorensen, *Kennedy.*
274. "Their stationing of nuclear armed ballistic missiles": William Kaufmann, *The McNamara Strategy.* New York: Harper & Row, 1964.
276. "There are many people": 26 June 1963, *Public Papers of the Presidents of the United States—John F. Kennedy.* Washington: United States Government Printing Office, 1962.
277. "We had to look for new ways": Author's interview with Willy Brandt.
277. "We had to adjust to reality": Author's interview with Egon Bahr.
278. "worked too hard on this": Author's interview with David Klein.
281. "Berlin Institute of Tunnelology": *The New York Times,* 7 April 1963.

Selected Bibliography

Brandt, Willy. *People and Politics.* Boston: Little, Brown & Company, 1978.

Cate, Curtis. *The Ides of August.* New York: M. Evans & Company, 1978.

Catudal, Honoré. *Kennedy and the Berlin Wall Crisis.* Berlin: Berlin Verlag, 1980.

Clay, Lucius. *Decision in Germany.* Garden City: Doubleday & Company, 1950.

Davison, W. Phillips. *The Berlin Blockade.* Princeton, N.J.: Princeton University Press, 1958.

Gavin, James. *On to Berlin.* New York: The Viking Press, 1978.

Honecker, Erich. *From My Life.* Oxford: Pergamon Press, 1980.

Howley, Frank. *Berlin Command.* New York: G. P. Putnam's Sons, 1950.

Khrushchev, Nikita. *Khrushchev Remembers.* Boston: Little, Brown & Company, 1970.

Klimov, Gregory. *The Terror Machine.* New York: Praeger Publishers, 1958.

Leonhard, Wolfgang. *Child of the Revolution.* Chicago: Regnery/Gateway, 1958.

O'Donnell, Kenneth and David Powers with Joe McCarthy. *Johnny, We Hardly Knew Ye.* Boston: Little, Brown & Company, 1972.

Schick, Jack M. *The Berlin Crisis 1958–1962.* Philadelphia: University of Pennsylvania Press, 1971.

Schlesinger, Jr., Arthur. *A Thousand Days.* Boston: Houghton Mifflin Company, 1965.

Sidey, Hugh. *John F. Kennedy, President.* New York: Atheneum Publishers, 1963.

Slusser, Robert. *The Berlin Crisis of 1961.* Baltimore: The Johns Hopkins University Press, 1973.

Smith, Jean. *The Defense of Berlin.* Baltimore: The Johns Hopkins University Press, 1963.
Sorensen, Theodore. *Kennedy.* New York: Harper & Row, Publishers, 1965.
Stern, Carola. *Ulbricht: A Political Biography.* London: Pall Mall Publishers, 1965.
Windsor, Philip. *City on Leave.* New York: Praeger Publishers, 1963.

Index